TO ORGANIZE THE SOVEREIGN PEOPLE

Early American Histories

Douglas Bradburn, John C. Coombs, and S. Max Edelson, Editors

To Organize the Sovereign People

Political Mobilization in Revolutionary Pennsylvania

David W. Houpt

University of Virginia Press
Charlottesville and London

University of Virginia Press

Printed in the United States of America on acid-free paper

First published 2023

1 3 5 7 9 8 6 4 2

Library of Congress Cataloging-in-Publication Data

Names: Houpt, David W., author.

Title: To organize the sovereign people : political mobilization in revolutionary Pennsylvania / David W. Houpt.
Other titles: Political mobilization in revolutionary Pennsylvania
Description: Charlottesville : University of Virginia Press, 2023. | Series: Early American histories | Includes bibliographical references and index.
Identifiers: LCCN 2023034107 (print) | LCCN 2023034108 (ebook) | ISBN 9780813950488 (hardcover) | ISBN 9780813950495 (paperback) | ISBN 9780813950518 (ebook)
Subjects: LCSH: Pennsylvania—Politics and government—1775–1865. | Pennsylvania—History—Revolution, 1775–1783 | Political participation—Pennsylvania—History—18th century. | Political participation—Pennsylvania—History—19th century. | Political culture—Pennsylvania—History—18th century. | Political culture—Pennsylvania—History—19th century.
Classification: LCC F153 .H775 2023 (print) | LCC F153 (ebook) | DDC 974.8/03—dc23/eng/20230811
LC record available at https://lccn.loc.gov/2023034107
LC ebook record available at https://lccn.loc.gov/2023034108

Cover art: Election Day in Philadelphia (1815) by John Lewis Krimmel.
(Courtesy of Winterthur Museum, Garden & Library)

To my family

CONTENTS

ACKNOWLEDGMENTS

I don't recall exactly when I started paying attention to the acknowledgments in books, but I do remember being amazed with all the different people authors tended to thank. Prior to undertaking the writing of a book, I always pictured the process as an inherently solitary endeavor—cloistering oneself in the archives, obsessing over seemingly trivial bits of information, wrestling with prose: these were activities, I presumed, to be done in isolation. Having now reached the other side, I can say with some confidence that I could not have been more wrong.

The genesis of this project dates to time I spent working as an undergraduate with the First Federal Congress Project at George Washington University. Ken Bowling, Charlene Bickford, Helen Veit, and Chuck diGiacomantonio introduced me to the joys of research and showed me how I could combine my interest in electoral politics with my passion for history. It was Ken who first turned me on to the rough-and-tumble world that was early Pennsylvania political culture. Following my time at GWU, I was incredibly fortunate to have the opportunity to work with Rosemarie Zagarri at George Mason University, who has been an invaluable source of support and knowledge ever since. At the CUNY Graduate Center, I benefited from the feedback and guidance of Jonathan Sassi, Martin Burke, and David Waldstreicher. I owe a special debt of gratitude to Andy Robertson, who in the wake of the Occupy Wall Street movement encouraged me to think about the efficacy of different forms of political mobilization. I have relied on his counsel and insights many times throughout this process. Andy Shankman has likewise always been generous with his time and knowledge.

While I was not wrong that doing history can be isolating, what I did not realize is that it is comradeship that makes success possible. To that end, in graduate school I benefited tremendously from the CUNY Early American Republic Seminar (EARS). The group created a supportive and intellectually stimulating environment. I especially want to thank Paul Polgar, Norah Slonimsky, John Blanton, Roy Rogers, and Alyssa Wade. I found a similar spirit of collegiality when I arrived at the University of North Carolina, Wilmington (UNCW). Nathan Crowe, Jennifer Le Zotte, and Nathan

Pilkington—original members of ju-fa (junior faculty)—provided timely feedback on portions of the manuscript. I had the opportunity to present parts of this research at the annual meetings of the Society of Historians of the Early American Republic and the Omohundro Institute, as well as to CUNY EARS, the Upstate Early American History Workshop, the Thomas Paine Institute, the Second Annual Roundtable on James Madison, and the Remaking Political History Conference.

Doing research can, as I have discovered, also cost money, and I have been fortunate to receive support from several places. My time at the CUNY Graduate Center was made possible by an Enhanced Chancellor's Fellowship and the Advanced Research Collaborative Knickerbocker Archival Research Grant in American Studies. I completed this project with the assistance of a Mosley Award through the History Department at UNCW. I also received a completion grant from the UNCW College of Arts and Sciences.

Of course, none of this research would have been possible if it had not been for the work of dedicated archivists. Over the ten years I have been working on this project, I have visited a number of different repositories. In particular, I would like to thank the staff at the Historical Society of Pennsylvania, the Library Company, the American Philosophical Society, the New York Public Library, and the Pennsylvania State Archives for their work in preserving and cataloging the sources that gave me access to the past. As part of this research was conducted during a global pandemic, which made access to the repositories themselves difficult, I also want to thank all those people who have worked so hard to make digital sources available.

Working with the University of Virginia Press has been a delight. I first began communicating about this project with Dick Holway, and when he retired the project was handed over to Nadine Zimmerli. I could not have asked for more from an editor. Nadine has been responsive, helpful, and supportive. The rigorous peer review process, which Nadine managed in a politic and professional manner, absolutely made this a stronger book. I especially want to thank Peter Onuf and the anonymous reader for trudging through the manuscript multiple times. Their detailed and thoughtful reports helped immensely. Additionally, I would like to acknowledge Margaret Hogan, whose close reading and keen editorial eye saved me from more than one embarrassment. Other people who contributed to this book's publication include Arthur McCormick, Bea Burton, Andrew Edwards, and Fernando Campos.

Above all else, I would like to thank my family. My parents have supported me at every step in this journey. My dad, Tim Houpt, is the one who taught me to value the past and showed me the importance of following your calling. My mother, Kate Woodworth, has been my writing buddy, and her skills as an author, editor, and cheerleader have helped in innumerable ways. Additionally, I want to thank my brothers, Joey and Danny, who have helped to ensure that at least once a week I did something other than think about Pennsylvania in the 1790s. I'd also like to express my gratitude to George Kocur and John and Nada Bahor for their love and support.

Last but not least is my wife and life partner, Loren. She has been there with me throughout this rocky ride that is the pursuit of a career in academia. She has help keep me grounded and shown me how to live rather than just work. Together, we have also created my greatest joy—our daughter, Mattea. Along with our furry children, Tolstoy, Sappho, Virginia, Woolf, Huxley, and Angelou, they make everything possible.

TO ORGANIZE THE SOVEREIGN PEOPLE

Introduction

A HEAT WAVE descended on Philadelphia in late June 1795. "The Sun is terrible here," complained Vice President John Adams. James Ross, one of Pennsylvania's two senators, collapsed after "walking a great deal about Town" in the sun and had to be "bled and vomited."[1] The summer months were often brutal in the nation's temporary capital, bringing an oppressive combination of humidity and heat that, when coupled with the stench from the open sewers, made the city nearly unbearable. The rising temperatures also brought an increased risk of yellow fever, which had killed nearly five thousand people two years earlier. Philadelphians who could afford to do so often sought refuge in the countryside, while those who remained were forced to seek shelter indoors. In a sweltering tavern on the outskirts of town, an elderly preacher named Herman Husband lay dying.

During his life, Husband had come to embody a particular strain of the American Revolution. Born and raised in the Anglican faith, in the Great Awakening he had become involved with the New Lights and had then converted to Quakerism. His commitment to free will and spiritual equality led him to embrace democratic principles and inspired him to dedicate his life to fighting for the landless and oppressed. Like many other Americans at the time, Husband had embraced an expansive definition of popular sovereignty that privileged free will and individual rights. According to this understanding, ultimate authority always rested with the people and, while they might delegate some responsibilities to their elected officials, the people always retained the right to assert their will directly. These principles had been enshrined in Pennsylvania's 1776 constitution, which gave residents an unprecedented amount of authority over the deliberative process. The state and nation had, however, begun to drift away from the ideals espoused by men like Husband in the years following the Revolution.[2]

With the adoption of the federal Constitution in 1787 and a new state constitution in 1790, Pennsylvania appeared headed toward a new definition of popular sovereignty that emphasized the rule of law and established voting as the only legitimate expression of the public will. In the face of these changes, Americans like Husband who remained committed to a more participatory form of politics mobilized to preserve their vision for the country. Inspired by events in France, these individuals used tactics ranging from public parades to targeted acts of violence in an attempt to protect the people's right to assert their will directly. These efforts had, however, failed to lead to any meaningful change. Instead, the violence had given the federal government an excuse to crack down on dissent. Husband was actually on his way home from Philadelphia after being arrested for his role in the Whiskey Rebellion when he collapsed and was taken to the tavern.

Husband's death came at a critical junction in the struggle to define the legacy of the American Revolution. Four days after he took his last breath, allies in his fight for a more democratic form of government suffered a stinging setback when the Senate ratified the Jay Treaty by a vote of twenty to ten. The treaty, which tethered the United States to Great Britain, represented a major blow to supporters of revolutionary France, who saw the agreement with the former mother country as an embarrassing capitulation and an insult to a sister republic. In an effort that would have made Husband proud, Philadelphians took to the streets on a scale not seen since the Revolution to try and convince President Washington to reject the treaty. Their pleas fell on deaf ears. As the chief executive of the new federal government, Washington was insulated from this type of popular pressure. Street protests might have played an important role during the Revolution, but by 1795 they no longer carried the same weight. Under the new federal and state constitutions, citizens had no direct role in the deliberative process, and elected officials were free to ignore public demonstrations. As Thomas Hartley, one of Pennsylvania's representatives to the First Congress, explained during a debate about the proper relationship between the people and their government, "when the passions of the people are excited," public opinion "has been known to be often wrong." As a result, "happy is the Government composed of men of firmness and wisdom to discover, and resist popular error."[3] If residents wanted a change, they would have to wait until the next election.

Husband's democratic utopia—in which average Americans had a direct voice in the governing process—had given way to a system in which the people spoke exclusively through the ballot box.[4]

But American democracy did not die with Husband. Instead, the violence of the Whiskey Rebellion and failure to stop the Jay Treaty convinced reformers to refocus their energy on winning elections rather than on engaging the people directly in the deliberative process. This shift in strategy led to the founding of the state's first political party and the rise of a new form of American democracy characterized by elections and mass parties.[5]

Using a close analysis of different forms of political mobilization in Pennsylvania, this book investigates how and why this transition from one form of democracy to another took place. Political mobilization, whether in the form of a vote, a petition, a parade, a town meeting, or a riot, is how the people engage in the deliberative process and exercise their authority. It is the connective tissue between the people and the political process, and questions about the nature of sovereignty often manifest as clashing conceptions of what constitutes a legitimate form of political mobilization. As a result, analyzing the evolution of different forms of mobilization can serve as a window into the larger struggle to define the meaning of self-government in the decades following the Declaration of Independence.[6]

A study of this sort requires state-level analysis. It is an axiom that all politics is local, and this was never truer than in the years following the separation with Great Britain. Americans in the late eighteenth century lacked a shared identity, and differences in culture, geography, economy, and religion made any sort of national political culture difficult to establish. A growing network of newspapers had begun to create spaces where Americans could fashion an "imagined community," but in the late eighteenth century this imagining had only just begun. Communication was unreliable, and travel, even along the populated eastern seaboard, could be both tedious and treacherous. Away from the ports and cities, many Americans remained isolated from much of the outside world. This provincialism shaped the political landscape. Voters seemed much more concerned with local matters, and turnout typically peaked during years when an important local office, such as sheriff, was on the ballot.[7]

In the absence of a national consensus, the states took the lead in defining the scope and meaning of the Revolution. Even after the ratification of the federal Constitution, the states retained control over who got to claim the rights and privileges of citizenship. As part of this power, each state had the right to adopt its own rules for regulating elections, and political practices varied widely across the country. While valuable for identifying broad trends, national-level studies tend to downplay these differences and exaggerate the degree to which Americans in the early republic thought of themselves as members of a national polity.[8]

Pennsylvania is a logical place to begin an analysis of the origins of America's political practices. Known as the "Cradle of Liberty" and the "Keystone in the Democratic Arch," it served as the backdrop to some of the most dramatic moments of the revolutionary era, including the signing of the Declaration of Independence and the drafting of the federal Constitution. The state also had a diverse electorate and a mixture of urban and rural regions that has led historians to describe it as an economic and social microcosm of the infant United States. Furthermore, Philadelphia, the largest and most cosmopolitan city in the country, hosted the federal government during the 1790s and acted as the political, economic, and cultural heart of the new nation.[9]

What happened in Pennsylvania did not, however, stay in Pennsylvania. Events there reverberated throughout the country. The state stood at the cutting edge of developments in political mobilization. Owing in part to their state's place in the national spotlight and its history of factionalism, Pennsylvanians were some of the first Americans to start organizing formal political parties. Additionally, two high-profile insurrections in the 1790s forced residents to take steps to more clearly define the limits of acceptable political action. Although each state would follow its own course, these developments in Pennsylvania foreshadowed changes that would occur throughout the nation. An exploration of the evolution of political mobilization in Pennsylvania can, therefore, provide insight into the larger story of the rise of American democracy.

The political history of the late eighteenth century is a well-trod path. Pennsylvania, in particular, has been the subject of a number of studies that have shed light on different facets of the state's political culture. Much of the existing scholarship on political mobilization has, however, tended to focus more narrowly on either the years surrounding the Declaration of Independence or on the period following the adoption of the Constitution.[10] Those historians who have looked at the era more broadly have usually focused on a single type of mobilization such as voluntary societies, petitions, celebrations, music, or popular violence.[11] While these studies have provided rich details about the origins of American political practices, their limited scope means that important questions about how the meaning of self-government changed as the country moved from revolution to republic remain unanswered. In particular, the existing scholarship does not fully account for how and why elections and parties came to define democracy in America.

This book provides a more complete portrait of how the boundaries of American political practices took shape by investigating the evolution of town meetings, voluntary societies, political rhetoric, petitioning, violence, celebrations, electioneering, and voting between 1776 and 1808. By following the trajectory of these different forms of mobilization between the Declaration of Independence and the end of the schism in the Pennsylvania Republican Party, *To Organize the Sovereign People* argues that citizens embraced political parties and elections because other, more direct ways of exercising their sovereignty proved unwieldy and ultimately ineffective at translating public opinion into public policy. The emergence of parties did not, however, mean that other forms of mobilization simply disappeared. Instead, as I demonstrate, parties succeeded in large part because of their ability to harness and repurpose existing forms of mobilization to establish themselves as agents of the people.

Scholars who have studied post-revolutionary political culture tend to fall into one of two camps. On the one hand, some historians see the years following 1776 as a steady retreat from a fleeting moment when the people had a real voice in their government. According to this interpretation, the adoption of new federal and state constitutions represented a "counter-revolution" that ensured elites would remain in control. These scholars often see the rise of parties in the same light and paint the political party as a tool designed to snuff out the remaining democratic embers. On the other hand, another group of historians has depicted the period following the Declaration as a slow but steady march toward greater rights and freedoms. The new constitutions, as they see it, represented a necessary correction to the excesses of the 1780s. Indeed, these scholars argue that, instead of being agents of oppression, the constitutions are what enabled American democracy to flourish. From this perspective, political parties are seen as the engine driving the rise of American democracy. While both narratives are compelling, the dichotomy oversimplifies the complexities Americans faced as they transitioned from a revolution to a republic.[12]

By focusing on the evolution of specific forms of mobilization, this book seeks to transcend the declension/democratization debate. There is no doubt that the new state and federal constitutions fundamentally redefined the relationship between the people and the deliberative process.

A golden age of democracy in Pennsylvania, however, never existed. Scholars who ascribe to the declension model have tended to focus on the state's 1776 constitution while overlooking the restrictions the regime placed on who could participate in the political process. Depicting the new constitutions as attacks on democracy also overlooks the fact that voters in Pennsylvania overwhelmingly endorsed the changes in government.[13] That said, the constitutions did place new limits on the ways citizens exercised their sovereignty. Moreover, some of the men who supported the change in government clearly favored a more deferential form of politics in which average Americans trusted affairs of government to their social betters.[14] The emergence of parties, however, helped to drive record numbers of Pennsylvanians to the polls on election day. While the process of building a successful electoral coalition forced some reformers to moderate their positions, parties ultimately enabled citizens to assert their will on a scale not previously possible. Instead of arguing about whether these changes represented a "good" or a "bad" development for American democracy, I am concerned with understanding how and why these changes took place. If, as Otto von Bismarck famously put it, "politics is the art of the possible, the attainable," this book describes how Pennsylvanians discovered what was possible.[15]

Charting the trajectory of political mobilization can also help to clarify what did, and did not, change following the Revolution and the adoption of the federal Constitution. Historians including Jessica Roney and Barbara Clark Smith have convincingly demonstrated that many forms of mobilization often associated with the Revolution can be traced back to the colonial period. Meanwhile, Kenneth Owen argues that the same strategies Patriots used during the Revolution were employed in the late 1790s as a way to ensure that government remained responsive to the will of the people. A focus on continuity, however, overlooks the fact that while forms of political mobilization may have remained consistent, their meanings changed. The Revolution imbued traditional forms of mobilization with new authority as the people gained the right to participate directly in the deliberative process. Thus, a voluntary society in colonial Philadelphia might have given residents the opportunity to participate in civic life, but it did not claim to represent the will of the people. The meanings of different forms of political mobilization shifted again after the Constitution established voting as the only way for citizens to exercise their sovereignty. As a result, a public meeting in 1779 might have followed a similar format to one held in 1799, but whereas the former served as an opportunity for citizens to participate directly in the deliberative process, the latter was merely an opportunity to rally support for a candidate.[16]

A greater understanding of the shifting approaches to mobilization contributes to the growing body of scholarship that focuses on state formation as well. As historians including Christopher Pearl and Patrick Spero have demonstrated, the Revolution in Pennsylvania was driven, at least in part, by the breakdown of the colonial state. Due to population growth, corruption, factional squabbling, and ongoing fights with the crown and proprietors, the prerevolutionary government was failing to fulfill even its most basic responsibilities. The absence of the state created a power vacuum, which opened the door for average Pennsylvanians to begin taking the law into their own hands. The Revolution was, therefore, about establishing more, not less, government. But as this book illustrates, while Pennsylvanians may have been united in their support for a functioning government, they divided when it came to the question of whether individual citizens had the right to intervene directly in the governing process. The expansive version of popular sovereignty that flourished in Pennsylvanian following the Revolution made it difficult for the state to assert its power. Ultimately, establishing a strong state—one that had the power to control the frontier, collect taxes, and generally enforce its will—required Pennsylvanians to redefine the role of the people. The creation of a powerful government, however, stoked fears of excessive centralization and led to the rise of an opposition movement that sought to give the people greater control over the political process. In the end, the emergence of parties helped to create a version of democracy that was compatible with state formation.[17]

To Organize the Sovereign People also bridges the gap between different generations of political historians. In the mid-twentieth century, the Pennsylvania Historical and Museum Commission published a trio of studies on revolutionary and early national Pennsylvania that defined the political history of the Keystone State for a generation. The books, authored by Robert Levere Brunhouse, Harry M. Tinkcom, and Sanford W. Higginbotham, provided a comprehensive overview of the debates surrounding the 1776 constitution, the rise of political parties, and the schism in the Republican Party. The studies are, however, top-down in nature and focus on a relatively narrow definition of what constituted politics.[18] Partially as a response to the perceived elite bias inherent in this approach, the "new political historians" began experimenting in the 1960s and 1970s with methodologies from political science as a way to gain insight into the political views of average Pennsylvanians. Often relying on quantitative evidence, these scholars offered new perspectives on constituents' behavior by studying voting returns and analyzing the socioeconomic conditions that led to the growth of parties.[19] The scope of political history expanded even further following the so-called cultural turn in history. The "new new political historians," who gained prominence during the 1990s and 2000s, concentrated more on political culture and utilized methodologies from anthropology and other disciplines to broaden the definition of what constituted "politics" and demonstrated that even the smallest of actions could reflect political choices. This approach opened the door for the exploration of the political lives of women and other groups who lacked access to the ballot box.[20] Each generation of political historians has uncovered rich new details about Pennsylvania during the Revolution and early republic.[21] There remains, however, a disconnect between what we know about politics indoors and what we know about politics out of doors. This study seeks to fill this void by considering both cultural and institutional perspectives to show how political practices shaped, and were shaped by, the debate over the meaning of popular sovereignty.

A history of democracy in revolutionary American faces a number of interpretative challenges, not the least of which is that no Americans would have described their society as a democracy before the 1790s. In fact, Americans rarely used the word, and when they did it was almost always in the context of a form of government to be avoided. Democracies, they believed, bred chaos and violence. Yet of all the states, Pennsylvania came the closest to what we would consider a democracy today. The 1776 constitution represented what one scholar has called a "radical manifesto" that granted near universal suffrage to adult males, provided for annual elections, established term limits, and gave citizens the right to issue binding instructions to their representatives. Even after the adoption of a new constitution in 1790, the commonwealth had some of the most liberal franchise laws in the nation.[22]

There are, however, significant qualifications to the notion of revolutionary Pennsylvania as a democracy. While Pennsylvanians spoke of a government founded on the consent of the people generally, in reality only a segment of the population could participate in the political process. Indeed, democracy and exclusion appeared to go hand in hand. Unlike neighboring New Jersey, where women with sufficient property could cast ballots, Pennsylvania election laws specified that only taxpaying men over the age of twenty-one (and their adult male children) could vote. Although the state adopted a gradual emancipation act in 1780, the 1800 census lists more than a thousand men and women who remained enslaved. Theoretically, free African American men who paid taxes could vote, but how many actually did so remains unclear.[23]

Despite these glaring limitations, the amorphous nature of "the people" that lay at the heart of the theory of popular sovereignty made it possible for a relatively small group of men to claim to speak for the people as a whole. As I show, political mobilization played a key role in this act of democratic transubstantiation. Public demonstrations of support such as a town meeting, a public celebration, or a petition drive helped to legitimize an individual's or a group's claims to represent the will of the people. In short, those who could mobilize the people could speak for the people.

"The people," of course, is a construct, and it can sometimes obscure more than it reveals. The term is rarely used to describe every single person. Instead, implicit and explicit limitations are usually placed on who exactly is part of the people. These restrictions take on extra importance in a democracy as they define whose voices matter. In fact, many times the same men who pushed for a more participatory form of politics also advocated for greater restrictions on who could participate. This apparent contradiction stemmed from one of the inherent challenges of establishing a government based on the principle of popular sovereignty: if the regime derived its authority from the people, then any dissent threatened to undermine its legitimacy. One way to address this problem was to focus on forms of mobilization that highlighted support while at the same time taking steps to define anyone who disagreed as being outside the boundaries of the people. Questions about how to define the people in Pennsylvania were, therefore, intertwined with changing approaches to political mobilization.[24]

In the early years of the Revolution, radicals defended their vision for the state by enforcing a limited definition of the people that prevented many critics of the 1776 constitution from taking part in the political process. In the 1780s, moderates seized on these restrictions as a way to undermine radicals' claims to speak for the people. In the process, moderates began to advance a more expansive version of "the people," and once in power, they restored the franchise to thousands of Pennsylvanians who had been barred from casting a ballot. Arguments continued over who was included within the boundaries of the people following the adoption of the new federal and state constitutions. In the wake of the French Revolution, some Federalists began arguing that political radicals and immigrants, who tended to support Federalists' opponents, posed a threat to the country. As a result, Federalists started pushing a new version of the people that included strict limits on which immigrants could be considered as part of the people. Republicans, by contrast, welcomed immigrants into their coalition, and recent arrivals played a key role in Republicans' success at the polls.[25]

Many Pennsylvanians were left out of this struggle to define who could be part of the people. Women, for example, occupied an ambiguous place in the debate. As 50 percent of the population, women were clearly part of the people. At the same time, however, women lacked a direct voice in the political process. As a result, activists seeking to speak for the people looked for ways to symbolically incorporate women by including them in public rituals and celebrations.[26] Black Pennsylvanians faced their own restrictions. Although some reformers in the 1780s and 1790s believed that African Americans could be incorporated into the people, most Pennsylvanians appeared content to define the people as only those who were white.[27] As Pennsylvanians came to accept elections and parties as the voice of the people, these racial boundaries on who was part of the people became clearer.[28]

Rather than an investigation of the people themselves, this book is about the individuals who used political mobilization to position themselves as the spokesmen of the people. As such, it focuses primarily on the work of mid-level political activists who connected the realms of formal and informal politics. Newspaper editors, as the disseminators of information, played a particularly important role, as did local and state officials who had to remain in regular communication with voters. These individuals were the thought leaders who drove the change in constitutions and who helped build the first political parties. Although these men (and they were all men) came from different backgrounds, they were hardly representative of average Pennsylvanians. By emphasizing their contributions, I do not mean to suggest that other voices did not matter. Far from it. Political practices were formed from the top-down, bottom-up, and middle-out, and as this book demonstrates, approaches to political mobilization were shaped by a push-pull between "elite" and "ordinary" Pennsylvanians. In the end, parties triumphed not because the few manipulated the many (although that may have been the case in some instances), but because the party structure yielded tangible results when other approaches had failed.[29]

NEAR THE END of his life, Herman Husband wrote about the importance of leaving "a true and free republican government to our posterity."[30] The version of self-government forged in Pennsylvania following the Declaration of Independence no doubt fell far short of what Husband had envisioned. The New Jerusalem never materialized. Pennsylvanians did, however, succeed in establishing a representative government that could be passed on to future generations. Citizens, working through a political party, had gained the ability to effectively assert their will in a way that was compatible with the construction of a nation. Ultimately, this process was a story of neither declension nor democratization. Focusing on whether people became more—or less—free in the decades following the Declaration of Independence obscures the struggles associated with translating the theory of popular sovereignty into a stable and effective political system that balanced liberty and order. Recapturing this process and gaining a better understanding of how and why political parties and elections emerged as the primary vehicles for the expression of the public will is not only an important part of understanding the history of revolutionary America, but at a time when America's democratic institutions and norms face unprecedented threats, it can also serve as an important reminder of what it takes to ensure that we continue to pass along a "true and free republican government to our posterity."

1

"The Mobility Triumphant"

The Revolutionary Regime

On 15 May 1776, a dejected James Allen confided in his diary that "peace is at a great distance & this will probably be a terrible Summer." A member of one of the most prominent families in Philadelphia, Allen had just learned that he had been selected as a member of the Colonial Assembly to represent Northampton County. Although the work of an assemblyman was not glamorous to begin with, Allen had a particularly good reason to dread the post. As the country appeared to careen toward independence, he, like most of the Pennsylvanian gentry, remained committed to the crown. Allen had, in fact, made himself "very obnoxious to the independents" because of his vocal opposition to a separation from Great Britain. Fearful of what kind of chaos a break from the mother country might unleash, Allen resolved to "oppose [independence] vehemently in the Assembly." As it turned out, however, members of the assembly would be relegated to the role of spectators. The people themselves would be leading the Revolution.[1]

This chapter explores how Patriots in Pennsylvania used popular mobilization to overcome opposition from a conservative Colonial Assembly and launch a revolutionary experiment in self-government. Following their split with Great Britain, Pennsylvanians adopted a radically democratic frame of government which established that, while citizens might select representatives, the people always retained the right to intervene in the governing process. This authority extended beyond what historian Barbara Clark Smith has identified as colonial Americans' right to consent "after the fact" by serving on a jury or participating in crowd action. Under the new constitution, the people would have the right to engage directly in the governing process through town meetings and binding instructions to elected officials.[2]

This expansive view of popular sovereignty provoked controversy from its inception. Political moderates attacked the new regime as unstable and dangerous, and they campaigned vigorously for reforms. In response, radicals employed a variety of mobilization strategies—including populist rhetoric, voluntary societies, petitions, town meetings, and violence—to defend their vision for the state. At the same time that they sought to enforce the will of the people, radicals also adopted a series of Test Laws designed to ensure that "the people" really only meant those who supported the new constitution. This approach to mobilization helped radicals establish themselves as the agents of the people and forestall attempts to change the constitution. The frequent appeals to the sovereign power of the people, however, created a turbulent political atmosphere that made the actual process of governing difficult. Although some Pennsylvanians appeared willing to tolerate these shortcomings in the name of democracy, the regime's failures became hard to ignore within a few years.

The Road to Revolution

Pennsylvania arrived late to the Revolution. Long after Americans in other colonies had decided to embrace independence, officials in the Pennsylvania Assembly remained committed to finding a way to reconcile with Great Britain. The colony had joined with its neighbors in the protest of the Stamp Act of 1765 and participated in the economic boycott of English goods following the Townshend Revenue Acts and Tea Acts, but no major widespread rioting or mob action had occurred. Thanks in part to the disproportionate number of men elected from the three original counties of Bucks, Chester, and Philadelphia, Quakers and men with commercial ties to Great Britain dominated the Colonial Assembly and managed to steer a middle course between condemning the actions of Parliament and advocating for a more confrontational stance. The Pennsylvania Assembly was, in fact, the only colonial legislature that did not establish a committee of correspondence.[3]

Beneath the colony's peaceful veneer, however, the seeds of the Revolution had begun to take root. The first stirrings of what would become the Revolution occurred in the western parts of the colony, where longstanding frustrations that stemmed from inadequate representation in the Colonial Assembly combined with simmering ethnic and religious rivalries to create a particularly tense environment. The region had been plagued by waves of violence since the outbreak of the French and Indian War in 1754. The Treaty of Paris that supposedly ended the war had done little to improve the situation. In fact, things had appeared to get worse as colonists and Native Americans engaged in a series of escalating attacks and counterattacks. The crown's efforts to secure peace along the frontier left many settlers feeling as though the king cared more about protecting Native Americans than ensuring the safety of his own subjects. The situation was exacerbated by widespread corruption, competing land claims, and local rivalries. The colonial state appeared helpless in the face of the growing crisis as pleas from desperate settlers for assistance from the assembly, which was controlled by pacifist Quakers, went unheeded. As a result, westerners felt they had no choice but to act themselves.[4]

In the mid-1760s, armed Pennsylvanians began using force to defend themselves against what they saw as an existential threat posed by the Native Americans. In 1763, the Paxton Boys massacred a group of Conestoga Native Americans and then marched toward Philadelphia. Two years later, the "Black Boys" attacked a supply wagon loaded with diplomatic presents for Native Americans. The group struck again in 1769. These disparate examples of a community taking the law into its own hands pointed to a growing dissatisfaction with the status quo and laid the foundation for what would happen next.[5]

In the 1770s, as the imperial crisis with England intensified, Pennsylvanians began forming Associations—volunteer militia companies—to, as one group from Lancaster put it, "learn the art of Military discipline, to enable them to support and defend their just Rights and Privileges, against all arbitrary and dispotic Invasions, by any Person or Persons whatsoever." Because these groups operated outside the established legal framework, their legitimacy hinged on establishing a broad base of support. Scots-Irish Presbyterians and other groups that had traditionally been excluded from the halls of power flocked to the companies. For these men, participation in the Associations offered a chance to assert their political power and push back against the Quaker and Anglican elite who typically monopolized colonial offices. Following tradition, each company elected its own officers, which helped to establish legitimacy and demonstrate the popular support for the movement.[6]

After first taking hold in the west, the Associator movement quickly spread throughout the colony. In Philadelphia, a central committee, which eventually grew to consist of one hundred men, emerged as the de facto head of the movement and helped coordinate protests with neighboring colonies. Although moderates and men of standing served on the Philadelphia Committee, their influence waned with every new report from England, resulting in leadership passing to a new group of men. As historian Richard A. Ryerson has demonstrated, the committee movement attracted a wide array of Philadelphians who had not participated in the colonial government. These individuals came from a diverse economic background and helped to infuse the movement with an energy and a willingness to challenge the status quo.[7]

The differences between the conservative assembly, whose authority stemmed from the colonial charter and the crown, and the more radical Associators, who derived their power from the people out of doors, came into stark relief in early 1776. Frustrations with colonial leadership and anger at the distribution of representatives in the assembly led the Associators and their allies to begin openly challenging the legitimacy of the colonial government. In February, the Philadelphia Committee issued a call for a provincial convention to discuss the adoption of a new constitution. In a last-ditch effort to stave off a revolution, the assembly responded by voting to enlarge itself by adding seventeen new members to be distributed among the various underrepresented portions of the colony. These seats would be filled by an off-cycle election scheduled for 1 May. Considering that moderates held a narrow majority in the assembly, the results of the election could very well tip the balance of power. As a result, the Philadelphia Committee agreed to postpone its call for a convention until after the May election. The future of independence in Pennsylvania, it appeared, hinged on the results of the upcoming contest.[8]

Populism and the Rhetoric of a Revolution

On the morning of 1 May 1776, Caesar Rodney, a delegate to the Second Continental Congress from Delaware, reported that "this day is like to produce as warm if not the warmest Election that ever was held in this City."[9] Given Pennsylvania's history of election-day riots, this was a telling statement.[10] The off-cycle election dominated political discussions for weeks. Newspaper articles imploring voters to turn out began appearing shortly after the assembly announced the date for the selection of the new members. The rhetoric, which had been ratcheting up for months, reached new levels as both sides looked for a way to galvanize their supporters. "Cato," writing in the *Pennsylvania Gazette,* assailed the members of the Philadelphia

Committee as agitators who peddled disinformation. "Like true quacks," Cato sneered, the Associators "are constantly pestering us with their additional doses till the stomachs of their patients begin wholly to revolt."[11] Writing as "The Forrester," Tom Paine responded by urging voters to "be not deceived. It is not a little that is at stake. Reconciliation will not now go down, even if it were offered." The truth about the monarchy had been revealed, he argued, and the question before voters was now whether they would choose slavery or freedom.[12]

Beyond simply revealing the stark ideological divide between the supporters and opponents of independence, the vigorous electioneering in the lead-up to the 1 May contest also brought to the surface festering class tensions. Colonial Pennsylvania had a reputation as the "best poor man's country" because of its relatively mild climate and fertile soil, but conditions had begun to change by the eve of the Revolution. In Philadelphia, wealth and property were becoming increasingly concentrated in the hands of a small number of rich merchants and financiers. Landlessness, meanwhile, was on the rise throughout the colony. An economic depression following the 1763 Treaty of Paris combined with Parliament's attempt to crack down on colonists' use of paper money exacerbated the colony's economic woes.[13]

Frustrations with the growing inequities and resentment toward the colonial elite erupted in the weeks before the contest. The heated rhetoric signaled a new phase in the march toward revolution as the debate progressively centered around which side actually represented the people of Pennsylvania. To help establish themselves as the true defenders of the people, proponents of independence increasingly relied on populist rhetoric.[14] "Independent" accused Cato and the other opponents of independence of representing the interests of the "better sort," who seemed to think that they "were made, ordained, constituted, appointed and predestined from the formation of the world to *govern*, and . . . *possess* the surface of this globe, and all its inhabitants."[15] Along similar lines, "Cassandra" claimed that opponents of independence comprised an "*aristocratical junto*" who sought to "make the common and middle class of people their *beasts of burden*." The people of Pennsylvania, however, had nobly refused "to be *ridden* by a *King, Lords* and *Commons*" and were not about "to take *Cato* and *his party* on their *backs*."[16] Another writer asserted that the men opposed to independence had "grown rich from *nothing at all*" and now sought to "keep every Thing" to themselves.[17] This type of rhetoric reduced the question of independence to a struggle between the many and the few, and encouraged Pennsylvanians to think of the battle with Great Britain as part of a larger campaign to prevent the elite from taking advantage of the people. Just as important, it established the Patriots as the real allies of the people.

Patriots also called into question whether the assembly actually reflected the will of the people by challenging the colony's suffrage laws. Colonial Pennsylvania had a relatively low property requirement of fifty acres, and scholars estimate that between 50 and 60 percent of adult males held the franchise.[18] Many of the Associators, however, appear not to have met this threshold. The fact that men who would willingly sacrifice their lives in defense of the colony could not cast a ballot while other Pennsylvanians who could vote refused to fight infuriated the partisans of independence. Patriots used this point to further emphasize that they stood for the rights of the people. "An Elector" declared "that every citizen who has armed and associated to defend the Commonwealth is, and should be an Elector; *and every non-associator and stickler for dependency on the power that is now in actual depredation of our Rights, Liberties, and all that is dear to us should be* KEPT FAR FROM OUR COUNCILS."[19] In other words, only those who were willing to stand up for the rights of the people should be able to vote. While couched as a matter of principle, the fact that such a change in the election law would also almost guarantee a pro-independence victory was likely not lost on anyone.[20]

The increasingly radical and classist tenor of the debate alarmed some Pennsylvanians. Even men who had originally been inclined to support independence began to worry about the direction of the movement. James Allen, who considered himself a moderate, found the "thinking people, uneasy, irresolute & inactive," which left the "the Mobility triumphant." Passion, rather than reason, appeared to drive most people. Allen professed that he continued to "love the Cause of liberty" but saw "the madness of the multitude [as] but one degree better than submission to the Tea-Act."[21] Men like Allen may have shared some of the same grievances as those who demanded independence, but they believed that political movements required strong leadership and top-down organization. Without proper direction, the "Cause of liberty" could spiral into anarchy.[22]

Pennsylvanians turned out in droves to cast their ballots in what had become a referendum on independence and the role of the people.[23] In Philadelphia, residents continued to line up at the State House well past dark, and a near riot ensued when the sheriff tried to shut the doors before everyone had had a chance to vote. When the ballots were finally tallied, neither side could claim a complete victory. Supporters of independence picked up seats in the west but suffered a stinging defeat in Philadelphia where moderates won three of the four open seats. Although Tom Paine and other proponents of independence claimed that they only lost the election in Philadelphia because the sheriff managed to prevent a number of people from voting, officials certified the results. Supporters of reconciliation would therefore maintain a small majority in the assembly. Patriots' attempts to use the election to establish themselves as the true spokesmen of the people had fallen short. Pennsylvania, it appeared, would not to be joining the Revolution.[24]

Taking It to the People: Town Meetings

The results of the 1 May election seemed to indicate that Pennsylvanians were not ready to challenge the status quo. Instead of admitting defeat, however, Patriots argued the election simply provided more evidence that the existing system privileged the elite. Building on the populist rhetoric employed during the campaign, radicals decided to ignore the results of the election and take the question of independence directly to the people.

A series of developments in the days following the vote helped to bolster the pro-independence movement. On 10 May, the Second Continental Congress began debating a resolution that called on Americans to adopt "such a government as shall in the best opinion of the representatives of the people, best conduce to the happiness and safety of their constituents in particular, and America in general." At the insistence of moderates, however, Congress had specified that the resolution applied only to colonies "where no government sufficient to the exigencies of their affairs have been hitherto established." Pennsylvania's conservative delegation felt confident that their assembly met these conditions and happily supported the resolution. But before its final passage, John Adams slipped in a preamble that declared the practice of swearing an oath to the king of England as "absolutely irreconcilable to reason and good conscience" and stated that it was "necessary that the exercise of every kind of authority under the said crown should be totally suppressed." Considering that members of the assembly swore allegiance to the king and derived their powers from the crown, the preamble left little doubt that Congress believed Pennsylvania needed a new government. The full resolution, including the preamble, passed on 15 May.[25]

Around the same time, Pennsylvanians also received reports that the king had hired Hessian mercenaries to help suppress the rebellion in the colonies. The news dealt a blow to the residents who had continued to see the king as an ally. Patriots pounced on the reports as evidence of the king's bloodlust.[26] Shortly thereafter, a British warship entered the Delaware River and exchanged fire with Pennsylvanian gunboats. Rumors had circulated that the British planned a massive operation to capture a coastal city, and residents panicked as the sound of cannon fire echoed throughout the City of Brotherly Love. Although the warship left without attacking Philadelphia, the incident left the city's inhabitants unnerved and brought the realities of the conflict with England home.[27]

Energized by these developments, supporters of independence immediately began discussing how to implement the congressional resolution. On 15 May, the day Congress officially adopted Adams's preamble, "a very large number of persons" met at the Philosophical Society in Philadelphia to discuss "the taking up & forming [of] new governments in ye Different Collonies." After deliberating for a day, the group "concluded to call a convention with speed" and agreed to "protest against the present Assembly's doing any business" in the interim. Before proceeding with their plan, however, they decided to call for a general town meeting to occur on 20 May so that they could "take the sense of the People" on the question of independence.[28]

Pennsylvanians had assembled to discuss important topics several times in the preceding years. With moderates and conservatives controlling politics indoors, radicals had frequently used public meetings to rally support for their causes. For example, close to eight thousand residents crammed into the State House Yard in 1774 to protest the Tea Act.[29] The meeting scheduled for 20 May 1776 was, however, different from those that had come before. Not only did it call on the public to specifically consider independence, but it effectively ignored the fact that "the sense of the People" had been expressed at the ballot box fewer than three weeks earlier. Calling for the town meeting to discuss the same subject, therefore, sent the message that the people could intervene directly in the deliberative process, even if that meant overruling the results of their own election.

The notion that the people could speak outside of the election was not totally unheard of at the time. Colonial Americans had established various informal ways of "consenting after the fact" to laws. Juries, for instance, could refuse to enforce a law deemed unjust. Similarly, a mob might prevent the collection of a tax seen as unfair. But the idea that a town meeting could address such an important question as independence, particularly when it involved ignoring the fact that voters had already spoken, represented something new and signaled a fundamental shift in how Pennsylvanians understood the role of the people.[30]

The Alarm, printed in both English and German, laid out the justification for using a town meeting to decide the future of the colony. The pamphlet argued that, although the assembly might claim to speak for the people, "the people have not *yet*, by any public act of theirs, transferred them" such power. In fact, according to the resolutions adopted in Congress, the assembly no longer exercised any power whatsoever. It was, therefore, "now high time to come to some settled point that we may call ourselves a people; for in the present unsettled state of things we are only a decent multitude." Pennsylvanians, the pamphlet declared, must join together "as a *legal people*" at the town meeting and assert their "natural rights" by calling for a "grand provincial convention to establish a government on the AUTHORITY of the PEOPLE."[31]

Despite heavy rain, thousands of Philadelphians turned out for the meeting on the morning of 20 May. A temporary stage had been erected for the occasion, and the crowd first listened to a series of speeches by prominent supporters of independence. Colonel Daniel Roberdeau, the moderator, then began to read the resolves of Congress. Before he finished the first sentence, however, the crowd burst into applause and cheers. This type of audience participation, which organizers included in printed accounts of the gathering, helped to legitimize the proceedings and reenforce the notion that the meeting represented the will of the people. Once the noise subsided, Roberdeau introduced a series of resolves which stated "that the Assembly was not a Body properly constituted, authorized and qualified to carry the Resolve for instituting a new Government into Execution and therefore that a Convention should be call'd." All but one of those in attendance voted to support the resolves. (The lone dissenter was "insulted and abused" for his refusal to vote with the majority, a warning to anyone with misgivings about independence.) With that, the crowd voted to overturn the colonial government.[32]

At the conclusion of the meeting, organizers dispatched riders to the backcountry to carry copies of the resolves and distribute broadsides and pamphlets. Patriots throughout the colony responded by holding their own meetings to endorse the resolves and select a delegate to attend a provincial conference. Perhaps more importantly, committees representing the Associators and various volunteer militia companies met and expressed their support for the plan. In Lancaster County, after the "resolves were deliberately read and approved by the battalion, [and] as a further testimony of their hearty approbation of the measures adopted gave three cheers." In Philadelphia, the Committee of Privates gathered on 6 June and voted unanimously in favor of establishing "a free and independent State."[33] Twelve days later, representatives from the different counties approved a plan to organize a constitutional convention to begin on 15 July.[34] The people, through direct participation in town meetings, had spoken. In so doing, they set the precedent that direct forms of mobilization such as town meetings carried more authority than indirect forms of mobilization such as the results of an election. As one writer in the *Pennsylvania Gazette* put it, "the revolution is now begun."[35]

The Radical Program

On 28 September 1776, delegates to Pennsylvania's constitutional convention, a motley crew of men with little governing experience, voted to adopt the country's most radically democratic form of government. The document opened with "A Declaration of the Rights of the Inhabitants of the Commonwealth of Pennsylvania" that laid out the principles undergirding the new regime. After establishing that "all men are born equally free and independent" and providing for freedom of religion, it stated "that the people of this State have the sole, exclusive and inherent right of governing and regulating the internal police of the same." Furthermore, the declaration asserted "that all power being originally inherent in, and consequently derived from, the people; therefore all officers of government, whether legislative or executive, are their trustees and servants, and at all times accountable to them." Citizens would, moreover, have "the right to assemble together, to consult for their common good, [and] to instruct their representatives." While much of the language in the rest of the Declaration of Rights had appeared in Virginia's Declaration of Rights (which had been adopted a few months earlier), the language granting Pennsylvanians the right to instruct their representatives was unique. Taken together, the declaration clearly established that ultimate authority always rested with the people and that, while they might delegate some authority to their elected officials, the people always had the right to assert their will directly.[36]

The actual frame of government that followed the Declaration of Rights reflected this expansive version of popular sovereignty. The constitution established a unicameral legislature, eliminated the office of the governor, called for annual elections, and set term limits for elected officials. Perhaps most notably, the constitution granted suffrage to "every freeman of the full age of twenty-one Years" who had paid taxes and lived in the state for a year.[37] The adult male children of freeholders could also vote even if they did not pay taxes. This change in suffrage would mean that approximately 90 percent of adult males in Pennsylvania would, at least according to the constitution, have access to the franchise. These features represented a sharp break from traditional republican theory, which favored restrictions on the popular branch of government and tied voting to property.[38]

The constitution included other measures designed to ensure that government remained responsive to the will of the people as well. Section 15 required that "all bills of public nature shall be printed for the consideration of the people," and that bills "shall not be passed into laws until the next session of the assembly" to ensure that the people had a chance to weigh in on the matter. As one supporter explained, although this rule made the process of adopting legislation slow and cumbersome, it ensured that citizens would "have the perusal, and consequent approbation of every law."[39]

As a final safeguard against corruption, the constitution stipulated that a specially elected Council of Censors would meet every seven years to "enquire whether the constitution has been preserved inviolate in every part" and to investigate whether elected officials had "performed their duty as guardians of the people."[40] The council would also have the exclusive power to propose amendments or call for a new convention. According to backers of the constitution, the existence of this type of independent body would help to prevent "rulers from embezzling your money, or employing it to corrupt your virtue, and undermine your liberties."[41]

For all its democratic features, however, it is unclear that the constitution actually reflected the will of the people of Pennsylvania. In the first place, voters had to swear an oath renouncing their allegiance to King George III and promise to support the establishment of an independent government in order to participate in the selection of delegates to the constitutional convention. This requirement effectively barred undecided or moderate voters, along with members of religious sects (such as the Society of Friends and German pietistic sects) opposed to the swearing of oaths, and ensured that radicals dominated the convention. Architects of the new constitution justified these exclusions by arguing that only those who stood ready to protect the state deserved the right to participate.

Delegates did not submit their work to the people for approval either. Instead, the convention simply proclaimed that the constitution would now be law of the land. Pennsylvanians would have to wait seven years for the Council of Censors to convene before they would have an opportunity to express their views.[42]

These undemocratic components did not end with the launching of the new government. The delegates also put restrictions on who would be able to participate in future elections. All voters would have to swear an oath promising to support the constitution before they could cast a ballot on election day. Additionally, all elected officials would have to swear that they would "not directly or indirectly do any act or thing prejudicial or injurious to the constitution or government thereof." Radicals would adopt a series of these "Test Laws" over the next few years. In theory, the restrictions would protect the regime from Loyalists who sought to sabotage the new government. In practice, the oaths had the effect of disenfranchising anyone uncomfortable with the direction of the Revolution or who had religious qualms about taking oaths. Although exact numbers are hard to come by, scholars have estimated that the Test Laws excluded up to one-half of the voters in some parts of the state.[43] In addition to being barred from voting, these non-jurors, as they were known, could not sit on juries, sue for debts, or legally purchase real estate. They were, however, still required to pay taxes and were subject to the same laws as everyone else. Non-jurors also faced constant harassment and ran the risk of being labeled traitors. If the constitution established that all power was "derived from, the people," then the Test Laws effectively defined the people as only those who supported the new regime. Pennsylvania's radical experiment in self-government was, therefore, built on the exclusion of large numbers of potential voters.[44]

The Moderate Counteroffensive

Not surprisingly, given its radicalism and the restrictions on who could participate, the publication of the new constitution in the fall of 1776 precipitated an immediate backlash from more moderate Patriots. Benjamin Rush declared that Pennsylvania had "substituted a mob government to one of the happiest governments of the world."[45] Even John Adams, who had helped engineer the overthrowing of the Colonial Assembly, expressed concern that the state would "be divided and weakened, and rendered much less vigorous in the Cause, by the wretched Idea of Government, which prevail, in the Minds of many People in it."[46] Men like Rush and Adams believed that the people should have the right to choose their own government, but they saw the state constitution as a reckless experiment that would lead to chaos and disorder. Liberty, they thought, required order, and in a representative government, popular passion had to be balanced with reason and good judgment. By not putting effective safeguards against the passions of the people, the constitution left the forces of democracy unchecked, a situation they feared could easily lead to the many taking advantage of the few. The Test Laws already signaled that the new regime cared little for the civil liberties of dissidents.[47]

Moderate Patriots, however, faced a challenge in developing a strategy for opposing the new constitution. Not only did they not want to take any action that might be deemed illegitimate or contrary to the will of the people as a whole, but they also had to contend with the ongoing war with Great Britain. As a result, moderates had to balance their concerns about the new government with the need to protect the larger revolutionary project.[48]

The campaign against the new constitution began with a series of town meetings. Like the meetings used to topple the Colonial Assembly, these gatherings helped to legitimize moderates' concerns. Residents assembled at the Court House in Carlisle on 8 October and resolved that they would not take the oath to support the new government.[49] A reported 1,500 people turned out for a meeting at the State House in Philadelphia on 21 October to discuss a series of resolutions that criticized the convention and constitution. After deliberating for a day, "a great Majority" of those in attendance voted to support thirty different resolutions that accused the convention of usurping "powers with which they were not entrusted by the people" and labeled the constitution "confused, inconsistent, and dangerous." Declaring that Pennsylvanians "did not desire such *strange innovations*," the resolutions demanded immediate amendments and called on all voters, judges, and elected officials to boycott the upcoming elections by refusing to take the oath supporting the new regime. Similar to what the Patriots had done following the May meeting, organizers formed committees tasked with distributing copies of the resolutions throughout the state at the conclusion of the assembly.[50]

The opposition to the new government quickly spread as a result of these coordinated mobilization efforts. Moderates in Cumberland County adopted a resolution declaring, "We are of the Opinion that the Constitution formed by the late Convention is Inconsistent with the principles of free government."[51] Election inspectors throughout the state ignored the Test Laws and allowed voters to cast ballots without taking the oath. In some areas, voters appear to have boycotted the election altogether. Judges and sheriffs likewise refused to take the oath, which effectively left those offices vacant. Moderates elected to the assembly agreed to take a compromise oath that left the door open for them to pursue changes to the constitution. Even then, the entire delegation from Bedford County walked out of the assembly, arguing that the body was "not representatives of the people" because of the number of voters excluded by the Test Laws. The widespread boycott of public offices left the new regime crippled, and basic government functions ground to a halt in some places.[52]

Political radicals, who stood united in support of the constitution, railed against their opponents and accused them of trying to sabotage the new government, but a government that claimed to represent the will of the people could not ignore the public outcry for long. In June 1777, the assembly, which radicals controlled by a wide margin, agreed to submit the question of a new convention to the people. The language of the resolution calling for a convention was telling and suggested that radicals worried about their ability to mobilize supporters. Instead of asking voters to cast a ballot on the question at their normal polling locations, the assembly directed each district to appoint a commissioner who would "go [to] the house or place of residence of each and every Freeman" and ask all legal voters "whether he desires another Convention be now called."[53] Even though supporters of the constitution would have a clear advantage because only those who had taken the oath would be allowed to participate, the requirement that commissioners visit residents' houses points to the fact that, while supporters of the constitution may have been able to mobilize supporters for a public rally, they appeared less confident when it came to translating these demonstrations into electoral victories.

Before the commissioners could begin to survey voters, however, the constitution faced a more immediate threat: on 26 September 1777, after defeating George Washington's forces at the Battle of Brandywine, the British Army under the command of General William Howe entered the City of Brotherly Love. The occupation forced moderates to put their crusade against the constitution on hold. Shortly before Howe's arrival, the assembly voted to give the Executive Council broad new powers and agreed to postpone the vote on a new convention.[54]

Although moderates had agreed to set their concerns with the constitution temporarily aside, the yearlong campaign against the new government underscored the challenges associated with founding a government based on the principle of popular sovereignty. The public displays of dissent threatened to undermine the legitimacy of the regime. In order to defend the constitution, radicals would need to find a way to mobilize their supporters to demonstrate that the government remained the voice of the people.

Conventions and Petitions: The Battle for the Constitution

Debates over the future of self-government in Pennsylvania resumed shortly after the British evacuated Philadelphia in June 1778. Moderates argued that the occupation more clearly laid bare the failures of the regime. The fact the British had so easily captured Philadelphia demonstrated the need for clear leadership and a government with the authority and power to protect its people. Radicals tried to deflect these attacks by portraying their critics as Loyalists and accusing them of consorting with the enemy, but support for a new convention continued to grow. In November 1778, moderates in the assembly managed to push through a resolution calling for a vote on the question of a convention the following April.[55]

Radicals had good reason to be concerned about the results of such a referendum. Unlike the previous resolution, this one would require voters to visit their polls and cast their ballots in person. Moderates had picked up a number of seats in the election of 1778, and radicals feared that they would be unable to mobilize enough voters to defeat the referendum at the ballot box. To simply boycott the vote, however, would only give moderates complete control over the drafting of a new constitution. A lopsided vote in favor of the moderates would also further erode public trust in the government. Backed into a corner, radicals responded by appealing directly to the people.

On 3 February 1779, the *Pennsylvania Gazette* printed an open letter addressed "to the INHABITANTS of PENNSYLVANIA" calling for a statewide petition campaign to force the assembly to cancel the referendum. Signed by "A MULTITUDE," the letter argued that the "former Convention was fairly and regularly chosen" and that the constitution it wrote reflected the will of the people. While admitting that no government is perfect, the writer accused "a few discontents" of trying to "unhinge what was done" and throw the state into chaos. Furthermore, the constitution already had a provision for making changes (the Council of Censors).

Calling a new convention would "cost the State a good many thousand pounds" and result in an increase in taxes. Given these difficulties, along with the persistent threat of another invasion, the letter writers urged Pennsylvanians to instruct their representatives to stop wasting "away our time in endless and frivolous disputes about the propriety or impropriety of a Convention" and instead focus on defeating the "vermin and British beasts of prey." The people, the letter concluded, must assert their will through a petition and demand that the assembly "rescind this resolve [calling for a referendum], and drop the affair."[56]

The petition was, of course, not a new form of mobilization. Pennsylvanians had been petitioning their leaders since the colony's founding in 1682. The 1701 Charter of Privileges granted the Colonial Assembly the right to "redress Grievances" expressed by residents. In the subsequent decades, Pennsylvanians sent petitions that covered a wide variety of topics. While many of the communications dealt with very specific concerns such as disputes over land or the placement of a road, others addressed larger issues. In 1728, for example, nearly two hundred residents living in the western parts of the colony signed a petition begging for the creation of a new county. These supplications, however, had no real authority, and colonial officials were free to ignore the requests.[57] Despite these restrictions, one Pennsylvanian reported in the years leading up to the Revolution that "town meetings (in imitation of the orderly republicans of Boston) have lately become a popular device for giving instructions" to elected officials.[58] The practice of issuing instructions gained legal sanction under the 1776 constitution, and although the details of what this right meant in practice remained vague, the petition seemed an obvious example of how the people could assert their authority over the deliberative process. For radicals, therefore, the petition offered an ideal way to short-circuit the convention movement by giving the people a chance to weigh in directly.[59]

To help oversee the public campaign to block a convention, radicals organized a new voluntary society called the Constitutional Society. Members of the group, which appears to have been a reconstituted version of the Whig Society (which formed in early 1777 but ceased to meet later the same year), pledged to "use our endeavors to prevent any infringements, violation, or illegal alteration" of "any rights" laid out in the constitution. The group also announced that it would establish a committee of correspondence with other parts of the state and began penning articles defending the democratic principles embodied in the constitution. Like petitioning, voluntary societies had a long history in Pennsylvania. Some of these organizations played important civic roles, but the establishment of the Constitutional Society, along with the more moderate Republican Society, marked the beginning of a new era of overtly partisan voluntary societies. These groups would play an increasingly important role in Pennsylvania politics in the coming decades.[60]

With the help of the Constitutional Society, remonstrances protesting the upcoming vote on a constitutional convention began pouring into the assembly. On a single day—27 February 1779—the legislature received petitions from Lancaster County (3,743 signatures), Germantown (310 signatures), Northumberland (192 signatures), Berks County (2,600 signatures), Cumberland County (357 signatures), and Northampton County (154 signatures). Many of the petitions echoed some of the same points made by "A Multitude." A remonstrance from York County, for example, argued that the call for a new convention "is Anticonstitutional and illegal and if Put into Execution would be Highly injurious to the common cause of liberty," while one from Lancaster warned that holding another constitutional convention would lead to nothing but "confusion and disorder."[61] Other petitions questioned the integrity of the members of the assembly who had supported the resolution calling for a new convention and suggested that they might be doing so for "the gratification of their own aspiring Ambition."[62]

Beyond just warning of the dangers of a convention and attacking the instigators, some of the petitions included a defense of the people's right to assert their will directly. A petition signed by "Sundry Inhabitants" explained that while some members of the assembly might think the state needed a stronger governor or an upper house, "we choose to retain the reins of Government in our own hands & Resolve that no other body of men, whatever wealth, influence or talents they may possess shall check, [or] control you" other than the "community at large." The people themselves, it explained, are as "competent Judges of the necessity & usefulness" of any proposed pieces of legislation. A petition from Bucks County put it more succinctly: "The power is radically with us." The petitions also made it clear that there would be consequences for ignoring the will of the people. One concluded by warning members of the assembly that if they "regard the tranquility of the state, or [their] own Honor & safety as members of it," then the body should immediately rescind the motion.[63]

The total number of signatures radicals gathered is staggering. In less than two months, supporters of the constitution collected more than sixteen thousand signatures.[64] A writer in the *Pennsylvania Packet* noted that this was "a far greater number than were ever known to manifest their dislike of any public proceedings by this mode heretofore."[65] Although remonstrances came from across the state, the largest number of signatures came from radical strongholds in the west. The sheer number of signatures collected in such a short time period, coupled with the fact that many of the petitions shared the same wording, served as a stark reminder of radicals' ability to harness popular forms of mobilization.

The deluge of petitions forced the assembly to take action. On Saturday, 27 February, noting that "a very considerable and respectable number of the Inhabitants of this Common-wealth" had expressed their opposition to the referendum, the assembly voted forty-seven to seven in favor of rescinding the original resolution. The seven voting in the minority, which included the archconservative Robert Morris, accused radicals of relying on "Solicitations, Misrepresentations, and other Artifices of designing Men" to dupe people into signing and suggested that many of the signatures might have been forged. They also protested that the number of Pennsylvanians who signed a petition represented only a fraction of the state's eligible voters and pointed out that some of the signers might not have had the right to vote. None of this appeared to matter to a majority of the assembly. The sovereign people had spoken.[66]

Committees and the Economy

Radicals may have managed to prevent the calling of a new convention, but the constitution still faced threats on several fronts. The war had wreaked havoc on the state's economy, and requisitions from both the British and Continental Armies left residents short on money and provisions. The increased demands and disruptions in trade had caused the cost of basic necessities and foodstuffs to increase steadily. By the winter, many residents had reached the point of desperation. Both urban and rural areas suffered. In January, more than one hundred armed sailors took to the streets of Philadelphia to demand higher wages. The same month, the people of Tincicum, a township in Bucks County, were forced to beg the assembly for relief because they could not even afford bread.[67] The constitution might have remained intact, but the people were suffering.

The crisis exposed the weaknesses of the government, and elected officials struggled with how to respond to the runaway inflation. Unwilling to confront the regime's shortcomings, radicals blamed merchants, who they accused of intentionally driving up the cost of goods to maximize profits. In January 1779, the Supreme Executive Council denounced the "heinously criminal" act of forestalling, or the buying up of goods to artificially raise prices and increase profits, and issued a proclamation "reprobating & prohibiting all such practices," but it also acknowledged that it lacked the power to take meaningful action. The assembly did not appear to have any answers either. Moderates, who held numerous seats, relied on merchants and traders for support, and they seemed determined to block any attempt to impose price controls. As a result, costs continued to rise, reaching new highs in early May.[68]

With elected officials seemingly powerless to help, residents decided to take matters into their own hands. On 22 May, a group of well-known radicals called for a general town meeting to discuss ways to rein in prices. Given the underlying tensions, some residents feared that the town meeting could lead to violence. Christopher Marshall, a prominent radical, went so far as to privately warn some officials that they should consider leaving town.[69] Elizabeth Drinker confided in her diary that a number of people were "apprehensive of a mob rising" targeting men accused of artificially inflating prices.[70] Her fears seemed justified when, the night before the meeting, someone blanketed the city with broadsides signed by "Come on Cooly" that warned, "We have turned out against the enemy and we will not be eaten up by monopolize[r]s and forestallers."[71]

Although the town meeting, which took place in the State House Yard on 24 May, did not degenerate into mob violence, the city's merchants and traders could hardly take comfort in what did occur. The meeting began with an address by General Roberdeau, the same man who had overseen the 20 May 1776 town meeting that led to the overthrowing of the Colonial Assembly. In his speech, Roberdeau blasted "monopolizers" for profiting from the misery of their countrymen and accused the state government of doing nothing to alleviate the suffering. Having energized the crowd, Roberdeau introduced a series of resolutions that called for the implementation of price controls. The costs of basic goods would be immediately returned to where they had been on 1 May and then gradually lowered until they reached their 1 January levels. To ensure that sellers adhered to these restrictions, the resolutions called for the creation of a series of committees composed of men elected by the community. These committees would wield broad powers and have the ability to investigate, and punish, anyone accused of price-gouging. They would also conduct investigations into what caused prices to increase in the first place and review how elected officials spent public money. Finally, the committees would be empowered to deal with anyone "who by sufficient testimony can be proved inimical to the interest and independence of the United States." Those in attendance unanimously agreed to the resolutions.[72]

Price control committees sprang into action throughout the state following the town meeting. Residents in York-Town, for example, gathered and voted to endorse the Philadelphia resolutions and called for the creation of "a Committee of three or more respectable persons" to oversee the implementation of price controls. Attendees then pledged to "support the Committee in the execution of their duty" and "suppress to the utmost of our power, and hazard of our lives, engrossing monopolizing, forestalling and depreciation."[73] In some cases, these meetings appear to have been the product of a grassroots movement; in others they were likely the work of a few well-connected men. Christopher Marshall, for example, participated in the Philadelphia town meeting before returning to Lancaster to serve as chair of a local committee. He later worked with local leaders to establish a committee in Northumberland County.[74]

Whether or not these price control committees formed organically, their rapid proliferation is one of the clearest examples of radicals' expansive definition of popular sovereignty. Elected officials had failed to control costs, and radicals argued that the time had come for the people to exercise their right to enforce the will of the community directly. It did not matter that the constitution did not specifically grant communities the right to regulate prices in this manner. According to radicals, in times of crisis the existing forms of justice proved "too slow in their operation." "We conceive," explained one writer, that there "can be no other [solution] than the discretionary power of the citizens, organized, and acting through a committee." It also did not matter that the assembly had not formally passed laws banning price-gouging. As one Philadelphia committee member put it, "There are offenses against a society which are not in all cases offenses against law." It was, he argued, a "maxim, that where the offence is publicly dangerous or injurious, and the laws unable to relieve or punish," the people had a right to act. The people, in short, always had the right to exercise their sovereignty directly.[75]

Some radicals went so far as to claim that the committees represented a purer expression of the public will, one that had not been filtered by the electoral process. "'Tis true their power is great," acknowledged "A Pennsylvanian," "but as they draw it immediately from the people," there was little chance that they would abuse it. In fact, because the committees gave more people an opportunity to participate in the governing process, "A Pennsylvanian" argued that they "encourage industry and patriotism" and "lay the foundations of tranquility and justice."[76] Far from representing a threat to the rule of law, for radicals this type of vigilantism was viewed as a sign of a healthy body politic.

While the price control committees claimed to derive their power from the sovereign will of the people, much of their actual authority came from the fact that they had the support of the militias. Local companies played a critical role in enforcing the dictates of the committees. For example, soldiers in Philadelphia arrested a dozen men accused of artificially inflating prices and/or sympathizing with the British following the 24 May town meeting. In a particularly brazen move, the militia even captured Levi Hollingsworth, one of the most prominent merchants in the city. After parading the prisoners throughout the city and subjecting them to various forms of painful and humiliating ritualized forms of punishment known as "rough music," soldiers deposited the prisoners at the jail to wait for the committee to convene. Some members of the militia appeared ready to go further than the traditional forms of rough music. One artillery company proclaimed, "We have arms in our hands, and know how to use them," and warned that "*our drums shall beat to arms*" if merchants and traders did not agree to the price controls.[77] These were not idle threats either. Elizabeth Drinker reported that "men with clubs &c. have been to several Stores obliging the people to lower their prices."[78]

Even with the threat of violence, some residents still resisted the price controls. Moderates condemned the committee movement and warned that the groups represented a dangerous step toward mob rule. As one critic put it, "Every man who takes a club in his hand to town meetings (which by-the-bye, have been very frequent of late) undertakes to be governor."[79] The committees also faced push-back from the business community. Artisans, in particular, balked at the attempts to regulate the prices of their wares. In early July, Philadelphia tanners, curriers, and cordwainers published an open letter complaining of "the extreme hardship and difficulty" they faced as a result of the price controls. They argued that because the cost of raw goods remained unchanged, the regulations would make it impossible for manufacturers and craftsmen to stay in business. Therefore, unless the committees lowered the prices of their materials, the artisans announced, "we do not consider ourselves bound by the regulated prices of our commodities."[80]

With support for the price controls wavering, radicals launched an even more ambitious campaign to save the economy. Once again bypassing the assembly, the Philadelphia committee called for a second town meeting to introduce "The Citizens Plan." Placing the blame for the state's economic woes on Congress, the plan called on the federal government to stop emitting paper money and gradually reduce the amount of currency in circulation. The plan was, in part, an acknowledgment of the limits of direct political action. While some unscrupulous sellers had likely used the economic situation to artificially raise their prices, Pennsylvania was part of an increasingly globalized economy, and costs were largely driven by market forces outside of the committees' control. Fixing the economy would require national coordination, something made difficult by the existing regime's emphasis on popular participation. Although those in attendance enthusiastically endorsed the plan "by a unanimous shew of hands," few people outside of Pennsylvania showed much interest in the idea. Ultimately, the Citizens Plan went nowhere, and Congress appears to have ignored the proposal entirely.[81]

Without the backing of Congress, the efforts to control prices collapsed. The committees did their best to punish anyone caught trying to evade the price controls, but their efforts proved futile. Merchants who wanted to avoid the price controls simply took their business elsewhere. Sensing the growing frustration with the committee, Philadelphia merchants and traders published an open letter on 10 September 1779 denouncing the price controls as "unjust" and a violation of "the laws of property." They agreed that the "deprecation of our money is the most capital inconvenience" but argued that committees had only exacerbated the problems.[82] Shortly thereafter, the Philadelphia committee announced that it would no longer try to enforce price controls and petitioned the assembly to request that it take action. The people, it appeared, could not fix this problem themselves.[83]

The experiment in popular control of the economy illustrates both strengths and weaknesses of a system that privileged direct political action. On the one hand, the committees provided Pennsylvanians with an opportunity to assert control over the cost of goods. On the other hand, the decentralized nature of the movement made it difficult, if not impossible, to address some of the larger national and international forces that shaped the economy. In the end, the price control committees did little more than exacerbate an already tense situation. The failure to regulate costs fueled the growing animosity between the laboring poor and the merchants and artisans, and increased tensions between radicals and moderates. The emphasis on direct political action combined with persistent economic hardship, lingering fears of Toryism, and supercharged rhetoric created an atmosphere ripe for violence.

Fort Wilson and the Threat of Popular Violence

The specter of political violence hung over Pennsylvania throughout the first years under the 1776 constitution. Independence was, after all, born out of a physical conflict with Great Britain, and violence remained one of the most potent forms of political mobilization. However, with the exception of the frontier, where white settlers and Native Americans frequently clashed, the Revolution in Pennsylvania was actually a relatively peaceful affair. Unlike the residents of Boston and New York City, Philadelphians had not participated in any major riots. The isolated examples of violence tended to be ritualized and directed at individuals suspected of aiding the British. Even in these instances, the attacks were limited, and with a few notable exceptions, no prominent moderates had been targeted. Critics of the regime still faced persecution but not violence. Even Robert Morris, a man reviled by many radicals and accused of price-gouging, was never assaulted. The political climate, however, changed following the collapse of the price controls.[84]

The first signs of an impending crisis came when a broadside appeared in Philadelphia in late August announcing that "the time has now arrived to prove whether the suffering friends of this country, are to be enslaved, ruined and starved, by a few overbearing Merchants, a swarm of Monopolizes and Speculators, an infernal gang of Tories." It called on all true Patriots "to rouse up as a Lyen out of his den" and punish those who had ignored the will of the community. Whereas the organizers of the original price-fixing meeting had urged residents to "Come on Cooly," this broadside ominously concluded "*Rouse! Rouse!* and COME ON WARMLY."[85]

On 27 September, two days after the price-fixing committee officially disbanded, members of the militia gathered in Philadelphia to discuss how to proceed. The cost of flour and other basic goods had spiked over the previous few weeks. Refusing to place the blame on the regime itself, the soldiers directed their ire toward British sympathizers and the families of exiled Loyalists. The fact that the families of men accused of siding with the British had been allowed to remain in Philadelphia had long been a point of contention, and some residents believed that the Loyalists had been using their wives to spy on the Patriots. The traditional rules of war, however, dictated that women and children were noncombatants. As a result, while they may have grumbled, most Patriots had accepted that the families of Loyalists would remain unmolested. With the city in crisis, however, the militia concluded that such tolerance could no longer be extended and decreed that the "wives and children of those men who had gone with the British or within British lines" should be immediately exiled. Desperate times called for desperate measures, and the people had the right to defend themselves.[86]

Even some leading radicals saw the militia's plot to target women and children as a reckless and dangerous provocation. When approached by the militia to oversee the operation, Charles Willson Peale, a captain and prominent member of the Constitutional Society, refused outright. He implored the soldiers to not go through with their plan and warned that "the taking of women and children from their homes would cause much affliction and grief." When his pleas failed to dissuade the militia, Peale left to collect two other well-known radicals to help try and talk the soldiers down. The three of them argued that exiling women and children was cruel and warned that such draconian measures could easily backfire and turn the public against the regime. The militia remained determined to press ahead, and Peale eventually concluded that "to reason with a multitude of devoted patriots assembled on such an occasion was in vain."[87]

The militia began rounding up suspected Tories on the afternoon of 4 October. A distraught Elizabeth Drinker reported that a mob seized her husband as she prepared supper. The soldiers then led him, along with other prisoners, "about the streets with the Drum after 'em beating the Rouges March."[88] The crowd swelled as the parade wound through town. Afraid that things would soon get out of control, General Thomas Mifflin, a widely respected political figure, attempted to intervene by speaking with one of the captains but was "struck or pushed" with a soldier's musket—a stunning act of insubordination and an indication that the men marching had no intention of listening to authorities.[89] The people themselves were now in charge.

As the militia continued to parade through the streets of Philadelphia, a group of outspoken critics of the radicals took shelter in the house of James Wilson, an outspoken moderate and member of the assembly. Afraid that they would become targets, Wilson and his compatriots had stockpiled muskets and barricaded themselves in the house. A militia captain sent word that he and his soldiers "had no intention to meddle with

Wilson or his house" and merely sought "to support the constitution, the laws, and the Committee of Trade," but the men remained holed up and ready to defend themselves if necessary. Even if the captain were telling the truth about his intentions, the men hunkered down knew there was no guarantee the rank and file would listen to their superiors. There was, therefore, an atmosphere of tense anticipation as the parade made its way toward the Wilson residence.[90]

There is a dispute about what happened next. According to eyewitnesses, the militia passed in front of the house and paused briefly to give "three cheers" as an assertion of their power. As the parade resumed, however, someone opened fire. One bystander reported that the shot came from inside the Wilson residence.[91] Another witness, however, claimed that someone had merely opened a window and waved a pistol, and that the first shot had come from the militia. Either way, the situation quickly escalated. Bystanders took shelter and a gunfight ensued between the soldiers in the street and the men at Wilson's house. Mifflin, who after the earlier incident had joined the other men hiding in Wilson's house, tried to order the soldiers to cease firing but was nearly hit by a bullet (the shooter later claimed that he had mistaken Mifflin "for some damned Tory").[92] After skirmishing for a few minutes, members of the militia began attempting to break down the door. When that effort failed, they called for a cannon. Some men did eventually make it into the house but were beaten back as they tried to go up the stairs. Before they could renew their attack, Joseph Reed, the president of the state, arrived with a cavalry and managed to restore order.[93] When the smoke finally cleared, six or seven men lay dead with another fourteen wounded. The majority of the casualties were among the militia.[94]

In many ways, the events of 4 October 1779, known as Fort Wilson's Riot, represented a logical outgrowth of radicals' approach to political mobilization. Radicals had repeatedly told Pennsylvanians that ultimate power rested with the people, and they had encouraged residents to take matters into their own hands on a number of occasions. It is no surprise either that the militia blamed Loyalists and their families for their suffering. Radicals had fed residents a regular diet of anti-Tory propaganda and often blamed the regime's shortcomings on the British. Defenders of the state constitution had also spent years portraying their opponents as closet Tories and enemies of the people. Still, the fact that the militia had so blatantly ignored the orders from Peale and other leading radicals set a dangerous precedent. Taken together, the incident served as a stern reminder of the dangers inherent in the regime's expansive version of popular sovereignty.[95]

Slavery, Race, and the People

In the short term, radicals did not appear to suffer any consequences following Fort Wilson's Riot. In fact, in the elections held a little more than a week after the incident, radicals won fifty-one of seventy-one seats in the assembly. The results are, however, a little misleading. In Philadelphia, many prominent moderates remained in hiding, and residents in other parts of the state may not have even learned of the incident before they went to the polls.[96] Whether the election results accurately reflected their popularity, radicals took the opportunity to enact sweeping legislation designed to reshape society. The 1779–80 assembly fulfilled several of the radicals' long-held wishes including seizing land that had belonged to the proprietors and gutting the College of Philadelphia, which had long been a thorn in the side of the radicals. The assembly's most lasting contribution, however, came with the adoption of a law providing for the gradual ending of slavery in Pennsylvania.[97]

In 1780, Pennsylvania became the first state in the nation to take steps to ban the practice of chattel slavery. Freedom for enslaved men and women would not, however, come at once. Instead, those born after the passage of the act would be held as indentured servants until the age of twenty-eight. The law said nothing about freeing enslaved people born before the law's passage. While the bill fell short of universal emancipation and contained loopholes that enslavers would later exploit, it nevertheless placed Pennsylvania at the forefront of the first emancipation movement.[98]

The Gradual Emancipation Act seemed to signal the beginning of a color-blind definition of the people in Pennsylvania. While the Test Laws had established that the people would only include those loyal to the regime, the status of free people of color had remained ambiguous during the first years of the Revolution. The 1776 constitution did not mention race, meaning that thousands of free African American men who lived in the state had the right to vote. Of course, free people of color still faced enormous social and economic challenges, and the new legislation did nothing to address these structural inequalities. As long as slavery remained legal in the United States, free Black men and women would also have to worry about being sold into slavery. Proponents of a biracial society recognized the limits of what could be accomplished with legislation alone. In the years following the Gradual Emancipation Act, groups like the Pennsylvania Abolition Society, which first formed in 1775, worked tirelessly to protect the rights of freedmen and -women and to promote Black citizenship. Members of the society imagined the Gradual Emancipation Act as the first step toward a future free of racial prejudice where Black and white joined together as a single people.[99]

Other forces, however, worked against this effort to break down prejudices and create a biracial version of "the people." Patriots relied heavily on racially charged propaganda to build support for "the common cause" of American independence. The press claimed that the British promoted and aided uprisings by enslaved people and Native Americans, and warned that a British victory would lead to a race war. Even though hundreds of African Americans joined the Continental Army and many Native American tribes either aligned with the United States or remained neutral, journalists depicted people of color as savage and a threat to civilized (white) people. This message appeared to resonate with some Pennsylvanians. The Test Laws, for instance, specified that only the "male white inhabitants of this state" needed to pledge their allegiance to the state. Similarly, the assembly specified that the requirement to register for militia service applied only to "every male white person capable of bearing arms." Although the laws did not explicitly bar Black men from taking the oath or serving in the militia, the inclusion of the word "white" in such important pieces of legislation suggested that people of color stood outside the normal boundaries of the people. This color line would become more apparent in the coming years.[100]

A Regime in Distress

Although Pennsylvania's Gradual Emancipation Act is often pointed to as evidence of the democratic promise of the Revolution in Pennsylvania, at the time its passage was overshadowed by the state's worsening economic condition. The winter of 1779–80 was especially difficult for Pennsylvanians. Below-average temperatures and harsh weather exacerbated preexisting problems. The cost of basic goods skyrocketed, and the value of paper money plummeted. Meanwhile, radicals in the assembly seemed unable to agree on how to respond. In the fall of 1779, the assembly passed a law aimed at preventing forestalling but reversed itself a month later. An attempt to revamp the militia law to ease the burden on the poor failed as well. The only relief came from voluntary societies run primarily by moderates, who seemed more than happy to demonstrate the failures of the regime.[101]

Radicals did their best to blame their opponents for the state's financial woes and accused moderates of intentionally destabilizing the regime for their own benefit. They also tried to turn Fort Wilson's Riot to their advantage and sought to portray Wilson as the leader of a violent cabal.[102] Voters, however, appeared unconvinced. Moderates picked up more than a dozen seats in the 1780 elections, and a number of high-profile radicals lost their reelection bids. The turnover was particularly apparent in Philadelphia City, where the archconservative boogeyman Robert Morris outpolled prominent radicals. Moderates built on their victories in the following election cycles, and by 1782 had taken control of the assembly. With the Council of Censors, which would have the authority to suggest changes to the state constitution, set to convene for the first time in 1783, the future of the constitution appeared very much in doubt.[103]

Taken as a whole, the years surrounding the Declaration of Independence demonstrated both the promises and perils of a regime built on an expansive version of popular sovereignty. In the years leading up to the Revolution, pro-independence Pennsylvanians had been largely shut out of the halls of power. As a result, they were forced to rely on popular mobilization to establish their legitimacy as spokesmen of the people. In the summer of 1776, despite voters appearing to favor reconciliation, Patriots joined together to use direct forms of mobilization to topple the Colonial Assembly. In so doing, they established the precedent that the people could intervene directly in the governing process. The new constitution codified this principle into law and established that ultimate authority always rested with the people. In the years that followed, radicals repeatedly turned to popular forms of mobilization to defend the constitution and protect the regime from moderates who called for reforms. The use of town meetings, petitions, committees, and violence gave Pennsylvanians an unprecedented amount of authority over the deliberative process. The same features that made the regime so democratic, however, also created instability. With the assembly seemingly incapable of managing a growing economic crisis, moderates sensed an opportunity to renew their call for a new constitution. In order to succeed, however, they would need a new strategy for mobilizing their supporters.

2

Mobilizing the Moderates

IN ANTICIPATION of the news of the official signing of the Peace of Paris, the Pennsylvania Assembly allotted six hundred pounds for the artist Charles Willson Peale to organize "public Demonstrations of Joy." The centerpiece of the festival was to be a triumphal arch, constructed on High Street between Sixth and Seventh Streets, that was more than fifty feet wide and thirty-five feet tall with an opening fourteen feet wide. The arch would be decorated with symbolic paintings that included the Temple of Janus with the doors firmly shut to signify peace, a bust of Louis XVI in honor of his assistance during the war, Pennsylvania's coat of arms, a picture of Native Americans building a church, and an image of Cincinnatus with "a striking Resemblance of General *Washington*." A balustrade "embellished with Figures representing the Cardinal Virtues, Justice, Prudence, Temperance, and Fortitude" would rest on top of the arch. Finally, the entire structure would be illuminated by approximately 1,200 lamps. Overall, the arch was meant to convey a sense that America was leaving behind its monarchical past and entering a new era.[1]

Like much about the first years of the Revolution in Pennsylvania, however, the unveiling of the arch did not go as planned. At first, the celebration seemed successful. Residents crammed into the city to witness the opening of the exhibit on 22 January 1784. Anticipating the crowds, organizers published detailed instructions for how visitors should approach the display and where they should stand to get the best view. They also warned that any unruly behavior would not be tolerated, and that "any Boys, or others, who disturb the Citizens . . . will be immediately apprehended and sent to Work-House." But what they did not foresee was problems in the actual design of the arch itself. With about an hour to go before the scheduled opening, workers began lighting the lamps.

Suddenly, one of the oil paintings that decorated the arch caught fire. Within a matter of minutes, flames engulfed the entire structure. As the fire spread, it consumed multiple boxes of fireworks, sending rockets into the crowd. In the resulting chaos, one person was killed and a number of others were wounded.[2]

While tragic, the burning of the arch was in some ways a fitting symbol for Pennsylvania's revolutionary regime. Like the men who built the arch, the architects of the 1776 constitution had sought to create something that would embody the spirt of the Revolution and serve as a testament to the principles of liberty and freedom. Just like the arch, however, Pennsylvania's experiment in self-government worked better in theory than it did in practice. The version of popular sovereignty enshrined in the constitution and promoted by the radicals gave average residents control over the deliberative process, but it also led to volatility, and officials found themselves helpless as the state spiraled into economic uncertainty and violence. The state might not have burned down, but by 1784 the regime appeared on the verge of collapse.

The signing of the Peace of Paris presented radicals with new problems as well. Defenders of the state constitution had, in part, relied on anti-Loyalist sentiment and warnings about the potential return of the British to fight off previous attempts to call a new convention. The cessation of hostilities meant that these arguments carried less weight. Peace also left the status of the Test Laws, which had allowed radicals to remain competitive in state elections, uncertain. The treaty stipulated that Loyalists should be allowed to rejoin their communities without persecution, and with the two countries no longer at war, there seemed to be little justification for depriving thousands of tax-paying citizens the right to vote. The most immediate threat to the radicals, however, came from an increasingly organized opposition.

Between 1783 and 1790, moderates (later federalists) built a coalition of voters who would eventually join together to topple the existing regime and redefine the meaning of self-government in Pennsylvania. Historians have pointed to a variety of factors to explain these developments including persistent economic challenges, ethnic and religious rivalries, and changing views on the role of government. As this chapter argues, however, in order to capitalize on the favorable environment, moderates needed to first develop a new approach to political mobilization.

In the early years of the Revolution, radicals had consistently outorganized their opponents. Even when the moderates appeared to be in the majority, radicals gained the upper hand by using populist rhetoric, petitions, public meetings, and committees to portray themselves as the true representatives of the people's will. Part of the problem was that some moderates remained uncomfortable with some of the most effective forms of popular politics. As William Bingham, a prominent moderate, explained, critics of the state constitution did not "possess half the activity & address which prevail amongst the factious leaders of the Opposition. These qualities are held but in little Respect amongst *Us*."[3]

In the mid-1780s, however, moderates began experimenting with a different approach to political mobilization that relied on some of the same democratic rhetoric and practices used by radicals. Moderates embraced anti-elitist messaging, public demonstrations, and petition drives to establish their legitimacy and draw a link between their crusade against the radicals and colonists' fight for independence. Using the language of popular sovereignty, moderates attacked the Test Laws as unjust and accused radicals of trying to thwart the will of the people. Moderates also started using holidays and celebrations to promote their message. These strategies helped moderates establish a broad base of support among groups that faced persecution by the radicals. In the face of these developments, radicals increasingly turned to popular violence to defend their version of democracy. The violence, however, served only to confirm moderates' warnings about the dangers of the existing regime. Ultimately, by adopting the popular forms of mobilization pioneered by the radicals, by the end of the decade moderates managed to establish themselves as the voice of the people.

The Council of Censors and Moderates' Rhetorical Moves

The early years of the Revolution had demonstrated the efficacy of populist rhetoric as a tool for shaping public opinion and mobilizing supporters. In the months surrounding the adoption of the Declaration of Independence, Patriots had used attacks on the elites and Loyalists to position themselves as the defenders of the public will. Radicals built on this strategy in the years following and cast their struggles with moderates as a battle between the many and the few. Moderates, in contrast, tended to eschew this type of emotionally charged hortatory rhetoric. Instead, they often relied on appeals to reason and focused their attention on pointing out the deficiencies of the 1776 constitution. Moderates also emphasized the importance of electing candidates with sound judgment and proper education. This type of laudatory rhetoric fit with their more conservative views on the role of the people, but it left them vulnerable to being labeled aristocrats and enemies of the people.[4]

Moderates' rhetoric, however, began to shift in the early 1780s. Instead of ceding the "friends of the people" label to the radicals, moderates began using some of the same populist tropes that Patriots and radicals had relied on during the early years of the Revolution. This shift is apparent when looking at the contest over the election of the first Council of Censors in 1783. The state constitution stipulated that every seven years a Council of Censors, composed of two members from each county, would convene to investigate whether the constitution had been violated at any point in the previous years. The censors had wide-ranging powers and could censure or order the impeachment of elected officials. More importantly, they could also recommend amendments and call for a new convention. The future of the radical agenda, therefore, hinged on the outcome of these elections. In approaching the campaign for censors, moderates framed their struggle as a continuation of the country's larger fight against tyranny rather than attacking the regime and focusing on the defects of the constitution.[5]

In the weeks leading up to the selection of censors, moderates launched a barrage of attacks designed to undermine radicals' claims to speak for the people. George Bryan, the prominent radical and former president of the state, was a favorite target. Moderates ridiculed Bryan and argued that he was "deeply involved in the enraged politics of a faction" and had "been the encourager of the heavy taxes" so he could line his own pockets. Other writers asserted that the radicals favored "rich and oppressive monopolizers" at the expense of the common folk and argued that the only men who opposed reform were "notorious public defaulters and plunderers."[6]

Moderates also portrayed their opponents as aristocrats who, like the former colonial officials, cared only for the rich. The moderate Philadelphia *Independent Gazetteer* printed a steady stream of articles that condemned the radicals as conmen who had taken advantage of average Pennsylvanians. "A Brother Mechanick," for example, warned his fellow workers not to be fooled by radicals' promises to fight for their interests. As soon as they were elected, he asserted, the radicals "will consider you as a useless set of beings."[7] A piece signed by "An Assemblyman" claimed that radicals "think that we country folks and middling sort of people are fools, and that we were made only to bellow . . . and vote for them at elections."[8] The time had come for the people to "think, see, and act yourselves," and just as the colonists had done in 1776, cast off the "chains of slavery" by overthrowing a corrupt and tyrannical government.[9]

Meanwhile, moderates presented themselves as the spokesmen of middling Pennsylvanians. Using pseudonyms including "A Chester County Farmer," "A Friend to All Mechanics," and "Rusticus," moderate writers emphasized their humble roots and often framed their attacks on the radicals as part of an effort to protect average citizens from fraud and abuse. According to one contributor to the *Independent Gazetteer*, the majority of elected officials did nothing more than waste the people's money by "idling away their time, and corrupting their morals in the city of Philadelphia." If given the opportunity, the writer assured readers, moderates would "recommend every plan of frugality and oeconomy."[10] In this way, moderates sought to present themselves as allies of the people in their struggle for freedom and liberty.

The shift in rhetoric did not necessarily mean that moderates' political positions had changed, and their more conservative views did shine through at times. In an article that appeared alongside that of "An Assemblyman," who asserted that the radicals viewed common Pennsylvanians with contempt, a piece signed "A Ranger" bemoaned the fact that under the existing regime, "ignorant, illiterate men without breeding or education" who were "utterly incapable of *spelling* a word, or dictating a single sentiment" aspired "to possess the first and most conspicuous stations in the community."[11] While the author was only trying to make the point that voters should select qualified men to serve, the condescending and pretentious tone undercut some of the moderates' attempts to distance themselves from their aristocratic reputations.

Even with the occasional rhetorical misstep, moderates' new strategy paid dividends, and they secured a majority of the seats on the Council of Censors. They did not, however, win a two-thirds majority, which meant that the radicals would be able to block any significant changes to the constitution and prevent the calling of a new convention. Frustrated but undeterred, the moderate majority used the meeting as an opportunity to force a discussion about the nature of self-government in Pennsylvania. A committee appointed to investigate "defects and alterations of the constitution" declared that the original frame of government was "materially defective" and proposed a series of amendments including the establishment of a bicameral legislature, creation of an annually elected governor, elimination of the requirement that bills be printed and circulated before being adopted, and removal of term limits. Although these changes amounted to an attack on some of the most democratic features of the state's constitution, moderates argued that they were necessary steps to ensure the survival of popular government.[12]

Not surprisingly, the radicals vigorously defended the constitution and accused their opponents of trying to hide their true intentions behind populist rhetoric. In their published reasons for dissenting with the majority, the radical members of the Council of Censors claimed that they spoke "not only the language of our constituents, but . . . also the voice of God and nature," and argued that the suggested additions would "introduce a form of government much more expensive, burthensome and complicated." Radicals cautioned Pennsylvanians that, despite what the moderates may say, the proposed plan for government would "introduce among the citizens new and aristocratic ranks, with a chief magistrate at their head, vested with powers exceeding those which fall to the ordinary lot of kings." The dissent concluded with a warning that if the moderates continued to push for changes to the constitution, "nothing will remain to the people, but the dreadful appeal to arms." The threat was a stern reminder that, at least according to some Pennsylvanians, residents had the right to use force to protect the will of the people.[13]

Instead of backing down or trying to reason with the radicals, moderates responded with their own appeals to the people. Rejecting radicals' claims to speak for the people, moderates called on Pennsylvanians to assemble and demand that their representatives support changes to the current constitution. In a printed public appeal that echoed some of the same language radicals had used in 1779 to try and block the calling of a new convention, the moderate majority urged the people as "the sovereigns of Pennsylvania" to protect their "birth right" and demand changes to the constitution. It was, they declared, now up to the people to "decide the great question whether Pennsylvania shall continue unhappy and distracted under her present constitution" or embrace a new constitution that would restore "harmony amongst yourselves and dignity to your government." With that, the moderates voted to suspend the Council of Censors in order to give the people "an opportunity to instruct" their representatives on how to proceed.[14]

The decision to turn the question over to the people underscored moderates' increasing comfort with popular mobilization, and over the next few weeks moderates blanketed the state with articles and pamphlets that built on the populist rhetoric used during the election of censors. They portrayed themselves as the voice of the people and accused the radicals of trying to undermine the democratic process by preventing the calling of a new convention. In one of the moderates' most well-circulated pamphlets, the well-known moderate Arthur St. Clair, writing under the pseudonym "One of the Majority," warned readers that, while they might present themselves as an ally, radicals believed that the average voter was "incapable of judging of what [they] read." Radicals would, he claimed, use "every artifice to engage you to support the [constitution]" and seek to blind reason by "inflaming your passions." In contrast, St. Clair asserted that the moderates had always "treated you as you ought to be, as reasonable creatures."[15]

Moderates' public opinion campaign appears to have influenced how some Pennsylvanians viewed the constitution. After communicating with the local population, Stephen Chambers, a moderate living in Lancaster, wrote that, thanks to the public opinion campaign, at least the "thinking part" of the community had started to turn against the constitution. He concluded that with a little more effort, "a great Majority of them will be for the Amendments," and urged his allies in Philadelphia to send both German and English copies of moderates' writings that he could distribute.[16]

Some Pennsylvanians, however, appeared less receptive to the moderates' message. After meeting with a group of voters and haranguing them about their drinking and need to support revisions to the constitution, Benjamin Rush was informed that the people "*will* have the *Constitution* & the *bottle* at any hazard whatever."[17] Despite these occasional rebukes from constituents, moderates still felt confident that they would have the votes needed to call a convention when the Council of Censors reconvened in June 1784. Such optimism, however, proved short-lived.

Between the adjournment of the first session of the council in January and the beginning of the second session in June 1784, moderates faced a series of unexpected setbacks that ultimately doomed their hopes of calling a new convention. First, a simmering scandal forced a moderate member of the council to resign. In his place, the voters selected George Bryan. Then, one of the moderates did not return for the second session, while one radical who had been absent in January arrived for the June meeting. As a result, when the Council of Censors reconvened, the moderates found themselves in the minority. The body deliberated for two months, but the results were a forgone conclusion. On 5 August 1784, the council voted against calling a convention.[18]

Although they ultimately failed in their efforts to change the constitution, moderates learned some valuable lessons during the fight over the Council of Censors. They had successfully appropriated some of the populist rhetoric usually associated with the radicals and had nearly succeeded in forcing a new convention. By attacking their opponents as elitists and claiming to speak for the people, moderates had found an effective way to rally support for their cause. At the same time, their inability to hold onto the majority underscored the need to reach a wider audience.

The Economy, the Confederation, and Public Meetings

Since the initial meeting that called for the overthrow of the Colonial Assembly, radicals had repeatedly turned to town meetings to block any attempts at reform. Not surprisingly, moderates tended to respond by rejecting the notion that a meeting could be representative of the will of the people. Radicals' use of town meetings, they argued, undermined the authority of the established government and invited anarchy. Why, they asked, even bother electing representatives if their decisions could be so easily overruled? As one correspondent explained, when important issues such as price controls or the return of Loyalists "are so easily discussed and carried into immediate execution at a town meeting," then the "legislature is an unnecessary expense to the public."[19]

The value of a public demonstration, however, could not be overlooked. In another sign of their evolving approach to mobilization, moderates in the mid-1780s began organizing more public assemblies. Unlike the radicals who used these meetings as opportunities for the people to participate directly in the governing process, moderates tended to use public gatherings as a way for interest groups to demonstrate support and promote a specific agenda. For example, in February 1785, a committee of merchants and traders criticized the "many abortive and ruinous attempts since the revolution" to create a stable economy.[20] Along similar lines, a "very numerous meeting of the master cordwainers of the city and liberties of Philadelphia" complained of the "pernicious consequence of such large importations of European manufactures."[21]

As the meetings of merchants and traders and master cordwainers suggest, the sluggish economy remained a top priority for moderates. In the years following the end of the war with Great Britain, the nation slid further into a depression, and moderates believed that the state and nation stood at the precipice of a disaster. Residents could not afford to pay even the most minimal taxes. As a result, many states struggled to pay off their debts or meet federal requisitions, which in turn meant that soldiers went unpaid and the nation's credit abroad shriveled. To make matters worse, British merchants flooded American markets at the end of the war, driving prices down. With the federal government unable to levy a protective tariff, American merchants and workers were left helpless. In Pennsylvania, the growing crisis led an increasing number of moderates to conclude that the cause of their suffering was "the supliness of Congress."[22] It would, in other words, take more than just a new state constitution to fix what radicals had broken.[23]

The Articles of Confederation, the country's first frame of government, was drafted shortly after the Declaration of Independence and reflected a fear of centralized authority. Similar to Pennsylvania's government, the Articles created a unicameral legislature and a weak executive. The national government, moreover, lacked the power to tax or compel the states to do much of anything. For moderates and opponents of the state's 1776 constitution, the federal government's failures were symptomatic of the larger problem of an excess of democracy and further evidence that the country needed a change.[24]

Moderates made the connection explicit between economic suffering and the weak central government at one of their largest public meetings held in Philadelphia on 20 June 1785. A broadside advertising the assembly called on citizens to attend in order to discuss "business of such general Importance to the Trade and Manufactures of this Country."[25] The meeting opened with a speech by Jared Ingersoll, a prominent critic of the existing regime. Addressing the crowd from a temporary stage, Ingersoll called on citizens to remember the "tumult and horror" of the war and reminded them of the great expectations they had for the country with the arrival of peace. Instead of thriving, however, the economy seemed to worsen following the end of the war. In his opinion, the cause of the suffering was clear: the impotence of the national government. The only remedy, he thundered, was to invest Congress with the powers to regulate trade. After Ingersoll finished, the crowd voted on a series of declarations stating, among other things, "that nothing but a full power in Congress, over the commerce of the United States, can relieve it from its present oppressions."[26]

Notably, although the printed account of the meeting stressed that the crowd had unanimously supported the resolutions, organizers never claimed that the body represented a gathering of the "legal people." This distinction reflected the fact that, although moderates had begun to embrace the importance of popular mobilization, they remained uncomfortable with the idea that the people could assert their will directly. As moderates saw it, only elected officials could represent the "legal people." Public meetings could help to establish legitimacy by demonstrating popular support, but the sentiments they expressed carried no legal authority. For moderates, therefore, the road to reform ultimately ran through the ballot box.

Voting for a Change

Although moderates had achieved some success at mobilizing voters, the Test Laws, which barred citizens who had not taken an oath to support the new government from voting, impeded their ability to build a stable coalition. As long as these laws remained in effect—disenfranchising thousands of potential supporters—the radicals would have an advantage. Moderates had tried to overturn the Test Laws multiple times since they went into effect in 1777. Each time, radicals had managed to defend the laws by arguing that oaths were necessary to prevent traitors from sabotaging the state. But with the country no longer at war, moderates saw an opening, and in 1785 they launched a multipronged campaign to overturn the laws.[27]

Building on their experiences with popular mobilization, moderates cast themselves as modern-day Patriots fighting on behalf of the people against a government that had become corrupt. Moderates used public rallies and printed appeals to highlight how the laws deprived non-jurors of their basic rights. At a Philadelphia meeting, for example, "a number of inhabitants" agreed to resolutions asserting that the Test Laws stripped law-abiding, tax-paying residents of their "inherent and unalienable rights" and "reduced [them] beneath the dignity of citizens."[28] Moderates argued that the laws undercut the very values propagated by the Revolution itself. A "large number of residents" signed a petition warning that, while the laws may have been necessary during a time of war, if they remained in operation much longer it "will fix a stain on the freeman of this state." The entire experiment in self-government would be revealed to "the whole world" as a farce driven by a lust for power.[29] The laws, explained one critic, put non-jurors in the same position colonists had been in when they raised arms against Great Britain: forced to pay taxes without the right to vote for a representative, effectively making them "*slaves* of a free state."[30]

While the moderates framed their attacks on the Test Laws as part of a principled crusade to uphold the values of the Revolution, they clearly saw how opposition to the laws would help build support for their campaign against the regime more broadly. Benjamin Rush confided that forcing the radicals to defend the acts might "rouse and irritate the sons and friends of the nonjurors" and cause them to turn against the constitution.[31] Another moderate explained that regardless of what happened with the laws, making the Test Laws a central issue might "yet fix [non-jurors'] Children . . . who are continually growing up & entitled to vote" to the moderates' side. "That body will soon be numerous," he noted, and their support might very well swing future elections.[32]

Moderates were not, however, content simply to wait until the children of non-jurors grew up. They made their opposition to the Test Laws a central part of their campaign strategy. In 1785, candidates ran under the "Friends of Equal Liberty" ticket, and electioneering articles relied heavily on populist messaging to implore voters to turn out to defend the rights of the oppressed. "A Non Juror" begged his fellow Pennsylvanians to "restore me the invaluable privilege of my birthright and of a land of liberty, of which I am tyrannically deprived." Other articles mocked the radicals' claims to speak for the people and accused them of advocating for virtual representation. Moderates, by contrast, were depicted as the defenders of the rights and freedoms of all Pennsylvanians.[33]

The Test Laws played a central part in the elections the following year as well. In the lead-up to the 1786 elections, moderates weaved criticism of the Test Laws into their longstanding accusations that the radicals were corrupt and took the people for granted. An article addressed "To the Mechanics of the City of Philadelphia," published on election day in 1786, argued that while the radicals' may have "APPEARED, in some instances, to consult your interest, their primary view has been their own emolument." Radicals' continued support for the Test Laws made it clear "that tyranny has been the ruling principle in their government, and despotism part of their political creed." The piece concluded with a stark message: "On your exertions this day depends either such a government as we have spent so much blood and treasure to obtain, or such a one as we opposed Britain to prevent."[34]

The vigorous campaigning and controversy surrounding the Test Laws contributed to a surge in ballots cast for moderate candidates in 1785 and 1786. Moderates even scored victories in traditional radical strongholds including Bucks County, where voters elected a slate of moderates for the first time. In 1785, moderates narrowly took control of the assembly with a thirty-eight-to-thirty-seven majority. In 1786, they increased their margin to forty-one to twenty-eight. Although historians generally agree that the elections of 1785 and 1786 marked a key moment in Pennsylvania politics, they disagree about what accounts for moderates' success. Some scholars argue that the election results reflected larger ideological shifts as Pennsylvanians increasingly soured on the democratic nature of the 1776 constitution.[35] Others, however, have suggested that moderates won because radicals became disillusioned with the assembly's failure to enact sweeping reforms and stayed home.[36] In contrast, Owen S. Ireland contends that the changes can be explained by hardening ethnic and religious divides.[37] Although each of these factors may have played a role in the shifting political tides, analysis of the election returns points to the fact that moderates triumphed primarily because of their ability to mobilize new voters. In fact, the number of people casting ballots for radicals remained relatively consistent throughout this period.[38] What changed was that moderates' increasingly sophisticated approach to electioneering led to more people voting. Ultimately, while ideological changes, frustrations with the assembly, and ethnic/religious tensions may have created a favorable political environment for moderates, none of that would have mattered if moderates had not found a way to turn out their supporters.

Once in control of the assembly, moderates moved swiftly to follow through on their promise to non-jurors. In March 1786, representatives gutted the Test Laws and restored the franchise to anyone who had previously been excluded because they had refused to take an oath in support of the regime. The following year, the assembly voted to remove the last vestiges of the Test Laws. The people would no longer be defined by an oath. Just as importantly, by adopting populist rhetoric, organizing popular demonstrations, and attacking the Test Laws as unjust, moderates had positioned themselves as the true spokesmen for this new, more expansive version of "the people."[39]

Violence and the Defense of the Radical Agenda

As moderates gained control over the state's formal political institutions, radicals increasingly turned to other forms of mobilization to protect their version of democracy. This was particularly the case in the western parts of the state. Citizens living in rural areas along the frontier had been some of the most ardent supporters of the 1776 constitution. For many of these men and women, the country's struggle for independence was intertwined with their individual quest to own land and become self-sufficient. They had high hopes that the end of the war would usher in a more economically egalitarian society. Instead, life had become harder. The economy sunk into a depression, and formerly prosperous farmers found themselves on the edge of destitution. Falling prices for crops—coupled with a scarcity of cash—led to chronic debt, which in turn led to foreclosure. Meanwhile, a small group of wealthy speculators took advantage of the crisis and purchased a vast amount of land for a fraction of what it was worth.[40]

Distressed residents in the western parts of the state initially sought redress through the formal political channels. The region sent outspoken radicals including William Findley and John Smilie to the assembly to fight for reforms that would make cheap land and credit readily available.[41] Poor communication coupled with ethnic and religious rivalries, however, impeded the ability of westerners to establish any stable coalitions. As moderates, who usually hailed from the eastern parts of the state, built majorities, westerners found themselves shut out of the formal governing process. Frustrated and on the brink of ruin, some residents felt they had no choice but to take matters into their own hands.[42]

Throughout the mid-1780s, men and women living in western Pennsylvania used extralegal means to defend their version of democracy. The historian Terry Bouton has described the variety of forms of protest residents used as "a series of concentric rings of protection" designed to "shield [residents] from the harmful effects of state policies" and defend "both property and popular notions of a just society." These rings, which began at the county level and moved down to the individual, encompassed many of the same forms of mobilization that colonists had employed against Great Britain, and their persistence reflected the state's expansive definition of popular sovereignty. Because all power flowed from, and remained with, the people, individuals felt they had the right to take the law into their own hands.[43]

Although resistance often took the form of nonviolent civil disobedience, violence remained an option. Tax collectors who attempted to do their job in western Pennsylvania regularly faced the wrath of aggrieved residents. Between 1784 and 1790, westerners forced at least three excise collectors to resign their positions. These incidents were ritualized and followed traditional patterns of "rough music" that could be traced back to England.[44] The ritualization helped establish that the attacks represented something larger than a random act of violence or a personal vendetta. Assailants, for example, often darkened their faces or wore disguises, not necessarily to obscure their identity or avoid punishment but to send the message that they acted symbolically on behalf of the community.[45] Targets typically received at least one warning and were given time to repent. Officials brave enough to continue were punished. In 1786, an angry crowd surrounded a Washington County official who had continued to collect taxes despite warnings and forced him to "imprecate curses on himself, the Commission and the Authority that gave it to him." The perpetrators then "cut off half his hair," put the other half in a pigtail, and paraded him through nearby towns. Finally, the crowd marched to the border of Westmoreland County and released the officer "with Threats of utter Desolution should he dare to return."[46]

While the "concentric rings of protection" tended to be successful in preventing the collection of debts or taxes in the short term, the popular uprisings also contributed to an already turbulent political atmosphere and may have hastened the collapse of the existing regime. Moderates argued that political violence had no place in a republic and pointed to the popular uprisings as symptoms of a larger problem of unchecked democracy. As they saw it, Patriots had been justified in using violence because they were fighting against a tyrannical government. Following the Revolution, however, the existence of a representative government removed the need for political violence. According to the moderates, in a republic mobs and crowds did not represent the will of the people; they were the tools of a disgruntled and lawless minority.

Celebrations and the Search for a National Identity

As radicals fought to protect the people's right to assert their will directly, moderates continued to experiment with different approaches to political mobilization. In the mid-1780s, moderates began turning to holidays and festivals as a means to promote their vision for the nation. Americans had a long tradition of gathering on holidays and days of celebration. The festivities, which were often rich in symbolism, offered residents from all backgrounds a chance to come together as a single people. In colonial America, public celebrations had also been a way to reenforce social hierarchies and instill loyalty to the king. The Revolution had, however, upended celebratory traditions. Americans, for example, would obviously no longer be gathering for the king's birthday. For moderates, this void presented an opportunity to use public celebrations to shape a new political identity.[47]

No holiday held as much symbolic importance as the Fourth of July. The anniversary of the adoption of the Declaration of Independence served as a time for Americans to reflect on the meaning of their Revolution. By extension, whoever controlled the Independence Day celebrations also got to control the meaning of the Revolution.[48] Pennsylvanians had, however, only sporadically recognized the anniversary of the Declaration of Independence in the early years of the Revolution. The highwater mark for celebrations came in 1777, when Philadelphians honored the day "with demonstrations of joy and festivity." Residents paraded ships "dressed in the gayest of manner with the colors of the United States." In the afternoon, members of Congress dined with members of the Pennsylvania Assembly and were entertained by a corps of British deserters and a "Hessian band of music" captured at the Battle of Trenton. Participants then drank toasts celebrating independence and honoring the "memories of those brave and worthy patriots" who died defending the country. That evening, many Philadelphians placed candles in their windows in observation of the anniversary (those who did not had their windows smashed).[49] In the years following, however, as the realities of war set in, the festivities became more muted. By 1780, the only celebration in Philadelphia on 4 July revolved around the commencement ceremonies at the University of Pennsylvania.[50]

Interest in the Fourth revived briefly following the official end of the war in 1783. The celebrations that year exuded optimism and reflected a sense of national pride. In Philadelphia, the day was "ushered in with the ringing of bells," and the ships in the harbor (excepting Great Britain's boats) displayed their flags. After a display of military maneuvers, members of the army joined state leaders in "an elegant entertainment."[51] A few blocks away, a group of Philadelphians hosted a dinner at the State House in honor of the federal army. Toasts to "The United States in Congress" and "New strength to the union, and new honors to its friends" were echoed with cannon fire and music from a military band. The guests, although hailing from "nearly every state in the union," behaved "like the members of one great and happy family."[52]

This burst of nascent nationalism, however, proved fleeting. The following year, instead of honoring the country on 4 July, celebrants focused on the state of Pennsylvania and showed little interest in the nation as a whole. Because the Fourth fell on a Sunday, all celebration except for the ringing of the bells of Christ Church occurred the following day. On that Monday, John Dickinson, president of the state, hosted a dinner for members of the Supreme Executive Council and other dignitaries. Meanwhile, the Confederate Congress did nothing to recognize the day, leading one disgusted correspondent to ask "O! INDEPENDENCE wither hast thou fled!" "Have the guardians and directors of our country forsaken thee?"[53]

According to moderates, the lackluster celebrations were symptomatic of the underlying weakness of the existing regime. Americans appeared adrift, and the moderates worried that the lack of a coherent national identity would prevent the country from ever reaching its potential. To guard against such an outcome, members of the Society of the Cincinnati, a hereditary organization consisting of former Revolutionary War officers, started organizing their own Independence Day celebrations. Although technically apolitical, the group's decision to make membership hereditary had made it a lightning rod as radicals saw it as a step toward aristocracy. The society's membership also included some of the most outspoken moderates who had been pushing for changes to the state and federal governments. These views were, in turn, reflected in how the group approached celebrating the Fourth.[54]

The first Fourth of July celebration hosted by the Society of the Cincinnati in Pennsylvania occurred in 1785. Festivities began with members of the society assembling at City Tavern, one of the most elegant buildings in Philadelphia. From there, the group proceeded to pay a formal visit to John Dickinson and Thomas McKean, the state's chief justice. This practice recalled deferential rituals associated with the British monarchy. Afterward, the celebrants returned to the City Tavern where they enjoyed an elegant dinner and drank toasts to honor the nation including "Prosperity to the United States" and "The United States Congress."[55] In this way, the society used the celebration to promote a vision of the country that stressed fidelity to elected officials and a reverence for the nation.[56]

Independence Day celebrations multiplied in the following years. In 1786, following the Society of the Cincinnati's example, citizens throughout the state gathered on the Fourth to honor the nation. In Germantown, for example, celebrants met at the falls of the Schuylkill River and drank to "The Day" and "The United States," while "the most respectable inhabitants of Dauphin County" gathered in Harrisburg and toasted "The United states of America in Congress assembled" along with "Our late glorious commander general Washington."[57]

The celebrations also became more overtly political. In 1786, members of the Philadelphia chapter of the Society of Cincinnati attended an Independence Day sermon that stressed the "indispensible necessity of strengthening the confidence in our continental councils, and encreasing the energy of our federal government." The speech, which was dedicated to the leading financier and prominent nationalist Robert Morris, concluded that "to attempt the repair of its feeble constitution, or to change the confederated system altogether, must soon become an unavoidable alternative." The toasts that night included "May the Union, Friendship, and Happiness of these States be forever uninterrupted by local prejudices, or local interests" and "Confidence in our Continental Councils, & an Increase of Energy in Our Federal Government."[58]

Taken together, the Independence Day celebrations served as another example of moderates' evolving relationship with popular mobilization. By controlling the anniversary of the Declaration of Independence, moderates hoped to sculpt what it meant to be an American and shape the future of the country. That future, they believed, began with a new national government.

A New Regime

By 1787, moderates in Pennsylvania felt confident enough in their approach to political mobilization to launch a campaign to establish a new central government. Adopting the name "federalists," they joined with allies from other states to craft a constitution that created a strong national government with a bicameral legislature and a powerful executive. The proposed frame of government represented a dramatic departure from the principles of the state's 1776 constitution. Whereas the existing regime gave residents numerous opportunities to engage in the governing process, the federal Constitution sought to insulate the deliberative process from the whims of popular passions by establishing elections as the only legitimate expression of the public will.[59] These changes reflected the fact that, while federalists believed in the principle of popular sovereignty, they rejected the notion that individual citizens could assert their will over the governing process at any point as both impractical and dangerous. As Benjamin Rush explained, Americans erred when they claimed that "'the sovereign and all other power is seated in the people.' It should be—'all the power is derived from the people.' They possess it only on the days of their elections. After this, it is the property of their rulers, nor can they exercise or resume it, unless it is abused." In other words, the public will could only be expressed through the ballot and the people should stay out of the governing process.[60]

Although the framers presented the proposed Constitution as the work of "We the people," the people had no direct role in the framing of the new government. The convention's business was conducted in the strictest secrecy and without input from the general public.[61] Therefore, in order for the claims of "We the people" to be credible, federalists would need to submit the document to the people for their consent. Of course, who got to be part of the people remained unclear, but by establishing that the people could speak exclusively through elections, the Constitution seemed to indicate that the people meant only individuals with access to the franchise.[62]

Recognizing that they faced an uphill battle in some parts of the country, federalists took several steps to tip the scales in favor of ratification. First, instead of following the Article of Confederation's policy that changes to the central government required unanimity, the delegates announced that only nine of the thirteen states would need to ratify in order for the Constitution to go into effect. Furthermore, instead of submitting the proposed government to the state legislatures, the framers called on each state to organize a special convention. Doing so accomplished two goals: first, it would further legitimize the claim of "We the people" by giving individual voters a chance to cast a ballot directly for or against a candidate who supported the Constitution, and second, and perhaps more importantly, it allowed the Constitution to bypass the state legislatures, which federalists believed were more likely to be hostile to the Constitution because it took power away from the states. Finally, the delegates announced that the states would only be allowed to vote for or against the Constitution as written. This meant that voters would have to choose between the new government or the status quo.[63]

Even though moderates had repeatedly demonstrated their skill at mobilizing supporters, federalists in Pennsylvania took no chances when it came to ratification. On 28 September 1787, before the state had even received an official copy of the new federal Constitution, federalist George Clymer introduced a resolution in the assembly calling for a ratifying convention to be held on 20 November, with elections scheduled for 6 November. This timeframe left a little more than a month for the people of Pennsylvania to digest and debate the contents of the proposed Constitution. For people living in the rural west, it might mean they would need to vote before even seeing a copy of the Constitution. Critics of the Constitution accused federalists of trying to force the new government on the people of Pennsylvania and did everything they could to stall. A contingent of anti-federalists even went into hiding to prevent a quorum. In response, federalists turned to a tactic traditionally favored by radicals: a mob. An angry crowd broke down the door of the house where two of the absent assemblymen had been hiding and dragged them back to the State House. Having achieved a quorum, the assembly adopted the motion calling for a ratifying convention.[64]

The subsequent campaign to rally support for the Constitution in Pennsylvania represented the culmination of years of experience mobilizing against the radicals. Just as the moderates had done, federalists focused their mobilization efforts on establishing themselves as the true spokesmen of the people. To that end, one of the first thing federalists did was start circulating petitions. One resident reported that petitions supporting ratification began "circulating in every ward of the City and thro' the County" within days of the conclusion of the Constitutional Convention.[65] A week after the delegates had finished their work, the assembly received a petition from Germantown signed by 250 residents that praised the proposed Constitution as "wisely calculated [to] form a perfect union of the states, as well as to secure to themselves and posterity the blessings of peace, liberty, and safety" and urged Pennsylvanians to move quickly to ratify.[66] Over the next month, nearly four thousand residents signed petitions expressing their support for the proposed frame of government. Although critics charged that the signers included "minors, foreigners, and old women," the petition blitz provided tangible evidence that large numbers of Pennsylvanians supported the proposed Constitution.[67]

Federalists followed up the petitions with a series of public rallies. These gatherings served a few purposes. First, they gave federalists a chance to legitimize their efforts by at least appearing to give the people a voice in the ratifying process. In Philadelphia, for example, federalists organized a public meeting so residents could endorse a preselected slate of candidates for the upcoming state ratifying convention. Even with a select committee picking the candidates, however, the organizers left nothing to chance and required each of the proposed candidates to publicly state support for the new Constitution.[68] Federalists outside of Philadelphia followed a similar strategy. A federalist meeting in Northampton County resolved that "each of the candidates, nominated . . . make [a] public declaration before this meeting that if it should be his lot to be elected as member of the said Convention, he will use his utmost endeavors that the said Constitution be ratified." In this way, federalists ensured that the desired candidates received the nominations while also ensuring that their candidates appeared to be supported by the people.[69]

The public assemblies also served as an opportunity to demonstrate popular support of their views. Published accounts of federalist rallies often stressed the size of the crowds to legitimize federalists' claims to represent the people and undercut any criticism that the Constitution represented some sort of coup d'état. The *Pennsylvania Packet,* for example, reported that an October 1787 federalist meeting in Carlisle "was the most large and respectable that has been in place since the Declaration of Independence."[70] Similarly, the *Pennsylvania Herald* noted that "a very great concourse of people" attended a pro-ratification meeting in Philadelphia.[71] These types of reports helped to create the impression that a vast majority of Pennsylvanians favored ratification.

Finally, the public meetings provided federalists with an opportunity to preach the virtues of the new government to a captive and friendly audience. At a rally in the Philadelphia State House Yard to build support for ratification, James Wilson, a delegate to the Constitutional Convention, "delivered a long and eloquent speech upon the principles of the Federal Constitution" that addressed many of the most common criticisms of the new government. Wilson conceded that he disagreed with some aspects of the proposed government but ultimately concluded that "anything nearer to perfection could not have been accomplished." The Constitution was, he claimed, "the best form of government which has ever been offered to the world."[72] Although the public did not get a chance to vote during this meeting, published accounts—which were carried in newspapers across the country—noted that Wilson was "frequently interrupted with loud and unanimous testimonies of approbation."[73] Like the references to crowd size, these asides worked to underscore the Constitution's popularity.

Federalists also built on moderates' use of populist rhetoric. Pro-ratification writers utilized many of the same rhetorical tropes first employed by the radicals and later embraced by the moderates. Journalists frequently chastised anti-federalists as modern-day Tories. A piece in the *Pennsylvania Gazette* compared the actions of the anti-federalists with the men who had remained loyal to the crown and concluded that "they are animals of the same breed." Just like the Loyalists, the article claimed, anti-federalists sought to thwart the will of the people. "The Tories despised the proceedings of conventions and town meetings and called them nothing but *mobs*—the Antifederalists despise the Convention of the United States and call the petitions and resolves of our citizens the acts of mobs and fools."[74] Federalist polemists also made liberal use of lingering resentments over the Test Laws and reminded recently enfranchised voters that it had been moderates who fought for equality.[75] Other articles dwelled on the flaws of Pennsylvania's revolutionary regime and accused leading critics of the federal Constitution of being power-hungry office-seekers who were only worried that the new government would cost them their lucrative government jobs.[76] These types of attacks reenforced the message that the federalists were the true friends of the people.

As they bombarded the public with pro-ratification pieces, federalists worked to undermine their opponents by controlling the distribution of messaging. The majority of newspaper editors in Pennsylvania supported the federalists, and anti-federalists faced difficulties in even getting their work published.[77] Federalist readers canceled subscriptions and boycotted newspapers that carried anti-federalist pieces.[78] Even when anti-federalists managed to get their criticisms of the Constitution printed, federalists at the post office prevented or delayed delivery.[79] Additionally, proponents of the new government waged a campaign to force journalists to use their real names when publishing articles. Federalists believed the stature of their supporters might lend the arguments greater weight. Perhaps more importantly, they hoped the move might scare anti-federalist authors in predominantly federalist parts of the state, such as Philadelphia, away from publishing comments critical of the Constitution because they might lose business or friends if their identities were revealed. The hope was not without basis. Benjamin Workman, for example, lost his job at the University of Pennsylvania after federalists unmasked him as the author of a series of anti-federalist articles signed by "Philadelphiensis."[80] Ultimately, the relative dearth of anti-federalist commentary in the newspapers worked to strengthen federalists' claims to speak for a majority of Pennsylvanians.

Federalists' most potent weapon, however, may have been George Washington. The former general of the Continental Army had risen to near mythic status, and his attendance at the Constitutional Convention and endorsement of the new government was one of federalists' most effective rebuttals to any critique of the new regime. Washington had led an outnumbered army to victory over the British, and then in a gesture of humility and patriotism, surrendered his post to return to his home. Americans trusted Washington, and it was widely understood that he would serve as the first president. Well aware of this fact, federalist writers frequently mentioned his name and reminded readers that "the illustrious SAVIOR OF HIS COUNTRY" had overseen the convention's proceedings. According to federalists, the fact that their opponents questioned a government approved by "the *immortal* WASHINGTON" provided further evidence that anti-federalists could not be trusted. Anti-federalists had little recourse in the face of these attacks, and the consistent appeals to Washington foreshadowed some of what would come over the next decade.[81]

Federalists' mobilization efforts led to a diverse coalition of voters turning out to support ratification. In the elections for delegates to the state ratifying convention, federalists won nearly twice as many seats as their anti-federalist opponents, all but guaranteeing that the state would endorse the Constitution. Positions on ratification tended to follow the radical/moderate divide: Anglicans, Quakers, Lutherans, and German sectarians who had been brought into the moderate camp during the fights over the Test Laws supported the Constitution, while Scots-Irish Presbyterians and Reformed Germans tended to side with the anti-federalists. Turnout was especially high in regions friendly to the Constitution, evidence of federalists' success at mobilizing voters. Although anti-federalists would go on to accuse federalists of a wide-ranging conspiracy to deprive the people of their rights, the reality is that moderates/federalists had convinced enough Pennsylvanians that they, not the radicals/anti-federalists, spoke for the people.[82]

When the state ratifying convention met, the anti-federalist minority railed against the proposed government, but the results were a foregone conclusion. On 17 December 1787, the delegates voted forty-six to twenty-three in favor of ratification, making Pennsylvania the second state to adopt the new Constitution. As would quickly become apparent, however, a change in government did not immediately translate into a change in political culture.

The Carlisle Riot and the Limits of Regime Change

The lopsided vote in favor of ratification obscured the extent to which the new government remained controversial in some parts of Pennsylvania. Federalists may have convinced a majority of voters to support the Constitution, but many Pennsylvanians remained committed to the notion that the people could exercise their will directly. The persistence of this version of self-government became clear less than a month after the state voted to ratify the Constitution.

In late December 1787, a group of federalists gathered in Carlisle to celebrate ratification and to "testify their approbation of the proceedings of the late Convention."[83] Carlisle had been a hotbed of anti-federalist sentiment, and the celebration infuriated residents who saw it as an affront to the will of the people. Festivities had just commenced when "a number of men armed with bludgeons" appeared and surrounded the celebrants. The mob, which included many of the area's most outspoken anti-federalists, demanded that the federalists immediately disperse because "their conduct was contrary to the minds of three-fourths the inhabitants." When James Wilson, one of the event's organizers, tried to respond, a few men attacked him, continuing to beat him even when he fell to the ground. Outnumbered and unarmed, the federalists helped Wilson to his feet and retreated. Meanwhile, the crowd built a large bonfire and burned a cannon along with a copy of the new Constitution.[84]

Federalists returned the following day carrying weapons, determined to have their celebration. Armed anti-federalists appeared during the festivities but made no attempt to interfere. After about two hours, the federalists concluded their celebration and went home. As soon as they had departed, however, someone began to beat a drum, and a crowd assembled. In addition to their weapons, the crowd carried effigies of Chief Justice Thomas McKean and James Wilson, both leading federalists. After marching through town, the demonstrators burned the effigies in the town square.[85]

The incident sent shockwaves throughout the state. Officials reacted with horror to the violence and condemned the burning of effigies. Chief Justice McKean took the incident seriously enough to issue warrants for the arrest of twenty-one men for engaging in riotous behavior, assault and battery, and causing "great terror and disturbance" to the residents of Carlisle.[86] The arrests, however, only inflamed public tensions and seemed to confirm suspicions that the federalists sought to deprive the people of their liberty. Allies of the charged men formed societies for the "purpose of opposing this detestable Fedrall conspiracy" and established committees of correspondence to coordinate resistance and alert the backcountry.[87] An anxious Carlisle federalist reported that each night after the jailing, "a party consisting chiefly of such boys and fellows of dissolute character" paraded through town banging drums.[88]

The standoff eventually came to a head when the militia decided to intervene. After a meeting of representatives from the various companies in the area, a delegation of soldiers visited the Carlisle jail and demanded that the sheriff immediately free the prisoners. Federalists initially debated whether "to oppose the rescuers by force" but ultimately concluded that doing so risked the loss of "many lives" and might plunge the region into a civil war. As a result, local federalists and town officials made no attempt to stop the militia from entering the city to free the prisoners. On 1 March 1788, companies from throughout the state marched into Carlisle to the sound of ringing bells and cheering crowds. Reports of the number of people who joined in the procession range from 250 to 1,500. The men paraded throughout town and assembled at the courthouse, where the sheriff delivered the prisoners. Having succeeded in their mission, the troops peacefully marched out of town.[89]

The "Carlisle Riot" illustrates that, despite federalists' success at the polls, at least some Pennsylvanians remained committed to an expansive version of popular sovereignty that gave residents the right to enforce the will of the people directly. Regardless of what the ratifying convention had done, the anti-federalists believed they spoke for the people of Carlisle. Because a majority of residents opposed the Constitution, the anti-federalists contended that the federalists had no right to celebrate in such a public manner. From this perspective, the attacks were a justified attempt to enforce the will of the community. The men arrested had, therefore, done nothing wrong, which meant that their arrests were illegitimate. Just as had been the case with the price-fixing committees, it was the will of the people, not the rule of law, that ultimately mattered. As far as the rioters were concerned, the ratification of the Constitution had done nothing to change that.[90]

The End or the Beginning?

Despite the pushback from anti-federalists, federalists proceeded with their campaign to reform the state. The fate of the 1776 constitution hung over the ratification debate in Pennsylvania. The new federal Constitution seemed to represent a repudiation of the principles of the state's revolutionary regime. Federalist writers made this point explicit in the months following ratification. The *Pennsylvania Mercury and Universal Advertiser* warned that unless Pennsylvanians "assume their native rights, and demand a state constitution . . . the federal government may yet be overset in this state. It is not fully established, 'till our state constitution is altered."[91] Although technically only the Council of Censors, next scheduled to meet in 1790, could suggest changes to the state constitution, federalists had no intention of waiting.

In March 1789, federalists in Philadelphia launched a carefully coordinated campaign to adopt a new constitution that once again relied on popular forms of mobilization to depict themselves as the voice of the people. Federalists began by presenting the question of a new convention as a matter of the people's right to self-government. In a public address, a group of thirty prominent federalists ridiculed the idea that only the Council of Censors could call a new convention and argued that the people "are not and cannot be limited to any certain rule or mode" for changing their government. To suggest that Pennsylvanians would need to wait until the Council of Censors met was an affront to the very idea of self-government.[92] Newspapers echoed these sentiments and argued that the Council of Censors "is better calculated for the reign of Charles I than for the present era of reason and liberty."[93] True liberty, explained another writer in the *Federal Gazette*, meant that the "the PEOPLE, who are sovereigns of the state, possess a power to alter [the constitution] *when* and in what *way* they please."[94]

In addition to depicting themselves as champions of the people's sovereignty, federalists turned to well-worn populist tropes to paint their opponents as corrupt and unprincipled. "One of the People" accused radicals of "gross ignorance, unparalleled stupidity, and factitious principles," and reminded readers that these same men had blocked efforts to repeal the Test Laws.[95] Ratification of the federal Constitution, explained another writer, had "banished the ignorance and heresies in which the constitution of Pennsylvania was wrapped by its friends" and opened the people's eyes to the fact that the state government had been nothing more than "a mass of folly and tyranny, forced on the people by usurpation and office-craft."[96]

Federalists reenforced their message that freedom came through constitutional revision at the annual Fourth of July celebrations. Reverend William Rogers, a professor at the College of Philadelphia, gave a speech that praised the Society of the Cincinnati for saving the county from the pitfalls of anarchy and despotism. "They knew," he explained, "that, although *independence* was the result of force, *good government* must be the child of reason."[97] Ashbel Green, the junior pastor of the Second Presbyterian Church, followed up the oration with a prayer thanking God for delivering "a righteous and energetic system of government" and requesting "to every rank and denomination of the people, a spirit of due submission to lawful authority." Other federalists joined for toasts to "the illustrious President and Congress of the United States of America" and "a speedy constitutional revision of our State Constitution."[98]

As they did during the ratification debate, federalists supplemented their rhetoric with a petition campaign to legitimize their claims to speak for the people. In 1779, radicals had managed to block a new convention by overwhelming the Pennsylvania Assembly with petitions. By 1789, the tables had turned. Petitions calling for a convention poured in when the assembly reconvened in September. Within a span of three weeks, federalists delivered at least twenty-nine petitions containing nearly ten thousand signatures. Radicals, who had mounted a half-hearted attempt to collect their own petitions defending the 1776 constitution, managed to gather a mere eight hundred names.[99]

Having effectively beaten radicals at their own game, federalists in the assembly proceeded to officially call for a new constitutional convention. The resolution announced that "having taken effectual measures for satisfying themselves of the sense of the good people of this commonwealth," the assembly could now "assume from the petitions referred to them . . . that a large majority of the citizens of this state" are in support of calling a new convention. In fact, federalists claimed that the only reason more people did not sign a petition was because the sentiment was so "generally agreeable." Radicals protested and argued that "a majority of the good people in this state are averse" to the idea, but it was all to no avail. By radicals' own rules, the people had spoken.[100]

In the fall of 1789, Pennsylvanians selected delegates to attend a constitutional convention. Not surprisingly, federalists dominated. The resulting frame of government, formally adopted in 1790, mirrored the federal Constitution: the state would have a bicameral legislature, a single executive with veto powers, and an independent judiciary.

The new state and federal constitutions, however, represented more than just a change in government. The moderate/federalist campaign against the radicals, coupled with adoption of new frames of government, effectively redefined the meaning of representative government in Pennsylvania. A comparison between the Declaration of Rights in the 1776 and 1790 state constitutions underscores this fundamental shift in the relationship between the people and their government. To begin with, in the 1776 constitution the "Declaration of the Rights of the Inhabitant of the Commonwealth or State of Pennsylvania" came before the "Plan or Frame of Government," implying that the preservation of individual rights and liberties was more important than the actual government. The framers of the

1790 constitution, by contrast, placed the declaration of individual rights (labeled simply article 9) at the end of the document, after the outlined structure of the new government. Symbolically, this change suggested that, under the new regime, the government is what made the preservation of individual rights possible rather than the other way around.[101]

The actual content of declarations differs in important ways as well. The 1776 declaration reads, "That all power being originally inherent in, and consequently derived from the people; therefore all officers of government . . . are their trusted servants, and at all times accountable to them." The 1790 version claims, "That all power is inherent in the people, and all free governments are founded on their authority," but it says nothing about elected officials being servants to the people. Additionally, while both declarations agree that the people have a right "to assemble together for their common good," the 1776 version states that citizens have a right to "instruct" their representatives, while the 1790 one notes the people could only "apply to those invested with powers of government." In other words, under the new constitution, the people could ask, not tell, elected officials to vote a certain way. In short, the 1790 declaration left no question that the new constitution represented a rejection of the version of democracy that flourished under the state's revolutionary regime.[102]

Although the new government represented a triumph for federalists, the debates during the constitutional convention revealed potential fault lines within the coalition. Some federalists had pushed for even more restrictions on average Pennsylvanians' voice in the governing process. William Lewis, a federalist delegate from Philadelphia, called for the indirect election of senators. Building on arguments that James Madison had made in the *Federalist Papers,* Lewis emphasized the need to filter public opinion. Instead of having voters cast ballots directly for a senator, he suggested that the state adopt a system akin to the federal Electoral College, where voters would cast ballots for two electors, who would then select the senators. Other federalists proposed apportioning seats based on a combination of wealth and population. Neither proposal garnered enough support to make it into the final constitution, and several prominent federalist delegates spoke out against the attempt to make the senate less democratic. The debate, however, foreshadowed future divides and demonstrated just how far some federalists hoped to go in rolling back the egalitarian forces unleashed by the Revolution.[103]

Despite these disagreements, the campaign to dismantle the state's revolutionary regime appeared complete by 1790. Although some historians have portrayed these changes as an elite counter-revolution, the reality is that voters overwhelmingly supported the new governments. By embracing popular forms of mobilization first associated with the radicals, moderates/federalists had established themselves as the true spokesmen of the people and built a diverse coalition of Pennsylvanians who were ready for change. The new regime, however, remained more of a theory than a reality, and important questions remained unanswered. If the people exercised their sovereignty exclusively through the ballot box, what role, if any, would they play in between elections? How would the new governments maintain their legitimacy? Would radicals accept the new restrictions on the role of the people? The boundaries of the people also remained opaque. The abolition of the Test Laws opened the door to a more ideologically diverse electorate, but it remained to be seen whether federalists would move to place new restrictions on who could be part of the people. The first years under the new state and federal constitutions would therefore be a critical period in the struggle to define the meaning of self-government.

3

Choppy Beginnings

Launching the Constitution

Federalists heralded the adoption of the new constitutions as the beginning of a new epoch in human history. The *Federal Gazette* jubilantly declared that the new regime would mark the end of "party spirit in Pennsylvania" and usher in an age of progress.[1] To celebrate the launching of the federal government, federalists in Philadelphia organized the largest parade the city had ever seen on 4 July 1788. Choreographed by Francis Hopkinson, a poet and signer of the Declaration of Independence, the Grand Federal Procession involved upward of five thousand participants, and another seventeen thousand gathered to watch. The parade—which included elected officials, members of the military, delegations from the city's different crafts, and a variety of elaborately decorated floats—was designed to project the image of a nation united in support of the new regime. One of the most popular floats, for instance, depicted the nation as a series of Corinthian columns held together by a dome symbolizing the national government. To drive the point home, the motto "In Union the Fabric Stands Firm" was carved into the base. Craftsmen also built a full-sized frigate dubbed the "Federal Ship," which horses dragged through the city. In sharp contrast to the unveiling of the triumphal arch in 1784, the parade went off without a hitch. No major accidents, disturbances, or serious problems with the crowd were reported. Even the weather cooperated. Providence, it appeared, favored the new regime.[2]

Federalists in Pennsylvania would have even more reason to celebrate when in 1790, as part of a grand bargain adopted the previous summer that involved the passage of Secretary of the Treasury Alexander Hamilton's Fiscal Plan and the selection of the Potomac River as the site for the future capital, Congress agreed to move the federal government from New York City to the City of Brotherly Love for a period of ten years. Philadelphia had not hosted Congress since 1783, and Pennsylvanians had lobbied aggressively to make the city the permanent home of the national government. Their efforts ultimately failed to win over southerners (including George Washington), who believed the new federal city had to be located somewhere below the Mason-Dixon Line, but some residents nevertheless held out hope that, once settled, government officials would find the amenities of what some observers described as the "Athens of America" too alluring to abandon.[3]

Federalists' honeymoon in Pennsylvania, however, proved short lived. Despite the new constitutions, residents remained deeply divided about the meaning of self-government. Some of the men who had supported the new state and federal constitutions thought that the change in government solved the underlying problems that existed under the previous regime, which meant their work was complete. Other members of the federalist coalition, however, saw the new federal and state constitutions as only part of the solution. These individuals, who retained the label "Federalists," concluded that broader social and cultural changes were necessary to ensure that the new governments succeeded. Rather than a formal political party, the Federalists were a coalition of likeminded men who believed that citizens would have to be taught to respect the power of the federal government. As part of this process, they argued that average Americans would need to learn to follow the guidance of a "natural aristocracy" composed of men of wealth, talent, and education. With these goals in mind, in the early 1790s these Federalists turned their attention away from the types of mobilization used to combat the radicals in the 1780s and instead began focusing on developing practices and institutions that would support and promote their vision for a deferential republic.[4]

The campaign to reshape the political culture provoked an immediate backlash. Federalists' efforts alienated some of the people who had originally supported the new constitutions and reenergized the radicals and anti-federalists. These Pennsylvanians became convinced that Federalists had plotted to deprive the people of their liberties, and an opposition movement began to coalesce around the belief that citizens had to play a more active role in the governing process. Galvanized by democratic uprisings in France and appalled with Federalists' apparent affinity for Great Britain, members of the fledgling opposition embraced popular forms of mobilization and portrayed themselves as members of an international campaign to protect the people's liberties and rights from the forces of aristocracy and tyranny. Federalists responded by denouncing their critics as radicals who, if given the chance, would plunge the country into an anarchic abyss. Both sides used popular mobilization to try and demonstrate that they represented the will of the people and attacked their opponents as enemies of the public good. As a result, instead of entering an age free of "party spirit," as the *Federal Gazette* had imagined, the country appeared to be careening toward a civil war.

The Election of 1790 and a New Strategy

The political fault lines underneath the new regime became apparent during the state's first gubernatorial election in 1790. The framers of the state's 1776 constitution had concluded that a governor represented a threat to the people's liberties and abolished the office. Moderates had viewed this action as a reckless and foolhardy decision that created confusion and inefficiencies. As a result, the new constitution established a strong executive who would control a vast patronage network and have the power to veto proposed legislation. Whoever held the office would therefore wield a significant amount of power over the workings of state government. The selection of the chief executive would also mark the first truly statewide election since the end of the revolutionary regime and serve as an important benchmark as Pennsylvanians began to come to grips with life under the new constitutions.

Federalists had dominated their opponents at the polls since the ratification of the Constitution. Supporters of the Constitution won six out of eight congressional seats during the first federal elections, and moderates/federalists held a comfortable majority in the assembly. In approaching these elections, federalists had adopted a strategy similar to the one the moderates had relied on against the radicals: they used popular forms of mobilization to portray their candidates as the people's choice. In 1788, for example, federalists organized meetings throughout the state to select delegates to attend the first ever statewide nominating convention in Lancaster. These gatherings gave the public a chance to participate indirectly in the nominating process. Newspaper articles underscored this point and argued that the Lancaster ticket represented the will of the people.[5]

Despite the success of this strategy, federalists took a different approach to electioneering in 1790. In preparation for the gubernatorial campaign, instead of organizing public meetings, a select group of prominent federalists known as the "Philadelphia junto" took it upon themselves to select General Arthur St. Clair, who was then serving as governor of the Northwest Territory, as their nominee. Although the public meetings held in preparation for the elections in 1787 and 1788 had been nothing more than a show and a way to legitimize the candidates that a small group of men had selected, the fact that members of the junto did not even bother to go through the motions of securing popular consent is revealing. In addition to demonstrating their confidence that the public would support whomever they nominated, the decision pointed to the fact that some federalists believed that average citizens should now step back and leave the business of governing to people who were more qualified.[6]

The rhetoric used to promote St. Clair further underscored federalists' evolving mobilization strategy. The broadside announcing St. Clair's candidacy, for example, made no mention of his popular appeal and did not try to present him as a champion of the people. Instead, it touted St. Clair as a man who possessed "amiable manners," "strict integrity," and a "comprehensive mind." Federalists did not, however, break entirely with the strategy used to promote the Constitution. The broadside emphasized that St. Clair "possesses the confidence of the PRESIDENT of the United States." As if to underscore that the public had not participated in the nomination process, the announcement concluded with the signatures of seven prominent men. The message was clear—all voters needed to know was that Washington trusted St. Clair and that he had the backing of these well-informed men.[7]

The flagrantly undemocratic nature of St. Clair's nomination offended the republican sensibilities of some Pennsylvanians and provided an opening for radicals and critics of the junto. With no viable radicals or antifederalists running, Thomas Mifflin, one of the most well-known political figures in Pennsylvania, quickly emerged as St. Clair's most formidable opponent. Mifflin had served in the colonial and state governments and had aligned with the moderates/federalists. Despite disagreeing on many points, radicals saw Mifflin as their best hope for defeating the junto. As one political observer noted, while Mifflin and St. Clair might have shared similar views, the radicals could at least take pride in the fact that Mifflin's candidacy would surely upset "the aristocrats."[8]

Mifflin's supporters went to great lengths to demonstrate that, unlike St. Clair, their nomination reflected the will of the people. Drawing on strategies federalists had employed during the ratification debate, pro-Mifflin activists organized meetings throughout the state that gave the public a chance to participate in the nominating process. To further underscore Mifflin's popularity, newspapers even took the unusual step of publishing the votes from these meetings. An assembly of residents near Philadelphia, for example, voted 229–3 in favor of Mifflin while a similar meeting in Bucks County endorsed Mifflin by a margin of 80–2. According to the published accounts, even these figures did not do justice to Mifflin's popularity, and the articles noted that the "great number present" who "did not avail themselves of the privilege of voting" cheered the results. Such numbers stood in stark contrast to the seven federalists who had endorsed St. Clair, and including such details in accounts of the meetings helped to create the impression that Mifflin was the people's candidate.[9]

Mifflin's allies reinforced this perception through the use of populist rhetoric. Unlike the broadside that stressed St. Clair's genteel manners and highlighted he had the support of a number of prominent men, pro-Mifflin articles focused on the candidate's firm commitment to republican principles. Mifflin had, explained one correspondent, always treated everyone equally because "no elevation of rank has been sufficient to warp his mind from its original democratical biases."[10] Along similar lines, a piece signed "One of the People" assured readers that Mifflin "converses with rich and poor with equal freedom," and that "there is not the smallest spark of aristocracy in his nature."[11] Other authors noted that while St. Clair might be a decent individual, the junto's nomination suggested that he would become a pawn to "men of known aristocratic principles." As for St. Clair's relationship with Washington, "A Republican" acknowledged that it was true St. Clair might indeed have the "confidence of the President of the United States" but "so did *Benedict Arnold*."[12]

The strategy of promoting Mifflin as the people's choice and depicting St. Clair as a puppet of the junto proved remarkably successful. On election day, Mifflin trounced St. Clair, winning in every county and receiving over 90 percent of the total vote.[13] Mifflin clearly attracted support from more than just the remnants of the radical coalition, and his victory was in no way a rejection of the principles of the new constitutions. Nevertheless, some federalists worried that the election might be a harbinger of things to come. Shortly before election day, St. Clair wrote to Thomas Fitzsimons, a member of the junto, that despite the change in government, the "[radical] party is not yet dissolved," and warned that it would "probably revive under a different name . . . but with the same views."[14] Pennsylvanian's revolutionary regime may have been defeated, but supporters of a more participatory form of politics had not given up.

Culture Warriors

The election of 1790 served as a stark reminder that a change in government did not automatically translate into a change in political culture. The backlash against St. Clair's nomination suggested that, even with new constitutions in place, Pennsylvanians still expected to play an active part in the governing process. According to members of the junto and their allies, the persistence of this democratic culture posed a threat to the health and longevity of the republic. In order for the nation to succeed, these "Federalists" believed that members of the public had to learn new customs and habits. To start with, citizens must be taught to defer to their elected officials, and ordinary Pennsylvanians needed to accept that they were not equipped to play a direct role in the deliberative process. Instead, commoners should leave the business of governing to their social and intellectual betters.

In addition to establishing a more deferential form of republicanism, Federalists also thought that Americans needed to develop a stronger national identity. In the 1770s and 1780s, state and local officials wielded the most power, and most residents rarely thought of themselves as part of a nation. Even after the adoption of the new constitutions, no real consensus existed on what it meant to be an American aside from a shared reverence for George Washington. Without a sense of nationalism, Federalists worried that the country would inevitably fall prey to internal squabbles. As they saw it, a strong national identity would not only cement the union but also help citizens to accept the legitimacy of the federal government.[15]

In an effort to mold the nation's political culture to fit their vision for the country, Federalists launched a campaign to instruct the public on the proper role of citizens through celebratory politics. Building on the efforts of the Society of the Cincinnati, Federalists used public spectacles and national holidays to create a space where Pennsylvanians could demonstrate their support for the new regime and symbolically participate in the governing process. These events also provided Federalists with opportunities to construct and promote their vision for the nation. As the Federalist James Wilson explained, "Public processions may be so planned and executed" so that "they may *instruct* and *improve*, while they *entertain* and *please*. . . . They may represent, with peculiar felicity and force, the *operation* and effects of great *political truths*."[16] For Federalists, therefore, public spectacles were an integral part of how Americans would learn how to be good citizens. Just as important, they could also be used to establish a national identity built around a reverence for the federal government.[17]

The Fourth of July played a particularly important role in Federalists' approach to celebratory politics. As had been the case for moderates in the 1780s, the annual commemoration of the signing of the Declaration of Independence presented an opportunity for Federalists to nurture a sense of nationalism. In 1792, for example, Philadelphia's Fourth of July festivities included, among other things, "a triumphal arch beautifully illuminated" (that did not burn down), "a sun, 37 round, beautifully illuminated," "3 fire pumps," "2 wings of brilliant fire," "2 globes beautifully illuminated," "2 ships of war to fight, 20 guns," "2 forts, 20 guns each, to fight the ships," "200 sky-rockets with stars and without," and "an angel presenting the Cap of Liberty to the President of the United States." With this type of symbolism, Federalists sought to portray the country as a rising superpower that stood ready to defend the principles of liberty and freedom. Notably, unlike the Grand Federal Procession, which included residents from all walks of life, in 1792 average Pennsylvanians were simply spectators in these festivities. In this way, the celebration also subtly promoted Federalists' idea of a more passive citizenry.[18]

Beyond promoting the power of the nation and teaching citizens to respect the federal government, Federalists also used the Fourth of July to link the adoption of the Constitution with the birth of the nation and to portray it as the fulfillment of the promises of the American Revolution. In 1790, a speaker proclaimed that "the day which the constitution of the United States was adopted, completed the great, the important event" that the Declaration of Independence had begun. "The 4th of July 1776," he continued, "gave independence but in name; the day on which the Federal Constitution was ratified, secured the reality."[19] John Fenno, editor of the influential Federalist newspaper the *Gazette of the United States*, proclaimed that it was "the glorious event of the adoption of the new Constitution" that enabled Americans to realize "what the word *Independence* imports—Laws and Rights—Peace and Prosperity—Credit and Confidence."[20] By denigrating (or simply ignoring) the years between 1776 and 1788, Federalists sought to erase the memory of the state's revolutionary regime and establish a direct line from the Declaration of Independence to the adoption of the federal Constitution.

Pennsylvanians appeared to be receptive to Federalists' Fourth of July message. Each year, the number of different groups gathering increased, and reports of various celebrations filled the newspapers for weeks. Towns across the state joined in the feting. In 1792, "a large number of gentlemen and ladies" in Wilksharre, Luzerne County, marked the day with "an elegant dinner" followed by cannon fire.[21] The number of people partaking in the festivities appears to have increased as well. In 1790, the *Carlisle Gazette* reported that "a greater number [of] most respectable citizens from town and country than had ever before" participated in the town's Fourth of July festivities. Taken together, the growing number of residents who gathered for Independence Day celebrations suggests that Federalists were succeeding at cultivating a greater sense of nationalism.[22]

As the reference to the "large number of gentlemen and ladies" who attended the celebration in Wilksharre indicates, it was not just men who attended these festivities. Indeed, women often featured prominently in Independence Day celebrations. Festivities at Gray's Garden outside Philadelphia in 1790 included "thirteen Young Ladies and the same Number of Gentlemen, dressed as Shepherds and Shepherdesses," who sang an "Ode on Liberty, by alternate Responses and a Chorus."[23] Celebrants also frequently raised their glasses in toasts such as "The American Fair" or "The Fair Daughters of America."[24] The inclusion of women in these celebrations served a few functions. First, it provided women, who could not vote, with a chance to symbolically participate in the political process. Second, it helped to legitimize Federalist claims to represent the people as a whole. Finally, the presence of women lent the festivities a degree of respectability and, at least theoretically, helped to prevent men in the crowd from getting too rowdy.[25]

Federalists had good reason to be concerned that celebrations might get out of hand, which would undercut their efforts to promote a more deferential culture. Festivities often included alcohol, and as the Carlisle Riot demonstrated, the line between a celebration and a riot was not always clear. To help guard against any mishaps, organizers began printing their plans for the Fourth of July ahead of time as a way to ensure that the public knew what to expect and to remind potential participants that the festivities depended on "order being preserved."[26] At the same time, leading Federalists implored Pennsylvanians to honor the day "with the decorum and harmony which ought to characterize a free people" and not get lost in the revelry.[27] These celebrations were meant to be instructive, not just entertaining. As a correspondent in the *Federal Gazette* explained, "The mere observation of [the Fourth of July] can answer no valuable purpose" if it does not also include a "rational re-examination" of the principles of the Revolution.[28]

Next to Independence Day, the most important day on Federalists' celebration calendar was George Washington's birthday. Unanimously elected as the first president, Washington remained the most popular figure in the country, and for many Americans he embodied the strength, hope, and promise of the young nation. His birthday provided Federalists with an annual opportunity to remind the public that the man who had once commanded the Continental Army now stood at the head of the new federal government. Pennsylvanians began gathering on 22 February to mark Washington's birthday as early as 1785, but the day did not gain much traction as a holiday until after the adoption of the federal Constitution. By the early 1790s, it had become one of the most widely observed holidays in the state.[29]

Volunteer militia companies, along with the Society of the Cincinnati, often took charge of planning for Washington's Birthday. These organizations, which also featured prominently in Fourth of July celebrations, served as models of the type of discipline and respect for rank that Federalists hoped to instill in all citizens. Festivities on Washington's Birthday typically began with a display of military maneuvers accompanied by the firing of cannons. The public drills were designed to inspire awe and promote national pride while also demonstrating the importance of good order. In Philadelphia, at the conclusion of these exercises, the militia, along with members of the public, would then take part in a ritual of deference by marching to Washington's residence to pay tribute to the "illustrious President." This type of ritual, which was described in detail in the local newspapers, helped to model the type of political culture Federalists hoped to inculcate.[30]

The rituals around Washington's Birthday also helped to reenforce social hierarchies. Newspaper accounts of the occasion often underscored the dignified and luxurious nature of the festivities. The *Federal Gazette*, for example, described a 1791 ball in Washington's honor as "the most elegant, numerous and splendid dancing assemblies ever exhibited in this city."[31] The following year, the same paper proclaimed the celebration "one of the most brilliant displays of beauty ever exhibited in this city." The paper also noted that in the evening, select participants retreated for dinners at the homes of local socialites.[32]

The emphasis on exclusivity and opulence of these gatherings was part of Federalists' larger campaign to establish what historians have dubbed a

"Republican Court" where the social and political elite could demonstrate their status through displays of wealth and power. Women played a particularly important role in these efforts. Events like Martha Washington's weekly levee, a rigidly formal reception reminiscent of monarchical rituals, provided elite women with an opportunity to model their understanding of proper behavior. At these gatherings, women practiced sociability and civility and demonstrated the importance of good manners. Outside of these private functions, upper-class men and women used dress and manners to establish and maintain the boundaries of the gentry.[33]

Despite the monarchical undertones of these practices, few Pennsylvanians questioned the celebration of Washington or the existence of a Republican Court. Even Benjamin Franklin Bache, the editor of the *General Advertiser* and one of the most outspoken critics of the Federalists, joined the celebrations. "The anniversary of our President's birth day," he wrote in 1792, "is the most suitable occasion for demonstrations of . . . manly joy and decent liberty. As long as Americans feel the blessing of Liberty, and of pure republican government, this day will be remembered as one of the most auspicious in their calendar."[34] Federalists, it appeared, had succeeded in developing an approach to celebrating national holidays that combined reverence for the new regime with a recognition of the importance of a social hierarchy. This cultural hegemony would, however, not remain unchallenged for long.

France and the Emergence of a Counterculture

The impetus for what would become an oppositional form of celebratory politics occurred thousands of miles away from Pennsylvania, on the other side of the Atlantic. The outbreak of the French Revolution in 1789 sent shockwaves throughout the Western world. When news of the uprising first began to trickle across the ocean, Pennsylvanians, like most Americans, cheered what appeared to be evidence that the seeds of liberty sown in America had taken root in Europe. Such unanimity proved fleeting. Following the outbreak of war between France and Great Britain in 1792 and the beheading of King Louis XVI in 1793, Federalists concluded that radicals had seized control in France. Reports of systematic attacks on the Catholic Church and mass executions seemed to confirm their belief that democracy bred violence and served as yet another reminder of the importance of constitutional checks on the will of the people.[35]

Other Pennsylvanians, however, saw events in France in a different light. Instead of viewing the revolutionaries as bloodthirsty fanatics, these men and women considered the French to be warriors on the frontlines of a global struggle against tyranny. Aghast that Federalists appeared to prefer a monarchical England over a republican France, these Pennsylvanians viewed the violence in France as a necessary, if perhaps regrettable, part of the process of uprooting the old regime. Moreover, they pointed out that America owed its very existence to France's decision to intervene on behalf of the Patriots during the Revolutionary War and argued that under the terms of the 1778 Treaty of Alliance, the United States was treaty-bound to aid the French.[36]

Washington initially sought to chart a middle course between the two sides. On 22 April 1793, he issued a Proclamation of Neutrality, which announced that the United States would "with sincerity and good faith adopt and pursue a conduct friendly and impartial toward" both Great Britain and France. He further warned that any American who tried to aid one of the belligerent powers would face legal repercussions. Instead of easing tensions, Washington's proclamation exacerbated the divide over the French Revolution. Allies of France accused Washington of abandoning a sister republic and saw claims of neutrality as a thinly veiled way of ensuring that Great Britain had the upper hand. Adding insult to injury, Washington made his decision unilaterally and had not consulted Congress, a move critics warned could set a dangerous precedent.[37]

Against the backdrop of these developments, Federalists' approach to celebratory politics began to take on a different hue. Some Pennsylvanians began to fear that perhaps Federalists opposed the French Revolution because they secretly hoped to return America to a monarchy. What else might explain their decision to abandon a fellow republic? Viewed from this perspective, the emphasis on the national government and the deferential rituals surrounding Federalists' celebrations on the Fourth of July and Washington's birthday combined with the establishment of the Republican Court began to look like a coordinated effort to undermine the people's sovereignty. Events like Martha Washington's formal levees and other exclusive gatherings might appear harmless, explained one correspondent, but they struck "a distinction between the public servant and his visitors, a distinction incompatible with a republican constitution."[38] The veneration of Washington, in particular, became a source of concern. To place any man on a pedestal, explained another writer, "is to destroy the equality which constitutes the essence of our sovereignty, and is a *degradation of freemen*."[39]

Even Pennsylvanians who had originally supported the celebration of Washington's birthday began to change their tune. Less than a year after he published the article praising the celebration of Washington's birthday, Bache printed a blistering satire addressed to "the Noblesse and Courtiers of the United States" advertising an opening for a "Poet laureate" to prepare some verse for the president's birthday. The successful candidate, he wrote, must be able to compose poetry praising "certain *monarchical prettiness* . . . such as LEVIES, DRAWING ROOMS, STATELY NODS INSTEAD OF SHAKING HANDS, TITLES OF OFFICE, SECLUSION FROM THE PEOPLE, &c. &c." Anybody interested in the position should also be ready to ridicule the idea of equality and poke fun at the absurd idea that the "*vulgar*, namely the people, should presume to think and judge for themselves."[40]

In addition to challenging the deification of Washington, some Pennsylvanians began to question Federalists' Independence Day celebrations. Liberty, it seemed, was under siege across the globe, and critics claimed that Federalists' rituals sent the wrong message. Instead of teaching Americans to remain vigilant in defense of freedom, Federalist celebrations promoted passivity and encouraged citizens to blindly follow the dictates of the federal government. Worse still, Federalist propaganda appeared to be having an effect. On 4 July 1792, the *National Gazette* worryingly observed that "some of our Citizens appear disposed to view Monarchial Power" in a manner that was different from the "way they viewed it in 1776." The Fourth of July, the paper noted, should serve as an annual reminder of the "principles and feelings of the Citizens of the United States in [1776]" and not as an opportunity to promote the power of the federal government and the president. In case anyone missed the point, the same issue also carried an article entitled "Rules for Changing a Limited Republican Government into an Unlimited Hereditary One," which suggested the best way to undermine a republican government was to teach the public to idolize elected officials.[41]

To counter what they saw as a trend away from a government based on the people's right to rule, members of the opposition began organizing their own celebrations. Like the Federalists, these Pennsylvanians gathered on the Fourth of July, but they also feted important French military victories and anniversaries. The imagery and rituals of these celebrations contrasted sharply with those organized by the Federalists. Whereas Federalists tended to rely on nationalistic symbols such as eagles and rising suns, the opposition used imagery associated with the French and

American Revolutions. For example, at one of the opposition's most extravagant festivals, labeled the "Feast of Reason," French and American dignitaries headed a massive procession that included "an obelisk on which were painted the attributes of liberty and equality, and surmounted by a Liberty cap." Women dressed in white and "adorned with three coloured ribbons" encircled the obelisk and spread flowers as the parade moved through the city. The procession ended at the gardens of Jean Fauchet, the French foreign minister, where celebrants "erected an altar to liberty, with an elegant statue of the goddess of liberty on it." Afterward, the crowd joined together in the singing of the "Marseillaise" and listened to a series of orations that extolled the virtues of liberty and equality. That evening, nearly five hundred residents dined at Richardet's Hotel, where they were treated to an elaborate display of fireworks before partaking of toasts that emphasized liberty and freedom including "Mankind: may they be no more the property of a few individuals," and "May death, like lightning, strike every hypocrite and false republican."[42]

Like the Federalists, members of the opposition hoped to use these spectacles to demonstrate popular support while simultaneously promoting the values and principles they deemed important.[43] In contrast to the Federalists, who used celebratory politics to instill a sense of nationalism and reinforce social hierarchies, members of the opposition promoted a more participatory culture that focused on a shared love of liberty. While spectators tended to play a passive role during Federalist celebrations, the opposition encouraged bystanders to join in the festivities at events like the Feast of Reason. In fact, organizers declared that simply by "participating in the celebration," residents would be "sensibly lending [their] aid to the cause of Liberty and equality throughout the Universe."[44]

Women also played an important role in the construction of this counterculture. Whereas women associated with the Republican Court worked to promote deference through aristocratic rituals, women in the opposition sought to cultivate a more participatory culture by drawing heavily on the styles of the French Revolution. In addition to taking part in celebrations such as the Feast of Reason, they began wearing neoclassical dresses and other clothing associated with the French Revolution. In France, clothing had become closely associated with political views, and by wearing a headscarf or a tricolored cockade, women in Pennsylvania demonstrated their allegiance to the principles of liberty and equality.[45]

The opposition's efforts to establish a more participatory political culture horrified Federalists. William Cobbett, for example, was appalled when throngs of adoring spectators greeted the arrival of the French foreign minister Edmond-Charles Genet before he had a chance to be formally welcomed by elected officials. The "sovereign people, [took] the liberty to act for themselves," Cobbett scoffed, "while their servants, the officers of government, [stood] looking on." What right, he demanded to know, "had the people of Philadelphia, even supposing them all assembled together, to acknowledge any man as a public minister, before he had been acknowledged and received as such by the General Government"? As he saw it, no matter how large the gathering, the people themselves could never act in such an official manner.[46]

Debating the Role of Citizens: The Democratic and Republican Societies

As Cobbett's criticism suggests, the dueling approaches to celebratory politics reflected an underlying disagreement about the nature of sovereignty. According to the Federalists, the new regime established that the public will could only be expressed through voting. As a result, only the duly elected government could claim to speak for the people. True liberty, explained one Federalist, did not consist of "the right of the populace to assemble and oversee the proceedings of the freely elected legislators of the nation." Instead, "liberty invests people with the right to elect their own rulers, whose task it is to enact laws for the general good."[47] Of course a private citizen or group of citizens could express opinions as long as they "do it with some little degree of modesty, . . . especially when the proper office of the government, entrusted by the constitution to speak the sense of the Union," had already acted. In other words, private citizens could speak their mind, but they should ultimately defer to their elected representatives.[48]

Critics of the Federalists rejected this form of representation and began to outline a different version of the role of citizens. Regardless of what Federalists might claim, members of the nascent opposition movement argued that the people always maintained authority. As James Madison explained in a series of influential essays in Philip Freneau's *National Gazette*, which emerged as the primary mouthpiece for the opposition, "PUBLIC opinion set bounds to every government, and is the real sovereign in every free one." Instead of deferring to elected officials, citizens had to remain vigilant and pay close attention to what happened in government. History, Madison explained, taught that republics often fail because the citizenry had grown complacent and allowed power and wealth to concentrate in the hands of the few. In order to prevent this from happening in America, the people had to remain involved in the governing process. The country should, therefore, promote "a general intercourse of sentiments" by establishing "good roads, domestic commerce, a free press, and particularly a *circulation of newspapers through the entire body of the people.*" Such open lines of communication would keep the citizenry informed and help serve as a check against possible abuses of power.[49]

As part of the effort to ensure that the people remained engaged and informed, members of the opposition began forming Democratic and Republican Societies. Between 1793 and 1794, Pennsylvanians organized nearly a half-dozen different groups throughout the state. Inspired by the Sons of Liberty and similar clubs in France and England, the Democratic and Republican Societies sought to "prevent abuses of power, and silent encroachments upon the liberties of the people" by "instructing the people in their natural and political rights." According to the members of the clubs, the Republican Court and cult-like worship of Washington were symptomatic of a larger problem facing the young nation. As the Philadelphia Democratic Society of Pennsylvania asserted in a circular announcing its creation, "the vigilance of the people has been too easily absorbed in victory." Citizens had become complacent, and as a result, "the seeds of Luxury appear to have taken root in our domestic soil." Echoing Madison's conclusions, the circular argued that the only real "antidote" to this "political poison" was a "constant circulation of information, and a liberal communication of republican sentiments." The society would, therefore, strive "to cultivate the just knowledge of rational liberty" and help to "facilitate the enjoyment and exercise of our civil rights."[50]

The type of political society advocated by the Democratic and Republican Societies stood in sharp contrast to the one offered by Federalists. Whereas the Federalists believed that a hierarchy was necessary to preserve order, the clubs promoted an egalitarian society free from social and economic distinctions. Although wealthier men tended to occupy leadership positions, the clubs attracted a socially diverse group of Pennsylvanians, and once initiated, every member had an equal vote on the initiation of potential members and on any proposed resolutions. The Philadelphia Democratic Society took the emphasis on equality even further and resolved to stop using the words "Sir" and "Humble Servants" in their communications. Members believed that such relics of aristocracy had no place in a republican society. Instead, following the example of revolutionaries in France, they would use the title "Citizen."[51]

When it came to the role of the people in the deliberative process, the Democratic and Republican Societies explicitly rejected Federalists' assertions that the people ceded sovereignty on election day. "It is," the Philadelphia Democratic Society argued, "the natural privilege of every free citizen to give his sentiments on all public measures, and not only on those which have operation, but on those also that are pending."[52] The dangers of not exercising this privilege had already become apparent. According to members of the clubs, Federalists had managed to lull citizens into "a general negligence of their political affairs," which allowed a cabal of "designing men" to seize control of the government.[53] The only way to combat such corruption was to encourage citizens to engage directly with the political process themselves. As one Democratic Society put it, "GOOD CITIZENS" and "PATRIOTS" must "constantly express our sentiments as well of OUR PUBLIC OFFICERS, as their MEASURES."[54] Regardless of what the Federalists might say or do, the societies believed, the people had both a right and a responsibility to regularly assert their sovereignty.

Although they challenged Federalists' version of representation, the Democratic and Republican Societies stopped short of calling for a regime change. The Philadelphia Democratic Society, for example, explicitly affirmed "that, the Republican Constitutions of the United States and of Pennsylvania, being framed and established by the people, it is our duty as good citizens to support them." The issue was what it actually meant to "support" the constitutions. For Federalists, support meant that citizens should defer to the judgment of their elected officials and support the government. For the Democratic and Republican Societies, it meant ensuring a space existed for "every freeman, to regard with attention, and discuss without fear, the conduct of the public servants in every department of government."[55]

The use of the term "freeman" hints at another way in which the Democratic and Republican Societies refrained from challenging the underlying status quo. For all their emphasis on creating a more participatory society, the clubs made no real attempt to radically alter the meaning of "the people." Although some members of the Democratic and Republican Societies also belonged to the Pennsylvania Society for Promoting the Abolition of Slavery, the club never addressed the fact that, even fourteen years after the adoption of a gradual emancipation law, many Black Pennsylvanians remained enslaved. In fact, according to William Cobbett, the Philadelphia chapter refused to admit a Black man who applied for membership because of the color of his skin.[56]

The Pennsylvania societies barred women from attending their meetings as well. Like Federalists, they included women in their celebrations, but members of the clubs seemed content with existing gender roles.[57]

There was, however, one marginalized group that the Democratic and Republican Societies encouraged to join: European immigrants. Thousands of immigrants had arrived in Pennsylvania since the adoption of the new constitutions, many of them fleeing the turmoil following the French Revolution. While Federalists viewed many of these new arrivals with suspicion, the opposition saw immigrants as potential allies in the struggle to establish a more participatory culture. The German Republican Society, for example, formed itself for the explicit purpose of engaging recent arrivals in the political process and conducted its business in German. Many of the officers of the Democratic Societies were also immigrants, and the club expressed hope that "the distinction of nation and of language [would] be lost in the association of Freedom and Friendship." This openness to immigrants would become a defining feature of the opposition in the coming years.[58]

The fact that the Democratic and Republican Societies explicitly stated they had no interest in regime change did not make much of a difference to Federalists, who saw the clubs as a threat to their version of deferential republicanism. Leading Federalists in Pennsylvania denounced the clubs as "self-created" (as opposed to elected) and accused them of promoting anarchy by claiming to speak for the people. The *Gazette of the United States* proclaimed that the mere existence of "any particular Democratic Society, rising in the midst of our great Democratic Government, and presuming to dictate to its constituted authorities," was not only "inimical to law and order" but also "highly insulting to the great body of the people" who trusted "the wisdom and virtue of *their own* delegates."[59] Tolerating any dissent, Federalists warned, could have dire consequences. "The very circumstance of allowing ourselves to speak against government," explained one correspondent, "has a tendency to bend our minds that way."[60]

In what would later become a major theme in the state's political divide, Federalists also criticized the Democratic and Republican Societies for catering to recent immigrants. Some Federalists accused the clubs of taking advantage of recent arrivals. The clubs, explained one correspondent, "have deceived as well as soured the minds of the ignorant and jealous, especially strangers and those who are sore from suffering in foreign countries."[61] Other Federalists blamed foreigners for the existence of the clubs and warned that radical immigrants were plotting to overthrow the government.[62]

On the whole, therefore, the forming of the Democratic and Republican Societies had the effect of amplifying the underlying disagreements about the meaning of self-government. While members of the clubs believed that the societies played an integral role in protecting the people's liberties by ensuring citizens remained informed and engaged, Federalists saw the societies as agents of chaos that encouraged citizens to challenge the federal government. This divide over the role of citizens would soon come into even sharper focus.

Regulation

Western Pennsylvania had remained a thorn in the side of Federalists since the ratification of the federal Constitution. Many of the residents in this area remained deeply suspicious of, if not outright hostile to, the federal government. Still harboring resentments stemming from the collapse of the 1776 constitution, these men believed that the regime privileged wealthy easterners at the expense of ordinary farmers in the west. Their concerns appeared justified when reports began to circulate that the new secretary of the treasury, Alexander Hamilton, planned to place a tax on distilled liquors, along with other items, to help fund the federal government and pay the interest on the national debt. The tax, which Congress officially adopted in 1791, hit Pennsylvania's western farmers, who relied on the sale of whiskey to supplement their earnings, particularly hard. Shipping grain and corn from the west was prohibitively expensive, and the only way to make a profit was to distill the grain into liquor, which was more easily transported. Adding insult to injury, much of the government's debt had ended up in the hands of wealthy speculators. These men now stood ready to earn a fortune thanks to Hamilton's fiscal plan. Many westerners, therefore, saw the tax as nothing more than taking money away from hardworking farmers and giving it to wealthy "stock-jobbers" who owned the debt.[63]

Aggrieved westerners divided on how to respond to the new tax. Some residents chose to work within the confines of the constitutional system and registered their disapproval through public meetings and petitions. In the fall of 1792, for example, delegates from the various western counties gathered in Pittsburgh and agreed to resolutions denouncing the excise tax and promising to take every "legal measure that may obstruct the operation of the Law until we are able to obtain its total repeal." Although the participants had gone out of their way to emphasize that they did not endorse the type of extralegal forms of protest associated with the Revolution, Federalists nevertheless condemned the meeting as "disgraceful to humanity, subversive of social happiness, and destructive of civil authority." Not surprisingly, the underlying complaints went unheeded.[64]

While some critics of the tax sought relief through their elected officials, others decided to take matters into their own hands. Although the adoption of the new federal and state constitutions supposedly obviated the need for popular violence, mobs attacked at least three men alleged to be related to the collection of the tax in 1791. The assailants relied on the same painful and humiliating forms of ritualized violence that Pennsylvanians had used in the 1770s and 1780s. A group of men, for example, abducted Robert Johnson, the collector for Allegheny and Washington Counties, and proceeded to cut off his hair and tar and feather him. The crowd then left Johnson, without his horse, miles from the nearest town. Johnson pressed charges against his attackers, but another mob seized the messenger tasked with delivering the warrant and subjected him to the same treatment as Johnson. The ritualized nature of these tactics sent the message that the violence reflected the will of the community rather than that of a few disgruntled residents and pointed to the persistence of radicals' expansive version of popular sovereignty.[65]

Unlike peaceful forms of protest, popular violence seemed to achieve results. Even after Congress adopted some changes designed to make the law more palatable, General John Neville, the inspector of the revenue, struggled to find anyone who would rent him space to open an office out of fear they would face retribution. As a result, the excise went uncollected. Just as they had under the previous regime, the people of western Pennsylvania asserted their right to reject laws deemed unjust.[66]

From the temporary seat of government in Philadelphia, Federalists followed the events in western Pennsylvania closely. With the federal government still in its infancy, many Federalists believed that the government had to stand firmly behind the rule of law and demonstrate that popular uprisings would not be tolerated—particularly those that occurred in such close proximity to the capital. Hamilton, who had emerged as one of the most prominent defenders of the new regime, warned President Washington that if he did not take steps to "exert the full force of the Law against the Offenders," then the "the spirit of disobedience . . . [would] naturally extend and the authority of the Government will be prostrate."[67]

Heeding Hamilton's advice, on 15 September 1792, Washington issued a presidential proclamation that called the recent attempts to obstruct tax collection "subversive of good order" and "dangerous to the very being of government." He went on to assert that popular uprisings, such as those that had occurred in the 1780s, would no longer be tolerated and ordered government officials to ensure that anyone breaking the law be brought to justice. For Washington and other Federalists, the attacks against excise collectors represented a direct challenge to the legitimacy of the new regime. The people, through their elected officials, had spoken in favor of the excise, and the aggrieved farmers, like everyone else, were bound to respect their will.[68]

A number of prominent Pennsylvanians agreed with Washington that popular violence had no place under the new constitutions. Governor Thomas Mifflin wrote that the constitutions and laws were expressions of the popular will and that "every irregular and illegal opposition to the existing laws will not only embarrass the operations of Government, but eventually undermine the only real security for the liberty and property of the individuals." If citizens had a problem with the law, they had every right to petition for redress. They could also try to elect new representatives. They could not, however, simply ignore the rule of law.[69] Along similar lines, Judge Alexander Addison urged westerners to "inculcate that constitutional resistance, which alone is justifiable in a free people."[70] William Findley, meanwhile, assured Governor Mifflin that the "leading Citizens" in the west rejected the "riotous opposition to the execution of the Excise Law."[71]

Regardless of what the "leading Citizens" might have thought, many westerners clearly believed that they had the right to assert their will directly. In April 1793, a group of men with darkened faces broke into the house of Robert Wells, a revenue collector in Fayette County. Finding Wells not at home, they terrorized his family. The sheriff, fearful of retribution, refused to deliver warrants against some of the men accused of participating in the attack. A few months later, the mob returned and forced Wells at gunpoint to surrender his account books and renounce his position. Once again, the mob suffered no consequences. Meanwhile, John Lynn, collector for Washington County, had his hair cut off, was tarred and feathered, and after being forced to swear that he would never take another position associated with the excise, was left naked and tied to a tree. Crowds also burned down the barns and destroyed farm equipment of distillers who cooperated with the law. By the spring of 1794, the situation had become so dire that the collection of taxes all but ceased in much of western Pennsylvania.[72]

The clashing views of sovereignty came to a head in the summer of 1794. Infuriated by the blatant disregard for the federal government's authority, Washington responded by calling for the arrest of tax evaders. The move backfired. After the inspector of the revenue John Neville, a man reviled by many in the west, began issuing warrants, rumors quickly spread that those arrested would be hauled to Philadelphia to face trial.[73] In response to what they perceived to be an attack on their liberty, nearly five hundred residents mobilized and descended on Neville's mansion, known as "Bower Hill." Neville managed to escape unscathed, but the attackers engaged in a brief skirmish with federal troops who had taken up position in the house. Although the outnumbered troops quickly surrendered, the gunfire left Captain James McFarland, one of the rebel leaders, dead.[74]

The violence at Bower Hill represented a significant escalation in the standoff between the opponents of the excise and the federal government. Even some of men who had originally supported the protest movement concluded that the attack on Neville's house and gunfight with federal troops exceeded the parameters of acceptable forms of political action. Other Pennsylvanians, however, saw the incident as further evidence of the dangers posed by the federal government. The death of Captain McFarland underscored the importance of the moment. The time had come, these men argued, for the people to rise up and reassert their authority. In a circular letter calling for a mass muster at Braddock's Field on 1 August, David Bradford and other leading insurgents proclaimed that it was time "that every citizen must express his sentiments not by his words, but by his actions." What had begun as a series of popular uprisings protesting a specific law had escalated into an open rebellion against the entire regime.[75]

Nearly seven thousand men turned out for the muster at Braddock's Field. Although organizers had not provided any details on what would happen once the crowd gathered, some of the attendees clearly viewed the muster as the first step in a second revolution. A group of insurgents had even created their own flag, which bore six stripes representing the counties of western Pennsylvania and Ohio County, Virginia, which supported the rebellion. There was talk of seizing a federal arsenal near Pittsburgh to help launch an armed rebellion. Cooler heads eventually prevailed. The arsenal was well-fortified, and many rebels lacked weapons. Instead, the men agreed to simply march through the streets of Pittsburgh as a demonstration of their power. When finished, the protesters dispersed and returned to their respective homes. No shots were fired, and nobody was injured.[76]

The threat of violence dissipated in the weeks following the muster. At an assembly of two hundred delegates from the six western counties on 14 August, political leaders Albert Gallatin, William Findley, and Hugh Henry Brackenridge successfully steered the opposition to the excise back into legal channels. While some of the delegates still favored more direct forms of protest, a majority agreed to appoint a committee to draft a petition to Congress outlining their opposition to the excise. The assembly also adopted a resolution calling on all citizens to work together to prevent "any violence or outrage against the property and persons of any individual." Attacks on excise collectors would no longer be tolerated.[77]

Although the rebellion collapsed and the majority of westerners pledged to support the federal government, Washington assembled a force of nearly thirteen thousand troops, matching the largest number of soldiers Washington ever had under his command at one time during the Revolutionary War, to march on western Pennsylvania. The massive show of force accomplished little more than upsetting locals. Civilians taunted the troops, and some residents raised liberty poles as a sign of their commitment to the principles of the Revolution, but the army met no organized opposition. Left with nothing else to do, soldiers contented themselves with harassing locals and making mass arrests. Many of the leading rebels, including David Bradford, managed to escape; others surrendered without incident.[78]

Although the troops may not have served much practical purpose, Washington's decision to call out the army did, however, send a clear message that the new regime would not tolerate challenges to the federal government's authority. Crowd action and popular violence were not viewed as expressions of the people's sovereignty, they were considered forms of rebellion.

Triangulation

The political fallout from the "Whiskey Rebellion" rippled throughout the state. Critics of the Federalists struggled with how to respond. Prominent members of the opposition had been outspoken in their opposition to Federalists' fiscal policies and had expressed support for the plight of westerners. On Independence Day in 1794, a mere two weeks before the insurrection, the Philadelphia Democratic Society drank a toast to "EXCISE, may this baneful exotic wither in the soil of freedom."[79] Members of the opposition also suggested that Pennsylvanians had a responsibility to resist the unjust law. The excise, they argued, served as one more example of the need for citizens to take an active role in the governing process. As "Agricola" warned readers, the public's response to the law would "demonstrate whether you are tame asses, who will submit to any load, which your new masters are pleased to lay on you." Although he did not call for violence, Agricola did suggest a "return to our good old way of giving instructions to our Delegates in Congress" to ensure that elected officials respected the will of the people.[80]

Federalists seized on these types of statements to blame the opposition for causing the rebellion. The Democratic and Republican Societies bore the brunt of the attacks. Federalists claimed that the societies' constant criticism of the federal government had laid the groundwork for insurrection. President Washington personally accused the groups of "laboring incessantly to sow the seeds of distrust, jealousy, and, of course discontent," and concluded "that they have been the fomenters of the western disturbances."[81] Echoing these claims, the *Gazette of the United States* proclaimed that "the mad conduct of the insurgents at Pittsburgh is the natural fruit of their democratic clubs."[82]

According to Federalists, however, it was not just the Democratic and Republican Societies that were at fault. Indeed, Federalists claimed that the uprising proved that organized opposition to the federal government of any sort bred violence. According to one correspondent, the whole affair could be blamed on "a sect of *leading partizans* . . . who, being originally opposed to the Constitution of the United States, have always maintained a systematic opposition to the matters of the government."[83] These men had allegedly fostered an environment where "a small portion of the community" felt entitled to ignore the law.[84] According to Federalists, these malcontents were just as responsible for what happened in western Pennsylvania as the men who refused to pay the excise, and if something did not change, the country would surely face another armed rebellion.

Blamed by the Federalists for provoking internal dissent and implicated in the rebellion by their opposition to the excise, members of the opposition responded by charting a middle course between the insurgents' use of violence and the Federalists' hostility to any criticism of the government. From the pages of the *Aurora* (the new name for the *General Advertiser*), Benjamin Bache declared that, although he may dislike it, the excise law had "received every constitutional sanction," and as such, it represented the "will of the majority."[85] Citizens might disagree with a particular policy or think a law was unwise, he argued, but they had no right to take the law into their own hands. Using force to overturn a law was "repugnant to true democratic principles."[86] Some members of the opposition went even further. According to one correspondent, the insurgents were actually promoting an aristocracy because they claimed to have the right to ignore the will of the people. "The first principle of democracy is that government is instituted for the happiness of the many," he explained. "The first step to aristocracy is to throw it into the hands of the few. Have not those citizens who oppose the execution of a law of the union by force of arms endeavoured to introduce this aristocratic principle into action?"[87]

But, while opposition journalists denounced the use of violence, they adamantly defended the right to organize and protest against laws deemed unjust. The problem with the insurgents had not been that they disagreed with the federal government. It was a matter of how the westerners went about expressing their dissatisfaction. Members of the opposition argued that the people were free to oppose any act of the federal government, but they must do so from within the confines of the constitutional system. "If a law is obnoxious," Bache explained, "let the citizens . . . petition for its repeal, expose its defects through the medium of the press; let them change their representation." If these approaches failed, however, it became a citizen's "duty to bear [the law's] burdins." The people had no right to take the law into their own hands.[88]

The opposition also sought to establish their commitment to the rule of law by joining Washington's army as it marched west. Many outspoken critics of the Federalists volunteered to help "subdue" the rebellion. Bache reported approvingly that a "universal ardour for military exertion seem[ed] . . . to pervade every rank of citizens in Philadelphia." These men, he noted, were not motivated by a "thirst of plunder or blood, but from the deliberate and just conviction that every thing dear to the commonwealth [was] at stake."[89] The Philadelphia Democratic Society likewise praised the "patriotic bands of Citizen-soldiers" who volunteered to march in defense of the principles of democracy, and prominent members volunteered their services. In fact, according to one observer, the "Democratic Society of Pennsylvania, could have made a quorum in the field."[90]

In the end, the Whiskey Rebellion may have actually helped the opposition gain legitimacy. By triangulating themselves against the Federalists on one side and the insurgents on the other, members of the opposition created space to carve out an identity as the friends of both liberty *and* order.

Critics of the Federalists did, however, experience one significant loss: the closing of Democratic and Republican Societies. The violence in western Pennsylvania, along with the barrage of attacks from George Washington and other Federalists, put an enormous amount of pressure on the clubs. In the wake of the Whiskey Rebellion, lurking ideological disagreements that had been masked behind a shared opposition to the Federalists began to surface. Tensions flared at a meeting of the Philadelphia Democratic Society, and nearly half of the attendees stormed out during a debate over a resolution censuring those who took part in the violence. The rupture proved to be the final straw, and the society withered in the following months. Sister clubs throughout the state met with similar fates, and by 1795 all the Democratic and Republican Societies in Pennsylvania had closed.[91]

Overall, the Whiskey Rebellion and subsequent collapse of the Democratic and Republican Societies marked an important turning point in Pennsylvania. Members of the clubs had promoted a version of civil society that stood in stark contrast to the one the Federalists hoped to establish. The clubs had advanced a more participatory political culture and defended the people's right to assert their sovereignty outside of election day. They had fought against aristocratic creep and worked to keep citizens actively engaged in the governing process. Now, justified or not, the clubs and their vision for the country had become associated with violence. From their ashes, however, critics of the Federalists begun to establish a more clearly defined role as a loyal opposition.

The Opposition Goes to the Polls

The first real evidence of how the Whiskey Rebellion would affect Pennsylvania's political landscape came when voters went to the polls in October 1794. Federalists consistently won a majority of state and federal elections during the first years of the new regime. The opposition had been gaining ground, however, and with the organizational structure provided by the Democratic and Republican Societies, they seemed poised to pick up additional seats in 1794. But the outbreak of the Whiskey Rebellion in late July followed by Washington's denunciation of the clubs in August threw everything into question. The elections would be the first time that voters could weigh in on the uprising, and the results could clarify how much blame the opposition would shoulder for the insurrection.

One of the most watched contests in 1794 occurred in the First Congressional District, which consisted of the city of Philadelphia and pitted incumbent Federalist Thomas Fitzsimons against John Swanwick. Fitzsimons had a long history in Pennsylvania politics. He had emigrated to Philadelphia from Ireland in the 1750s and helped to organize a militia company to fight against the British during the Revolutionary War. Afterward, he served in the Continental Congress and then as a delegate to the U.S. Constitutional Convention. He was first elected to the House of Representatives in 1788 and had been reelected twice by wide margins. Although Fitzsimons remained a popular figure, a federal excise on manufactured goods adopted in the spring of 1794 had damaged his standing in Philadelphia and left him vulnerable to a challenge.[92]

Swanwick, like Fitzsimons, was an immigrant. Born in Liverpool, England, he moved to America in the 1770s, where he went to work for Robert Morris as an apprentice. Swanwick eventually served during the Revolutionary War but only after being accused of sharing secrets with the British. Following the war, he aligned himself with the moderates and supported federalist candidates in 1788 and 1790. Like some of the other members of the original federalist coalition, however, Swanwick became disillusioned with efforts to reform the nation's political culture. He was elected to the state assembly as a member of the opposition in 1792 and quickly earned a reputation for being an outspoken (and loquacious) critic of the Federalists. Exactly when the opposition settled on Swanwick as their candidate in 1794 is unclear, but by the late summer he had emerged as the favorite to take on Fitzsimons.[93]

The Whiskey Rebellion and Washington's attacks on the Democratic and Republican Societies put Swanwick in an especially difficult position. He had joined the Philadelphia Democratic Society in April 1794 and played a prominent role in some of their celebrations. The Federalist *Gazette of the United States* seized on the connection and labeled him "AMBASSADOR EXTRAORDINARY to the Insurgents."[94] Swanwick responded in the assembly by denouncing the insurgents for ignoring the rule of law. In a speech that was subsequently printed in many of the local papers, Swanwick claimed that he had been working through constitutional channels to secure the repeal of the excise prior to the uprising. In fact, he argued that the uprising had "greatly injured" the chances of accomplishing anything. Worse still, he believed that the insurgents had "armed the friends of the system with new reasons for enforcing [the tax], deduced from the necessity of firmness in government."[95] In other words,

Swanwick sought to draw a clear distinction between his legal efforts to repeal the tax and the unconstitutional violence in the west.

Swanwick and his allies launched an aggressive campaign to mobilize their supporters in the weeks before the election. The opposition held a series of meetings designed to give the public an opportunity to ratify Swanwick as the nominee and establish his credentials as the people's choice. Although these types of meeting had become commonplace, the number and location of the pro-Swanwick assemblies point to the opposition's increasingly sophisticated approach to mobilizing voters. Many of these gatherings occurred in lower-class neighborhoods that were home to large numbers of artisans, laborers, and recent immigrants. At least two meetings occurred at the German Lutheran Church, located on the corner of Fourth and Cherry Streets in North Mulberry Ward. A densely populated area, North Mulberry was one of the fastest growing parts of Philadelphia, and low property values and cheap rent made it popular among recent immigrants and unskilled laborers. These were key constituencies, and Swanwick would need them to turn out in order to overcome Fitzsimons's base of support among the gentry.[96]

In addition to the rallies, local dignitaries, including Thomas McKean, chief justice of the state supreme court, were seen canvassing voters in the days before the election. Swanwick treated members of the State House to an extravagant lunch at Oeller's Hotel and purportedly agreed to make a generous donation to St. Mary's Catholic Church in an attempt to win over Catholic voters. On election day, supporters were supplied with ample quantities of grog at one of Swanwick's taverns.[97]

This type of overt solicitation of votes horrified Federalists' deferential sensibilities. The *Gazette of the United States* charged Swanwick with pioneering a "new style" of politics that threatened to undermine the basic values of the republic.[98] Although Swanwick's tactics were not particularly new, they had never been practiced on such a scale. What was new, and particularly troubling to Federalists, was that Swanwick made no attempt to hide his ambition. Candidates were supposed to remain above the fray and let supporters do the canvassing. Not only did Swanwick personally solicit votes but he seemed to target poor and uneducated voters with slogans such as "Swanwick and no excise."[99]

Although they condemned Swanwick for openly courting voters, Federalists also took steps to bolster Fitzsimons by calling for their own nominating meeting to occur on Saturday, 11 October—three days before the election. The meeting was nearly a disaster. In an effort to secure the proper outcome, Federalists scheduled the assembly at a time that would make it difficult for artisans and laborers, who tended to align with the opposition, to attend. Aware that it would be the last meeting before the election, Benjamin Bache urged members of the opposition to attend. His appeals seem to have worked because when it came time for the meeting to vote on a nominee, the chairman had to take two votes before he could declare that the majority of those in attendance endorsed Fitzsimons. Although Federalists avoided humiliation, the fact that it was even close was an ominous sign.[100]

The election returns point to the effectiveness of Swanwick's approach to electioneering. At least two hundred more people voted in 1794 than had in 1792, an increase of approximately 4 percent. When the votes were tallied, Swanwick came out on top by a vote of 1,240 to 1,182 or 51 to 49 percent. Swanwick received the highest percentage of votes from the ethnically diverse working-class neighborhoods of North and South Mulberry. Turnout was also particularly high in these wards, suggesting that the rallies may have succeeded in mobilizing these voters. Swanwick's courting of the lower classes did not prevent him from making inroads in other areas either. Although High and Dock Wards, home to some of the most prestigious families and wealthiest merchants, supported the Federalist candidate, Swanwick made a good showing. It is also worth noting that Swanwick received over 30 percent of the votes cast by the army and militia. His strong backing from men committed to quelling the Whiskey Rebellion suggests that he had successfully distanced himself from the rebels.[101]

Ultimately, Swanwick's victory in 1794 seemed to indicate a path forward for critics of the Federalists. By affirming their willingness to remain within the confines of the constitutional system and engaging in targeted forms of electioneering, the opposition could slowly chip away at Federalist majorities. Of course, this strategy would mean they would have to accept the regime's limits on the role of citizens and commit to working through elections rather than direct political action. As would become clear, some members of the opposition were not yet prepared to make that concession.

The People Out of Doors versus the Jay Treaty

Before the dust from the Whiskey Rebellion had settled, Pennsylvanians faced the next crisis that brought to the surface festering disagreements about the role of the people. The fight over America's relationship with

Revolutionary France had continued to rage since Washington had issued his Neutrality Proclamation. The declaration that the United States would not take sides in the war between Great Britain and France had not only failed to keep domestic peace; it had also done nothing to stop both powers from harassing American merchant vessels on the open seas. With the country divided and the economy suffering, Washington appointed Chief Justice John Jay, a prominent Federalist, as special envoy to Great Britain in the spring of 1794. Although the United States technically remained neutral, Jay's appointment seemed to signal that the new nation would be casting its lot with the former mother country.

On one level, the decision to side with England made practical sense. The U.S. economy remained deeply enmeshed with Great Britain, and Americans traded with the British much more than they did with the French. While in England, Jay could also address American concerns about British violations of the Peace of Paris and deal with outstanding debts dating back to the Revolution. Critics of the Washington administration, however, reacted to the appointment with outrage because it seemed to confirm their suspicions that Federalists had betrayed the spirit of the Revolution. Philadelphians burned Jay in effigy before he had even set sail.[102]

Members of the opposition were therefore on edge when rumors of a signed treaty first began circulating in early 1795. President Washington received the official terms in March and promptly submitted the treaty to the Senate for consideration. Contents of the treaty remained secret throughout this process, and senators discussed the provisions in closed-door sessions. Although this was standard procedure for sensitive information, the clandestine nature of the deliberations infuriated the opposition, who argued that concealing the details of such an important treaty from the public and debating its contents in secret amounted to a bastardization of the meaning of representation. "Franklin" raged that, although the Constitution granted the president and the Senate the right to negotiate treaties, these powers were "derived from *the People,*" and as such, they had to be consulted before decisions were made.[103] To suggest that elected officials could act without knowing the will of the people, explained another correspondent, would mean "representation is a paradox—it is only a name."[104] The protestations fell on deaf ears. Federalists in the Senate narrowly ratified the treaty on 24 June with a vote of twenty to ten, just barely meeting the two-thirds threshold required for treaties, and sent it to Washington for his signature.[105]

But, as the country waited to learn what Washington would do, a senator leaked a copy of the treaty to Benjamin Bache, who printed it on 1 July 1795.[106] The contents inflamed public opinion. Under the proposed treaty, Americans would have to accept severe restrictions on tonnage and settle prewar debts owed to British merchants. In exchange, the country received some minor concessions relating to disputed forts in the Northwest and trade opportunities with British territories. The treaty said nothing about Britain's repeated violations of America's maritime rights.[107]

The opposition responded to the publication of the Jay Treaty by feverishly denouncing what they saw as an attempt to make America subservient to Great Britain, and they immediately set about organizing a series of public protests designed to force Washington to withhold his signature. Regardless of what the Senate had done, the opposition believed that a massive outcry against the treaty would surely convince Washington that a majority of the American people opposed it. Critics adopted many of the approaches to mobilization the opposition had been developing throughout the early 1790s. Protestors, for example, used the Fourth of July to condemn the agreement. Instead of the typical festivities, the opposition "celebrated" the day by donning mourning attire and staging a mock funeral procession to mark what they described as the "*last* anniversary of American *Independence*."[108] At the end of the procession, "amid the acclamation of hundreds of citizens," the crowd burned an effigy of Jay.[109] Opponents also filled the newspapers with impassioned articles that depicted the treaty as an attack on the people's rights and a threat to their independence. One particularly provocative piece described it as an "illegitimate imp, the abortion of liberty," and asserted that its ratification would mean America had "*virtually*, tho' not formally, become a party in the confederacy of despots against liberty, and surrendered the rights of an independent nation into the hands of Great Britain."[110]

The opposition's efforts to use popular mobilization to kill the treaty culminated with a decision to call a general town meeting in Philadelphia. The authority of these gatherings remained somewhat ambiguous during the first years of the new regime. Both Pennsylvania's Declaration of Rights and the recently ratified First Amendment to the federal Constitution specifically guaranteed the people the right to assemble and petition their elected officials. The constitutions did not, however, specify that government officials were bound to follow their constituents' advice. Federalists in the House of Representatives had, in fact, explicitly rejected a proposed motion to give voters the right to instruct their representatives. George Clymer, a representative from Philadelphia, spoke for many Federalists when he dismissed the idea of instructions as a "most dangerous principle" that was "utterly destructive of all ideas of an independent and deliberate body." According to Federalists, citizens expressed their will exclusively through the ballot box and were otherwise expected to defer to the judgment of their elected officials.[111]

Given their understanding of the relationship between the people and their government, Federalists denounced the opposition's decision to call a town meeting to discuss the Jay Treaty. Such a gathering, Federalists argued, would do nothing more than create controversy and could easily lead to violence. As one writer explained, "The administration of the commonwealth is in the hands of men of approved wisdom and virtue. What necessity therefore can there be to disturb or interrupt this safe and enviable state by the convulsive operations of town meetings; where neither order wisdom, or safety can be expected?"[112]

The opposition had a different perspective on the role of the people. Regardless of what the Federalists might say about the new constitutions, critics believed that citizens had both a right and a responsibility to mobilize in defense of the principles of the Revolution. Handbills announcing the meeting emphasized what was at stake and called on all citizens to attend to "discuss the Momentous Question, viz: Are the People the Legitimate Fountain of Government?"[113] Bache urged his readers to attend and proclaimed that no "real republican" could possible question the "right of the citizens to meet and deliberate on measures which so intimately concern their welfare and property."[114] The people, he asserted, always had the right to express their views, and Federalist attacks on the town meeting only proved they were enemies of self-government.[115]

Whether motivated by the larger questions of the nature of sovereignty or concerned primarily with the treaty, more than 1,400 people crammed into the State House Yard on 23 July, making it one of the largest public gatherings in Philadelphia to that date.[116] Organizers set the meeting for 5:00 p.m. to maximize attendance and to ensure that the city's laborers and mechanics could attend. After coming to order, the meeting followed the traditional format and opened with the selection of a chairman and a brief period of deliberation. According to published reports, the assembled then "UNANIMOUSLY" adopted a statement that affirmed "the constitutional right and patriotic duty of the Citizens of the United

States, to express on every important occasion, the public sense of public measures," and stated that "the citizens of Philadelphia *in judgment and in feeling,* disapprove of the Treaty." After agreeing to the resolutions, participants selected a committee to draft a memorial to President Washington that would "respectfully but forcibly" assert the people's opposition to the treaty. The meeting then concluded with an agreement that everyone would reconvene in two days to discuss the committee's work.[117]

An even larger crowd turned out for the subsequent meeting, which took place on a Saturday. The *Aurora* estimated the crowd at between five and six thousand people, which would have made it the largest town meeting since the Revolution. Speaking from a temporary stage built for the occasion, members of the committee read through their memorial, pausing to allow the crowd to vote on each paragraph individually. At the conclusion, the chair asked if the meeting was prepared to adopt the memorial, and the audience cheered, stomped their feet, and waved their hats to demonstrate their approval. Bache reported that while "*one* and *two* hands were up in the negative" for specific paragraphs, "*one* and but *one*" voted against the final memorial. According to him, "The greatest order prevailed" throughout the entire proceeding. Emphasizing the deliberative nature of the assembly, he reported that the crowd remained absolutely silent "so that each citizen present could hear every word distinctly." Furthermore, "not the least violence was attempted" against the lone dissenter to the final memorial.[118]

Had the crowd dispersed at the conclusion of the meeting, the spectacle of more than five thousand residents peaceably expressing their disapproval of the treaty would have served as an important demonstration of how the people could participate in the governing process in an orderly and controlled manner. Unfortunately for the organizers, that did not happen. The crowd remained energized after agreeing to the memorial and showed no signs of disbanding. Sensing an opportunity as the chairman and committee exited, Blair McClenachan, the former president of the Democratic Society of Pennsylvania, jumped on stage, and while waving a copy of the treaty above his head, bellowed that he "had one more motion to make to my fellow countrymen, and that is, that you kick this damn treaty to hell!" With that, McClenachan threw the treaty into the sea of onlookers. Members of the crowd seized it, stuck it to the top of a pike, and then paraded to the French minister's house where they held another ceremony to denounce the treaty. Later that evening, between two and three hundred residents assembled in front of the houses of prominent Federalist Philadelphians where they burned copies of the treaty and broke windows.[119]

Federalists pounced on this uproar to dismiss both meetings as the work of malcontents and radicals. The pandemonium, they argued, clearly demonstrated that the crowd did not actually represent the will of the American people. Oliver Wolcott, a Federalist from Connecticut, concluded that the "actors generally were an ignorant mob, of that class which is most disaffected and violent."[120] Echoing these sentiments, Secretary of State Timothy Pickering reported to Washington that the majority of people in attendance had been mere spectators and that virtually nobody in the crowd had actually read the treaty.[121] Other writers claimed that most of the people who turned out were immigrants who had only recently stepped off the boat.[122] Federalists also challenged the *Aurora*'s estimate on the size of the crowd. One correspondent even measured the space in the State House Yard and then divided it by the average space a single person needs to stand in order to mathematically prove that there could not have been more than about two thousand people in attendance.[123]

In addition to delegitimizing the meeting by focusing on the violence and attacking the size and composition of the crowd, Federalist journalists also reminded the public that, under the current regime, "the constituted authorities of the country are the only organs of the national will." Town meetings, regardless of their makeup, could never represent the public will.[124] In fact, Federalists claimed that by appealing directly to the people and challenging the authority of the elected officials, critics of the treaty had acted "contrary to their duties as members of a civil society" and given "artful demagogues" an opportunity to prey on the "idle" and "turbulent" masses.[125] Ultimately, Federalists argued that the entire experience confirmed their belief that town meetings tended to "subvert all government, and introduce anarchy and confusion." It was, therefore, "the duty of every well disposed citizen, to discourage town-meetings."[126]

Members of the opposition defended the authority of the meeting and accused Federalists of committing "a libel on the Federal, and every free Constitution" by attacking the people's right to exercise their sovereignty at a town meeting, but the mayhem helped give Washington enough political cover to ignore the public outcry. On 14 August 1795, he signed the Jay Treaty.[127]

With this stroke of his pen, Washington dashed the opposition's efforts to use town meetings to intervene in the deliberative process. His signature was a reminder that under the Constitution, town meetings, no matter what their size, could not speak for the people. That power rested exclusively with elected officials. Critics howled in protest and accused Washington of blatantly disregarding public opinion. There was, however, little they could do. Washington had made his decision. According to the Constitution, the people had spoken.[128]

Federalists and the Power of Petitions

Washington may have been able to ignore the town meetings, but Federalists could not simply ignore public opinion. The regime remained fragile, and its legitimacy still depended on the extent to which Americans accepted it as the embodiment of the public will. As a result, Federalists had to continue to find ways to demonstrate their popularity. To that end, in the aftermath of the controversy surrounding the signing of the Jay Treaty, Federalists turned to another well-established form of mobilization to reaffirm their status as the spokesmen of the people: the petition.

Having failed to stop the Jay Treaty through town meetings, members of the opposition in the U.S. House of Representatives mounted a last-ditch effort to block its implementation by demanding to see diplomatic correspondence and refusing to appropriate the necessary funding. The move backfired. Drawing on lessons learned by moderates in the 1780s, Federalists responded by flooding Congress with petitions and memorials in support of the treaty. Federalists across Pennsylvania organized meetings and created committees to go door to door collecting signatures. Over a period of approximately three months, Pennsylvanians sent Congress at least 44 pro-treaty petitions signed by more than 6,400 citizens. Federalists in other states followed suit.[129]

Unlike a riot or the opposition's efforts to instruct Washington on how to vote, a petition fit with Federalists' vision for a deferential republic. Framed as a request rather than a demand, these petitions carried an implicit acknowledgment that the people could not participate directly in the deliberative process and that elected officials ultimately had the only real power. The language of the petitions reinforced this message. "Waiving all questions of the merits of the Treaty with Britain, it has acquired the sanction of the American Constitution," explained one petition from western Pennsylvania. The treaty was therefore the law of the land, and the people had no right to try and stop its implementation.[130] Petitioners did not make any claims about representing the will of the people as a whole either. Thus, when a group of Philadelphia merchants declared "that the faith, honor and interest of the nation, may be preserved by making necessary provisions for carrying the Treaty into fair and honorable effect," they spoke only as individual citizens rather than as the sovereign people.[131]

The Federalists' petition drive caught members of the opposition somewhat off guard. A belated attempt to collect signatures in opposition to the Jay Treaty in Pennsylvania yielded only 10 petitions with approximately 2,600 names—less than half the number Federalists gathered.[132] Critics of the treaty, who believed that they spoke for the majority of the people, struggled with how to make sense of how Federalists had produced so many petitions in such a short period. Reviving some of the same accusations lobbed at radicals during their petition drives in defense of the revolutionary regime, members of the opposition claimed that Federalists must have used fraud and deceit. Reports circulated that bank directors had threatened to cut credit if people did not sign the petitions.[133] One correspondent claimed that he was told to "EITHER SIGN THIS PETITION OR YOU WILL HAVE A WAR" and was never informed that the petition had to do with the treaty.[134]

Despite these claims, the barrage of petitions proved overwhelming. Even William Findley, one of Pennsylvania's most prominent critics of the administration, bowed to the pressure. Forced to choose between abandoning his principles or facing a potential backlash from his constituents, Findley conveniently stepped out of the room during the final vote. Two of the representatives from Pennsylvania who had originally been in favor of blocking the treaty reversed their positions as well. The final vote on the treaty was fifty-one to forty-eight, meaning that the opposition could have prevailed if the three Pennsylvanians had held their ground.[135]

The failure to block the Jay Treaty followed by Federalists' petition campaign dealt the opposition and their vision for a more participatory form of politics a devastating blow. For years, the opposition had regularly accused Federalists of trying to deprive the people of their rights and secretly establish an aristocracy. They had used celebratory politics in an attempt to foster an environment more conducive to the principles of liberty and equality, and they had fought to engage the public more directly in the deliberative process by organizing Democratic and Republican Societies and staging town meetings. These efforts had, however, failed to bring about any meaningful changes. Instead, the Whiskey Rebellion and

Jay Treaty debates had given Washington and the Federalists a chance to clearly establish the limits of direct forms of mobilization. Under the Constitution, the people spoke through the ballot box. At the same time, the Federalists' successful petition campaign served as a reminder of the value of some forms of popular politics. For the opposition, this meant that they would either need to accept Federalists' rule or change their approach to mobilizing their supporters.

4

From Opposition to Party

ON 19 SEPTEMBER 1796, *Claypoole's American Daily Advertiser* printed an open letter to "*the* PEOPLE *of the* UNITED STATES" by George Washington making official what most political observers had already concluded: the president would not seek a third term in office. Looking back on his eight years in office, Washington had plenty he could be proud of. He had overseen the birth of a new regime that promised to usher in an age of freedom and prosperity. Thanks to Secretary of the Treasury Alexander Hamilton's handiwork, the country's economy appeared to be rebounding. Just as importantly, the recently implemented Jay Treaty ensured that America would not be dragged into another war and helped to cement the relationship between the United Kingdom and the United States.

As bright as the country's future looked, however, Washington still found cause for concern. During his time in office, clashes over the Republican Court and the French Revolution had exposed deep ideological rifts between the Federalists and their opponents. Washington worried that, if left unchecked, these divisions would eat away at the social fabric of the republic and sap the strength of the federal government. As a result, he dedicated a substantial part of his Farewell Address to warning his fellow citizens of the dangers of factionalism. Organized resistance to the government, he cautioned, "agitates the community with ill-founded jealousies and false alarms, kindles the animosity of one part against another," and, as had happened in western Pennsylvania, "foments occasionally riot and insurrection." To guard against such pitfalls, he called on citizens to "discountenance irregular oppositions to [the government's] acknowledged authority" and "resist with care the spirit of innovation upon its principles." In other words, Americans should accept the realities the new regime.[1]

By 1796, even members of the opposition appeared to agree with Washington on this point. Their attempts to use popular politics to force change had failed. Recognition of this fact did not, however, mean that members of the opposition embraced Federalists' vision for the nation. Instead, as this chapter argues, critics of the Federalists abandoned efforts to engage the people directly in the deliberative process in the wake of the Whiskey Rebellion and Jay Treaty defeats and instead started focusing on winning elections. This shift marked the beginning of the opposition's transition from a disparate coalition without any clear structure to an organized political party.

Adopting the label "Republicans," members of this emerging party remained committed to keeping the public engaged and informed but focused their efforts on achieving change through electoral victories rather than through direct political action. Although Republicans continued to criticize Federalists' version of deferential republicanism, the construction of a party apparatus came with the implicit acceptance of the idea that the people spoke exclusively through the ballot box. Nonetheless, popular mobilization remained a key part of Republicans' strategy. Rather than trying to engage the people directly in the deliberative process, Republicans used rallies, parades, meetings, and voluntary societies to drive voter turnout and establish themselves as agents of the people.

As the Republican Party took shape, Federalists in Pennsylvania continued to rely on the same types of mobilization that they had successfully employed throughout the early 1790s. With threat of a war with France looming, they turned to celebratory politics and public meetings to rally support for the federal government. Convinced that any organized opposition posed a threat to the country, Federalists also embarked on a campaign to silence their critics using legislation and violence. These measures helped Federalists maintain their grip on power for a few years, but they also bred resentment and eventually opened the door for Republicans to position themselves as the guardians of the Constitution and the true spokesmen of the people.

State of the State

The social, economic, and political conditions in Pennsylvania help to explain the emergence of the Republican Party in the late 1790s. State and national politics remained intimately intertwined. The City of Brotherly Love continued to function as the political heart of the nation. State and federal representatives regularly intermingled, and Philadelphia's newspapers remained the best source of information about what was happening in the national government. The *Gazette of the United States* and the *Aurora* served as the primary mouthpieces of the leading political factions, and the two papers often set the tone for the political debates throughout the country. These papers were also joined by new journals, including William Cobbett's *Porcupine's Gazette*, which contributed to the increasingly polarized environment.[2]

Philadelphia also remained the nation's most cosmopolitan city. In addition to hosting a steady stream of diplomats and dignitaries, the city had become home to an increasing number of foreign refugees. Pennsylvania had always been a popular destination for immigrants, but the wars in Europe led to a surge in immigration. The French Revolution and failed Irish uprising in particular produced a flood of political refugees in need of asylum. While some of these men and women moved on to look for permanent homes in other parts of the country, many chose to stay, and some of these individuals, including William Duane and James T. Callender, would play important roles in the emerging Republican organization.[3]

Outside of Philadelphia, the state continued to grow as well. Following the Battle of Fallen Timbers in 1794, where U.S. forces defeated a coalition of Native American tribes living in the Ohio River Valley, settlers flocked to the western parts of the state. Pennsylvania's population increased nearly 40 percent between 1790 and 1800, and the state carved out four new counties to accommodate the increasing number of people living in rural areas. This growth, fueled by both immigration and natural reproduction, resulted in an already heterogenous population becoming even more diverse. As more people moved westward, the number of newspapers published outside of Philadelphia also increased, and between 1795 and 1800 more than a dozen new papers began circulating throughout the state—a majority of which opposed the Federalists. These papers and their editors would in turn help to shape the state's political landscape.[4]

The state's economy remained robust throughout this period. A burgeoning manufacturing sector combined with healthy agricultural production, and a strong import/export business helped solidify Pennsylvania's position as the most developed economy in the new nation. Advances in the economy, however, occurred unevenly. While the eastern parts of the state moved toward a more commercial economy, the west remained predominately rural and agricultural. The emerging market economy also led to an increase in social stratification and a concentration of wealth. This growing disparity between east and west and rich and poor exacerbated underlying social and cultural differences and helped to create a combustible political atmosphere.[5]

Getting the Party Started: The Election of 1796

The 1796 presidential election came at a critical junction in Pennsylvania politics. Historian Jeffrey L. Pasley has dubbed the election "the first real presidential contest" because, for the first time in the new nation, some question existed about who would win. George Washington had been re-elected unanimously in 1792, and despite suffering some political damage during the Jay Treaty debates, he seemed a shoo-in for a third term. Washington's decision to retire, however, meant that Americans would have to find a new commander in chief.[6] Still reeling from the Whiskey Rebellion and the failure to block the Jay Treaty, the opposition recognized that the election of a new president presented an opportunity to recapture some momentum and demonstrate their ability to work within the confines of the Constitution. A strong showing could also help legitimize their claims to represent the people and serve as a roadmap for the future.

No real mystery surrounded possible candidates who might succeed Washington. For Federalists, Vice President John Adams was the logical heir. Although he had a strained relationship with some prominent Federalists, Adams had a long history of public service and had diligently fulfilled his duties as vice president. For the opposition, Thomas Jefferson stood as the obvious candidate. Having clashed frequently with Alexander Hamilton while a member of Washington's cabinet, Jefferson worked closely with his Virginia ally James Madison to push back against Federalists' efforts to reform the national political culture. By the time he retired from public life in 1793, Jefferson had emerged as the *de facto* head of the opposition. The "Sage of Monticello" professed to have no interest in being president, but few people seem to have taken that assertion seriously.[7]

Although Washington did not officially announce his retirement until September 1796, the contest between Jefferson and Adams in Pennsylvania had actually begun months earlier with a struggle over the laws that would govern how the state would select presidential electors. As another safeguard against the whims of popular opinion, the architects of the Constitution ensured that the people would not be given a chance to vote directly for the president. Instead, voters would select "electors" who would make up the Electoral College, which would then select a president and vice president. The allotment of electoral votes followed the earlier compromises over representation and gave each state the same weight it had in Congress, which meant that Pennsylvania would be entitled to the selection of fifteen electors. The Constitution left it up to each state to determine on its own how the electors would be selected. Because Washington had been the obvious choice in 1788 and 1792, the method for selecting electors had not elicited much controversy. In the spring of 1796, however, with Washington's decision to retire an open secret, the rules for selecting electors might affect the outcome of the next presidential election. As it happened, the laws would also serve as the impetus for the creation of the Republican Party in Pennsylvania.[8]

The legislature began discussing the laws governing the upcoming presidential election in March 1796, when some of Jefferson's allies proposed dividing the state into districts. Although framed as a question of representation and fairness, the call for districts was also driven by strategic considerations. Dividing the state this way would ensure that the vote from the sparsely populated western parts of the state where Jefferson was popular was not diluted by the more populated—and Federalist—east. Not surprisingly, Federalists favored a statewide approach in the hope that their majorities in the eastern part of the state would ensure they controlled the selection of electors. After a heated debate, Federalists eventually triumphed and pushed through a law calling for statewide elections. Voters would therefore be able to pick up to fifteen people when they cast their ballots. Federalists also selected 4 November, a month after the regular elections, as the day Pennsylvanians would vote for electors. The decision would likely give Federalists the upper hand by suppressing turnout in more Jefferson-friendly rural areas where voters had to travel long distances to reach their polling locations.[9]

Federalists may have succeeded in framing the election law, but their strategy ultimately backfired because the challenge of coordinating a statewide election and convincing voters to go to the polls a second time is what ultimately drove the opposition to take steps to create a more formal and organized party structure. Prior to the election of 1796, the opposition in Pennsylvania had approached electioneering in a haphazard manner. Individual candidates had some success, but the coalition had never developed a coherent statewide strategy. The lack of organization was, in part, a product of the fact that elections remained primarily local affairs. Voters tended to turn out in higher numbers during elections that included the selection of a sheriff or another important local official. Additionally, the handful of statewide elections that did occur had been relatively one-sided affairs. As a result, activists had little incentive to coordinate with potential allies in other regions. The election of 1796, by contrast, was expected to be closely contested and would require a sophisticated organization capable of ensuring that voters from across the state cast ballots for the same fifteen men.[10]

The outlines of what would become the Republican Party in Pennsylvania took shape on 4 April 1796 when a coalition of state and national representatives gathered in Philadelphia for what historians have identified as the first real party caucus. The assembly, which consisted of some of the most prominent and outspoken critics of the Washington administration, signaled a shift in how the opposition would approach mobilization. Instead of trying to engage the people in their deliberations, these men took it upon themselves to develop a strategy for delivering the states' electoral votes to Thomas Jefferson.[11]

The first step would be selecting a slate of candidates who had statewide appeal. Pennsylvania election law banned the use of printed tickets, so nominees had to have statewide name recognition (it also helped if their names were easy to spell). With this in mind, the caucus filled their ticket with well-known state officials with distinguished careers including Chief Justice Thomas McKean, Congressman William Irvine, former Senator William Maclay, and the widely popular German politicians Peter Muhlenberg and Joseph Heister.[12] This all-star slate represented a significant change from the second-tier politicians who had been chosen as electors in the previous presidential contests and was a sign of how seriously the caucus took the upcoming election.[13] In contrast, John Adams's supporters—who were unaware of their adversaries' maneuvers—followed tradition by selecting lesser-known individuals.[14]

At the conclusion of its caucus, Republicans took the unprecedented step of selecting a committee, headed by veteran of the Pennsylvania Democratic Society Michael Leib, to coordinate the campaign and disseminate relevant information throughout the state.[15] The campaign would be conducted from both the top down and the bottom up. Although a central committee in Philadelphia would supervise statewide electioneering activities, party leaders intended to let local leaders do most of the heavy lifting. As John Beckley, who functioned something like a campaign manager, explained in a letter to an ally, "A little exertion by a few good active republicans in each *county* would bring the people out."[16]

In addition to lessening the burden of party leaders in Philadelphia, this approach allowed local activists to tailor their electioneering efforts and ensured that communities felt some connection to the campaign.

Jefferson's allies sprang into action following Washington's Farewell Address. Federalist Fisher Ames described the announcement as "a signal, like dropping a hat, for the party races to start."[17] Now free to openly promote Jefferson, Republicans began organizing public meetings throughout the state to publicize their candidate list and give the public a chance to formally endorse the slate. A "number of Citizens, from different parts of the County of Philadelphia," for example, gathered in the Northern Liberties on 2 October and unanimously agreed to the slate of electors.[18] Notably, organizers made no attempt to hide that a select few individuals had developed the list of names, and members of the public were not invited to suggest other potential candidates. These meetings were, therefore, not actually about giving the people a chance to participate in the nominating process. Instead, they were primarily an opportunity to rally voters and legitimize the preselected slate of candidates.[19]

In addition to the public meetings, the Republican campaign committee blanketed the state with handbills and newspaper articles that portrayed Jefferson as the people's candidate. Adopting familiar populist tropes, Republicans attacked their adversaries as undemocratic and accused them of working to undermine the will of the people. Partisans pointed to passages from John Adams's *Defense of the Constitutions of the United States* as well as his *Discourses on Davila* as supposed proof that the signer of the Declaration of Independence harbored monarchical ambitions. As one handbill stated succinctly: "Thomas Jefferson is a firm REPUBLICAN—John Adams is an avowed MONARCHIST."[20]

The Republican campaign committee also worked to ensure that voters would cast their ballots for the correct slate of candidates. Jefferson's allies distributed pocket-sized election guides that voters could bring with them to the polls. To circumvent the ban on printed tickets, Beckley, along with other activists, transcribed nearly fifty thousand ballots that were then passed to express riders to deliver throughout the state. One rider, Major John Smith, recalled covering more than six hundred miles and riding from before the sun rose until after dark for nearly three weeks straight to distribute tickets and campaign literature. Beckley even asked that his riders begin delivering tickets in the western parts of the state and slowly work their way back to Philadelphia, thereby preventing leading Federalists from learning of their star-studded list of nominees until insufficient time remained to respond. This type of coordination underscored the budding party's organizational capacity.[21]

Republicans began incorporating other forms of political mobilization into their electioneering strategy as well. In the early 1790s, the opposition had used holidays and fetes to promote a broad ideology and to challenge Federalists' deferential vision for the country. In 1796, Jefferson's supporters employed similar public rituals and celebrations as a way to drive voters to the polls. A day before the election, Republicans organized a parade consisting of a crowd of upward of 150 sailors carrying a flag that proclaimed Jefferson "the man of the People" and chanting, "Jefferson and no king weaved through the streets of Philadelphia."[22] Throngs of Jefferson's supporters reportedly also donned tricolored cockades as they went to cast their ballots. Such outward displays of partisanships helped to establish a shared Republican identity and linked a vote for Jefferson with the larger struggle against tyranny.[23]

Despite a relatively low turnout, the network of Republican activists managed to mobilize enough voters to swing the state in Jefferson's favor by the narrowest of margins. Statewide, electors backing Jefferson received 50.6 percent to Adams's 49.4 percent. The election returns indicate a particularly high level of ticket voting as well. In a testament to Republicans' success at publicizing and promoting their slate, only 133 votes separated Thomas McKean, the Republican elector who received the most votes, from James Edgar, the Republican who received the least votes.

Republicans' joy at winning Pennsylvania, however, proved short-lived. Although the state would deliver Jefferson fourteen of its fifteen electoral votes, Federalist John Adams won a majority of the electors nationwide and became the nation's second president. As runner-up, Jefferson served as the vice president.[24]

Despite failing to capture the presidency, Republicans could take solace in the fact that Jefferson had bested Adams less than a year after the embarrassing culmination of the debate over the Jay Treaty. The focus on coalition-building and the mobilization of voters also provided Republicans with a potential guide for challenging Federalists in the future. Although this approach meant giving up attempts to engage the people directly in the deliberative process, the results suggested that it might be a trade worth making. Federalists, however, had no intention of giving up on their quest to establish a culture of republican deference. A diplomatic dustup would soon give them the opportunity to recapture the initiative.

Federalists' Cultural Counteroffensive

Revolutionary France continued to exert a powerful influence over American politics. France had initially held out hope that George Washington's retirement would open the door to a new administration that favored friendlier relations, but John Adams's victory seemed to foreclose any hope of rapprochement. Shortly after the election, French privateers began attacking American merchant vessels. President Adams resisted calls from fellow Federalists to respond with a declaration of war and dispatched an envoy to negotiate with the French Directory. Instead of welcoming the overture, French officials issued a series of demands, including for a bribe to the French foreign minister Charles Maurice de Talleyrand, which had to be met before discussions could even begin. Horrified by such a wanton breach of diplomatic protocols and etiquette, the stunned American diplomats dashed off reports to Adams inquiring how to proceed. Adams initially sought to keep news of the French demands secret, but after receiving pressure from Republicans who believed that the news from France would benefit them, he released the reports to the public. To protect anonymity, the names of some of the French officials involved in the demands were substituted with the letters "W," "X," "Y," and "Z."[25]

In the aftermath of the "XYZ Affair," as it became known, political momentum swung decisively in favor of the Federalists. Writing from Philadelphia, Abigail Adams reported that "the publick opinion is changeing here very fast, and the people begin to see who have been their firm unshaken Friends, steady to their interests and defenders of their Rights and Liberties."[26] The Directory's actions seemed to confirm everything Federalists had said about the dangers associated with the French Revolution. Just as importantly, the news left Republicans, who had remained steadfast in their support for France, humiliated. The incident presented Federalists with an ideal opportunity to reaffirm the strength of the federal government and reassert their vision for the country.[27]

Pennsylvania Federalists moved quickly to capitalize on the publication of the dispatches. Building on their established mobilization strategies, they began by organizing a series of public meetings. Shortly after news of the XYZ Affair broke, Federalists in Philadelphia gathered at an upscale tavern where attendees unanimously adopted resolutions praising Adams's actions surrounding the negotiations with France as "wise, just, liberal, and sincere." In order to engage as many citizens as possible, the meeting also agreed to draft a memorial that would circulate throughout the city and state.[28]

Federalists throughout Pennsylvania followed the example set by the Philadelphia meeting. In the town of Reading, for example, "the largest meeting ever known to inhabitants" approved resolutions thanking Adams.[29] Federalists in the towns of Canonsburg, Harrisburg, Huntington, and Shippensburg echoed these sentiments. In Philadelphia, meanwhile, Federalists appointed a committee to go door to door collecting signatures. As had been the case with earlier Federalist mobilization efforts, these gatherings made no attempt to instruct elected officials. Instead, the rallies and memorials served as opportunities for Americans to express their support for the administration and demonstrate their loyalty to the regime. As such, they fit within Federalists' version of deferential republicanism.[30]

Federalists' public demonstrations culminated on 7 May 1798, when a crowd—estimated at nearly ten thousand—assembled to watch eleven thousand young men deliver a petition to President Adams, who donned a military uniform for the occasion. John Fenno, editor of the *Gazette of the United States,* called the spectacle the most "affecting, pleasing, and animating scene" he ever witnessed. The orderly procession, which concluded with the men pledging their support for the nation and the Adams administration, embodied Federalists' vision for the country and exemplified their understanding of the proper relationship between the people and their government.[31]

Federalists reenforced this message by organizing volunteer militia companies. The XYZ Affair had led to a surge in nationalism, and hordes of young Pennsylvanians rushed to join militia companies following the creation of a volunteer army. Although technically apolitical, Federalists dominated these groups. The officers of MacPherson's Blues, one of the largest companies, even screened applicants to ensure that only men with a firm commitment to Federalism would join their ranks. This practice of "exclusionary patriotism" implied that Republicans could not be trusted to protect the interests of the nation.[32]

With no actual combat occurring, the new volunteer militia companies spent their time mustering and patrolling the streets. At the behest of William Cobbett, some companies even began wearing black cockades in their hats. The cockade, he explained, would serve as a symbol of the troops' commitment to the regime that "will be seen by the whole city, by the friends and the *foes* of the wearer." In other words, it would serve as both a reminder of Federalists' popularity and as a warning to any potential critics. Overall, the presence of troops worked to reaffirm Federalists' strength and solidify their role as the defenders of the people.[33]

In addition to the public meetings and militia companies, Federalists used patriotic songs and odes with titles including "Adams and Liberty" and "God Save George Washington" to promote nationalism and encourage reverence for the federal government. The most popular of these songs was "Hail Columbia," written by the Philadelphia attorney Joseph Hopkinson in early 1798. Set to the tune of the "President's March," the song invoked imagery of heroic soldiers defeating the British during the Revolutionary War, praised President Adams as "the rock on which the storm will break," and called on "immortal patriots [to] rise once more" and "defend your rights, defend your shore!" The song was met with "unbounded and repeated plaudits" when it debuted in Philadelphia. According to one witness, there had never been such excitement "witnessed in a public place; not even in France at the commencement of the revolution."[34] Subsequently dubbed the "Philadelphia Patriotic Song," "Hail Columbia" became something of a theme song for the Federalists. In addition to rallying supporters, Federalists used it to taunt Republicans. After Albert Gallatin gave a speech in Reading that criticized the Adams administration, members of the MacPherson's Blues surrounded his boardinghouse and spent the night "singing Hail Columbia and other good patriotic songs."[35]

Although most of their efforts tended to center around mobilizing men, Federalists also found ways to engage women. In his description of the parade of young men that delivered Adams the petition, Cobbett made sure to note, "Every female in the city, with a face worth looking at, gladdened the way with their smiles."[36] Other women donned black cockades to advertise their support for the regime and made banners and flags, which they then presented to Federalist militia companies. As had been the case in the early 1790s, the inclusion of women in these rituals reinforced Federalists' claims to speak for the people.[37]

The Federalists' cultural offensive put Republicans in a difficult position. Support for Revolutionary France had been one of the bedrocks of the opposition, and critics of the Federalists had embraced French symbolism as part of their campaign to establish a new type of celebratory politics. The tricolored cockade in particular had become an emblem of those who fought against Federalists' deferential republicanism. Even after reports of the Reign of Terror began trickling in, members of the opposition continued to sing "Ça Ira" and the "Marseillaise," and to dance the

"Carmagnole." Following the XYZ Affair, however, such outward displays of Francophilia increasingly became a political, and even physical, liability. Theatergoers, for example, hissed and booed when the Philadelphia orchestra played "Ça Ira," and a correspondent subsequently cautioned the orchestra to avoid any song "that bears the least tincture of French principles."[38]

In response to the changing political landscape, Republicans in Pennsylvania began to alter their approach to mobilization. For starters, they worked to sever their symbolic ties to Revolutionary France. Although Benjamin Bache had once urged all Republicans to wear tricolored cockades, in 1798 he proclaimed that "citizens have no business with cockades." They were "a military emblem which ought only to be worn by a soldier." He, therefore, "earnestly recommended to the Republicans, the real friends of order, not to think of assuming any badge liable to misconstruction."[39] Along the same lines, members of the "True Republican Society," a new Republican voluntary society, flatly rejected a suggestion that the group display both American and French flags.[40] By symbolically abandoning France, Republicans sought to distance themselves from the actions of the French government and to reaffirm their loyalty to the United States.

Republicans also began organizing their own partisan volunteer militia companies. Although prominent members of the opposition coalition had marched against the Whiskey Rebels in 1794, Republicans had never formed into their own companies. Some critics of the regime had gone so far as to challenge the existence of the volunteer militia and warn that it might lead to a standing army.[41] In the wake of the XYZ Affair, however, Republicans began to see the potential value of organizing a volunteer militia company. In 1798, leading Philadelphia Republicans including Blair McClenachan, one of the officers of the Democratic Society of Pennsylvania, and William Bache, the brother of the editor of the *Aurora*, formed the Republican Blues to serve as a counterweight to MacPherson's Blues. Like the Federalist companies, Republicans made their politics apparent. An advertisement recruiting new members for the Southwark Light Infantry stated that "REPUBLICANS ONLY are admitted." Applicants were also required to declare their support for the principles of the Republican Party.[42]

The new Republican militia companies served a few purposes. First, they gave Republicans a chance to demonstrate their patriotism and refute Federalist charges that they posed a threat to law and order. Second, with the Democratic and Republican Societies defunct, the volunteer militia companies could help oversee and direct partisan activities at the local level.[43] Finally, as would become increasingly necessary, the new militia companies could provide protection from Federalists.[44]

Taken together, the XYZ Affair pushed Republicans to move farther away from the types of mobilization the opposition had used in the early 1790s. Instead of looking for ways to engage the people in the deliberative process, Republicans began to adopt strategies typically associated with the Federalists. These changes reflected a broader moderating of the Republicans' views that took place following the XYZ Affair. As historian Seth Cotlar has shown, Republicans began moving away from more radical positions on issues such as the abolition of slavery and the pursuit of economic equality in the late 1790s. Given the state of public opinion, Republicans recognized that, in order to remain competitive at the ballot box, they would have to set aside some of their more ambitious goals and instead focus on demonstrating their commitment to the regime.[45]

Federalist Repression and Republican Response

Despite their efforts to distance themselves from France, voters punished Republicans at the polls. Federalists' cultural offensive effectively wiped out whatever gains the party had made since 1796, and in the elections of 1798 Federalists received majorities in both houses at the state and national levels. Firmly in control of the reins of power and with the Republicans badly weakened, Federalists used the opportunity to push through a series of controversial pieces of legislation designed to institutionalize their vision for the nation and prepare the nation for war with France.

First, convinced that America faced an imminent threat, Federalists passed a series of bills designed to strengthen national security. Beyond keeping America safe, the measures also fit with Federalists' larger goal of instilling order and ensuring that the federal government had the resources necessary to assert its will. The total price tag for the new legislation, which included money for a volunteer army, amounted to over $10.5 million—nearly $4 million more than Congress usually allotted for the entire government. To pay for these measures, Federalists adopted a series of new taxes, including the nation's first direct tax on houses.[46]

At the same time, Federalists pushed through the Alien and Sedition Acts. The Alien Acts, which consisted of three different parts, extended the time it took for an immigrant to become naturalized and gave the president the power to expel any immigrant (regardless of naturalization status) deemed a threat to the nation. The Sedition Act, meanwhile, sought to tamp down on public criticism of the federal government. The law made it a crime, punishable by a fine up to $2,000 and/or two years in jail, to "write, print, utter, [or] publish . . . any false, scandalous and malicious writing or writings against the government of the United States."[47] Although these laws clearly represented an assault on the people's liberties, Federalists justified the measures as necessary steps designed to keep American safe from internal enemies.[48]

More broadly, the Alien and Sedition Acts reflected Federalists' increasingly narrow understanding of who got to be part of "the people." Although the Alien Acts did not bar immigrants from becoming citizens, they made it much more difficult and, when coupled with the constant threat of deportation, sent the message that only native-born Americans could truly be considered part of the people. For its part, the Sedition Act's blatant disregard for the First Amendment's protection of freedom of speech suggested that Federalists saw their critics as somehow no longer part of the people and therefore not entitled to basic rights. Federalists' embrace of this type of reactionary populism would only become more pronounced in the coming months.[49]

The new legislation infuriated Republicans, who saw the laws as a naked power grab by the Federalists. Americans had long seen a standing army as one of the biggest threats to liberty, and Federalists had already demonstrated a willingness to use troops to send a political message. Beyond that, it was lost on no one that recent immigrants tended to vote Republican and that the only people likely to face punishment under the Sedition Act were Republican journalists. As Federalists held majorities in both the Senate and the House, however, Republicans in Congress were powerless to prevent the passage of the laws. Left with no other option, Republicans took their campaign against Federalists out of doors.[50]

Instead of turning to violence or trying to assert the will of the people directly through town meetings, however, Republicans in Pennsylvania responded to the war measures by organizing a petition drive. Using the emerging statewide party structure, Republicans in each county began to establish committees to write and circulate petitions condemning the recent legislation. By January 1799, Pennsylvania representatives were being swamped by petitions denouncing the new taxes and the Alien and Sedition Acts. Nearly every county sent at least one petition, with the largest number of signatures coming from Montgomery, York, and Franklin Counties. In total, at least 15,200 Pennsylvanians signed petitions calling on Congress to reconsider the war measures, more than double the number of signatures Federalists collected during the debate over the Jay Treaty. The number of signatures was a testament to the burgeoning Republican Party's strength and a reflection of their commitment to channeling anger at the laws into constitutional forms of resistance.[51]

The language of the petitions underscored Republicans' efforts to establish themselves as a loyal opposition. Unlike the petition drives associated with the states' revolutionary regime, which included threats of what would happen if officials did not abide by the will of the people, Republicans' petitions protesting the war measures adopted a deferential tone. The petitioners defended their right to assemble and express their opinions, but they also emphasized that they would ultimately defer to the judgment of elected officials. Far from claiming that the people should have a direct voice in the deliberative process, a memorial from Washington County stated that "on ordinary occasions we deem it inexpedient to interrupt with petitions and remonstrances, the public deliberations of the Nation."[52] Some of the petitions even included language praising the regime. Instead of asserting the right to exercise sovereignty directly, residents from Cumberland County proclaimed that "the welfare of the county almost wholly depends on a rigid adherence of the citizens to the principles of their government and constitution."[53] In fact, some petitioners framed their opposition to the legislation as an effort to protect the regime and argued that the war measures were "directly-opposed to the spirit and even letter of the constitution."[54]

By February 1799, Republicans' petition campaign seemed to be working. Although Federalists tried to prevent the House of Representatives from formally accepting the memorials on the grounds that the public had no right to criticize the government, Congress agreed to revisit the measures. In the end, however, Republicans in the House came up short. The petitions could not overcome Federalists' majority. By a vote of fifty-two to forty-eight, the Federalist-controlled House adopted a resolution stating that it was "inexpedient to repeal" the Alien and Sedition Acts. A subsequent resolution defending the increases in military spending passed as well.[55]

The rebuke served as a stern reminder of the limits of popular politics under the Constitution. The Republicans' petition drive galvanized supporters and may have helped strengthen party ties, but it could not overcome the reality of a Federalist majority. Change would have to wait for the next election. Some Pennsylvanians, however, were not willing to wait that long.

Popular Nullification and the Limits of the Constitutional Resistance

The failure to repeal Federalists' war measures added fuel to a brewing crisis in the northeastern part of the state. In the fall of 1798, residents began erecting liberty poles as a sign of their opposition to the laws. Some communities went even further and began signing pledges to prevent any tax collectors from assessing their property. But while the use of liberty poles and the boycott of taxes deemed unjust harkened back to forms of mobilization associated with the Revolution, these protestors did not see their actions as a direct challenge to the existing regime. Instead, they saw resistance to the Federalist war measures as a way to defend the Constitution. According to these residents, Federalists in Congress had overstepped their authority by adopting the laws, and true supporters of the Constitution had a responsibility to prevent the laws from going into effect. The liberty poles carried flags that made this point explicit with slogans including "The Constitution Sacred, No Gagg Laws, Liberty or Death" and "The United States of America, Free, Sovereign, and Independent."[56]

The notion that a citizen had the right to ignore a law deemed unconstitutional raised two related questions that the architects of the regime had left unanswered: who gets to interpret the Constitution and what happens if the federal government tries to do something that may be unconstitutional? In the late 1790s, most Americans would have agreed that citizens should not be bound by an unconstitutional law. Even Alexander Hamilton had written in Federalist no. 78 that "no legislature act . . . contrary to the Constitution, can be valid."[57] Controversies arose, however, when it came to who had the authority to declare a law unconstitutional. While Hamilton and most Federalists envisioned the judiciary as the arbitrator of questions involving a law's constitutionality, many Republicans believed that, as the source of sovereignty, the people always retained the right to reject laws deemed illegal. For some Republicans this meant that the states, acting on behalf of the people, could nullify an unconstitutional federal law. This was the position that Thomas Jefferson and James Madison would take in the Kentucky and Virginia Resolutions. The protestors in Pennsylvania went one step further. In framing their boycott of the taxes and opposition to the Alien and Sedition Acts as an attempt to block unconstitutional laws from taking effect, they asserted that the people themselves had the right to intervene to protect the Constitution.[58]

Instances of this type of "popular nullification" first began in Northumberland County in late 1798, but by early 1799 the unrest had spread to neighboring Bucks County. Assessors began assessing property in February and quickly found that the inhabitants of Bucks had no more interest in submitting to the new laws than had their brethren in Northumberland. The decision to appoint a few Quakers, whom some residents still viewed with suspicion because of their pacifism during the Revolutionary War, and the choice to employ one of the wealthiest men in the area as assessors only exacerbated the situation. As news of the assessors spread, communities began gathering to form associations and to sign pledges agreeing to take whatever steps were necessary to stop officials from doing their jobs. Like their neighbors in Northumberland, citizens in Bucks framed their actions as part of an effort to defend the Constitution, not as a challenge to the regime itself.[59]

The spreading resistance to the excise forced President Adams to act. Committed to the principle that Americans had surrendered their right to intervene directly in the governing process, Adams tasked Marshal William Nichols with apprehending the ringleaders and enforcing the rule of law. On 1 March 1799, Nichols set up an office in Bethlehem, a town that bordered Northumberland and Bucks Counties, and began making arrests. Although some of the suspects fled, Nichols managed to take a few men into custody and brought them to the jail in Bethlehem, where they would wait for transportation to Philadelphia for trial.[60]

The situation quickly escalated following news of the arrests. Residents were particularly upset with the fact that the prisoners would face trial in Philadelphia, which they saw as a violation of the suspects' right to a jury of their peers. In response, on 7 March, a force of about four hundred men mobilized to free the prisoners. Some of the assembled wore tricolored cockades, suggesting that they saw the effort as part of a larger campaign to establish a more participatory culture. John Fries, a Revolutionary War veteran who had assumed command of the company, however, wore a black feather in his hat. Fries had once aligned himself with the Federalists and had marched against the Whiskey Rebels. While he had recently grown disillusioned with the Adams administration, his decision to don the black feather, which was associated with Federalists, sent the message that he had no intention of challenging the regime itself. Instead, he saw the jailbreak as a necessary response to an act of injustice.[61]

When the posse arrived in Bethlehem, Fries initially sought to avoid any controversy and offered to free the prisoners legally by paying their bail. The marshal, however, refused the money. As a result, Fries gave the order to storm the jail and take the prisoners by force. As he did so, Fries implored the troops to "please, for God's sake, don't fire *except* [if] we are fired on first."[62] The soldiers appear to have largely followed his order, and the jailbreak proceeded in the most orderly fashion possible. Officials did not put up much of a fight, and the prisoners were freed without violence. Having achieved its goal, the posse left town without further incident.

"Fries's Rebellion" reignited the debate about what constituted a legitimate form of political expression under the Constitution. Although Fries may have believed he had acted within his rights, Federalists denounced the jailbreak as treason. They reiterated their rejection of the entire concept of constitutional resistance. In their view, the uprising represented an existential threat to the stability of the republic. William Cobbett warned that tolerating such lawlessness would lead to "a *civil war* or *surrender of Independence*."[63] Federalists were particularly troubled by the tricolored cockades, which they believed demonstrated that the rebellion was inspired by the French Revolution. Overlooking Fries's black feather, the *Gazette of the United States* declared that the uprising was "directly related to the political posture between this county and France."[64] Other Federalists blamed the French outright and declared that Fries and the other insurgents were trying to "imitate their revolutionary brethren in other parts of the world."[65]

President Adams appeared to agree with his fellow Federalists about the dangers associated with the uprising. On 11 March he issued a proclamation ordering the "insurgents of Northampton, Montgomery and Bucks counties" to end their "treasonable proceedings . . . [and] to disperse and retire peaceably to their respective abodes" within a week. To ensure that his orders were followed, Adams also called up the newly created army and, in a particularly brazen move, appointed Federalist William MacPherson, who led the Federalist militia corps MacPherson's Blues, as commander.[66]

Fries's Rebellion served as another important inflection point for Republicans. The rhetoric coming from the party was partially responsible for creating such a combustible atmosphere. Prior to the incident, Republicans had been issuing increasingly dire warnings about what might happen if Federalists remained in power. Blair McClenachan, a Republican member of the U.S. House of Representatives, reportedly traveled throughout the northeast part of the state claiming that Federalists "wished to oppress the people" by taking land and reducing the residents to serfdom. "The President," he cautioned, "would make himself to be king of the County!"[67] Some Republicans had even publicly flirted with popular nullification. Republican congressman Robert Brown, for example, applauded the initial efforts to block tax collectors and urged Pennsylvanians "to keep the assessors back so that the rates should not be taken before the new congress met."[68]

Following the jailbreak, however, Republicans moved quickly to distance themselves from what had happened. The incident seemed to justify Federalists' hysteria and threatened to undermine Republicans' efforts to establish themselves as a legitimate opposition. As a result, Republican editors wasted no time in condemning Fries and his compatriots, and they went to great lengths to show that Republicans had not been involved in the jailbreak. Jacob Schneider, editor of the *Reading Adler*, proclaimed that "none of the perpetrators of violence" subscribed to his paper.[69] In Philadelphia, William Duane, who had assumed the position of editor of the *Aurora* following Benjamin Bache's death from yellow fever in late 1798, pointed out that Fries was a known Federalist and assured readers that no "Republican can justify the conduct of those people who resisted the marshal in the execution of his duty."[70] Republicans, he suggested, would never endorse the idea that the people could take the law into their own hands. Even Thomas Jefferson, who had once claimed that "a little rebellion now and then is a good thing," wrote that Fries's actions were "not the kind of opposition the American people will permit." Indeed, he warned that any indication that Republicans supported the use of force "would check the progress of public opinion."[71]

In the end, Fries's Rebellion forced Republicans to recommit to seeking change through the ballot box. As the Republican *Farmers Register* lectured, no matter how bad a law might be, "mobs, riots, and hostile oppositions are not the way and means" to see it overturned. Following the adoption of the new constitutions, the paper explained, "a more effectual and orderly method can be pursued by *ELECTIONS*."[72] Ironically, as Republicans emphasized their commitment to using only constitutionally sanctioned forms of mobilization, Federalists increasingly turned to extralegal tactics.

Will the Real Friends of Order Please Stand Up?

Federalists had long styled themselves as the "friends of order" and sought to portray their opponents as obstreperous and a threat to society. Despite these assertions, it was Federalists who were more likely to use violence as a political tool in the late 1790s. While Republicans in Pennsylvania were developing a party structure that could channel popular outrage into constructive forms of mobilization, Federalists' top-down approach to mobilization left supporters with no real opportunity to vent their passions. As a result, whipped into a frenzy by reports of internal enemies and dire warnings about the threats posed by Republicans, Federalists began taking matters into their own hands.[73]

In the weeks following the XYZ Affair, Federalists roamed the streets of Philadelphia looking for an excuse to fight. Federalists beat a group of men caught wearing tricolored cockades and attacked Republicans trying to collect signatures on a petition opposing the Alien Acts. The whole city seemed consumed with partisan violence. One congressman claimed that he saw women "meet at the church door and violently pluck the badges [displaying partisan allegiance] from one another's bosoms."[74] Even a meeting of the local society for free debate degenerated into a brawl. Angry readers assaulted Bache twice in 1798. Each time, despite professing to be the friends of order, Federalist leaders looked the other way. In fact, President Adams seemed to encourage the violence and rewarded one of Bache's assailants with a diplomatic position.[75]

Federalist attacks on Republicans differed from the type of political violence associated with the state's revolutionary regime. Unlike the mobs that harassed excise officers throughout western Pennsylvania, the violence against Republicans was not ritualized—nobody wore disguises or blackened their faces, and victims were not tarred and feathered. Perpetrators made no attempt to justify their actions as the will of the community. Instead, Federalists argued that Republicans posed a threat to the country, which meant that the normal rules of engagement did not apply. Rather than political opponents, Republicans were enemy combatants. The violence, therefore, was not only justified but necessary to protect the country. As one General William MacPherson explained, the federal government "must be obeyed; otherwise the Constitution must be destroyed, with it all government, law and order must perish, and disunion, civil war, and anarchy must ensue."[76]

The apogee of Federalist violence occurred following Fries's Rebellion. Given Federalists' paranoia, President Adams's decision to call out the army with MacPherson at the helm seemed to invite trouble. Even though residents of northeastern Pennsylvania adopted resolutions promising "to desist from opposing any public officer in the execution of his office . . . and give due submission to the laws of the United States," MacPherson led a force of nearly a thousand men to "restore" law and order to northern Pennsylvania in early April 1799.[77] The deployment, while considerably smaller than the one sent to suppress the Whiskey Rebellion, nevertheless represented a substantial show of force.

As had been the case in 1794, however, when the troops arrived, they found that the people had no intention of resisting. Instead of combat, the troops occupied their time by cutting down "sedition poles" that had been erected to protest the war measures. Although the raising of a liberty pole did not violate any laws, Federalists viewed them as a direct challenge to the authority and legitimacy of the federal government. According to MacPherson, they could "be considered in no other light than as rallying points for the disaffected."[78] It was, therefore, imperative that they come down.

Members of the Lancaster Troop of Horses appear to have taken MacPherson's criticism of the liberty poles to heart. As they began their march through the northeast, one of the soldiers purportedly boasted that he planned to "not only cut down all liberty trees" but also to "burn and destroy everything where such poles had stood and been erected."[79] Although they refrained from starting fires, the Lancaster Troops began waging a campaign of terror throughout the areas surrounding Reading in early April. Soldiers even charged at a pregnant woman with drawn swords and terrorized a group of children who had erected a miniature liberty pole.[80]

The aggressive tactics infuriated locals who defended the poles as a form of peaceful and legal resistance. Schneider's *Reading Adler* published an article signed "A Friend to Truth" that accused the Lancaster Troops of violating the "laws of the land." Their actions, he declared, "would be more apt to excite the people to insurrection and raise them against the government, than to enforce obedience."[81] The public criticism of the troops, however, only made things worse.

Shortly after the publication of "A Friend to Truth," a group of soldiers led by Robert Goodloe Harper, a Federalist member of the U.S. House of Representatives, visited Schneider's office. After Schneider confessed to authoring the piece, the posse beat and dragged him to the town square where the captain ordered that the already bloodied Schneider receive twenty-five lashes with a knotted rope across his bare back. The goal was not only to punish Schneider but also to send a message to the broader public that dissent would not be tolerated. Fortunately for Schneider, a company of the Philadelphia cavalry arrived and stopped the lashing at six. The troops involved in the attack, however, received no discipline for their actions.[82]

News of Schneider's beating rippled throughout the state. In Philadelphia, William Duane printed a detailed account of the incident and mocked Federalists' claims to represent the rule of law. According to Duane, such a savage attack clearly demonstrated "who are the insurgents, who are the violators of our laws, [and] who are the enemies of our Constitution." The violence could not simply be blamed on a few rogue soldiers either. General MacPherson, after all, was a known partisan and had allowed the perpetrators to escape without facing any real consequences. Duane went on to warn that if something were not done, "every citizen in Philadelphia, who was obnoxious to Macpherson's Blues" might soon suffer the same fate. His prediction proved to be more accurate than he might have imagined.[83]

On the morning of 15 May, a few days after Duane first published details of the assault, members of various Federalist militia companies confronted the editor at his office. Never one to back down, Duane initially announced that he would be happy to fight any of the soldiers individually. When nobody stepped forward, he returned to his paperwork. Incensed by Duane's flippancy, the soldiers responded by seizing him and dragging him outside. In front of the office, the troops encircled the editor and took turns beating him. When Duane could no longer stand, the group turned to whipping. By the time they were done, Duane lay barely conscious and covered in blood and dirt.[84]

The violence, however, did little to silence the Republicans who used the attacks as proof that Federalists could not be trusted with power. Duane was back at work a day after the attack and published an account of the assault under the headline "More of Good Order and Regular Government." "The *lovers of good order and regular government,*" he proclaimed, had tried to silence him for his commitment to fighting against "the intrigues and the injustices of arbitrary men."[85] Other Republicans warned that accepting such a "gross violation of the laws of the United States" would inevitably lead to more violence. "If an armed band can drag one citizen from his family and punish him at discretion, another band may do the same," reasoned one contributor to the *Aurora*. "If such things are tolerated," he mused, "will not the bayonet soon become the test by which we are to be governed?"[86]

Republicans had, in effect, turned the tables on the Federalists. When combined with their condemnation of Fries's Rebellion, the attacks on

Schneider and Duane gave Republicans the opportunity to present themselves as the real friends of order. They were the ones who were loyal to the regime and who protected the Constitution. It was Federalists who had become blinded by the "inveteracy and fury of party spirit." As Republicans had learned, however, none of that would matter if they did not start winning elections.[87]

Party Maturation

Republicans in Pennsylvania had significantly expanded their organizational efforts since Adams's election as members of the party worked to harness frustrations with the Federalists and channel popular outrage into electoral victories. Between 1796 and 1798, Republicans established standing committees in every county. In some regions, the party set up committees at the township level as well. The creation of these committees represented an important step in the development of a formal political party apparatus. Pennsylvanians had formed ad-hoc electioneering committees in previous years, but they had always disbanded following election day. In contrast, these committees were a permanent fixture and would meet year-round. The process of organizing the committees occurred from both the top down and the bottom up. In places where a committee did not already exist, party leaders appointed members, but once the committee became more established, these posts became elected positions. This approach allowed more people to take part in the process and helped to legitimize Republicans' claims that the party spoke for the people. In addition to overseeing electioneering activities, the committees served as liaisons between the general public and party leaders. Committees also helped to organize party celebrations for the Fourth of July and other holidays. Taken together, the emerging party structure worked to ensure that citizens remained engaged and energized while at the same time emphasizing change through the ballot box rather than having people take matters into their own hands.[88]

A growing network of newspapers aided the work of the committees. Despite Federalists' attempt to silence criticism of the federal government with the Sedition Act, eight new Republican newspapers began circulating in Pennsylvania between 1797 and 1799.[89] The editors of these papers were an integral part of the party organization. They served as nodes in a statewide communication network that worked to keep Republicans connected and informed. In addition to reprinting articles from the *Aurora* and other Republican outlets, editors also tailored their papers for their local audiences. This meant that Republicans could adopt targeted messaging to appeal to different constituencies.[90]

Notably, while many of the men who opposed the Federalists welcomed the emerging party structure, some politicians worried about the increasingly polarized nature of politics. Alexander James Dallas, for example, initially refused to participate in the Republican organization. As secretary of the commonwealth under Governor Thomas Mifflin, Dallas had been a leading member of the opposition in the early 1790s, but he broke with them in 1796 over the campaign to block appropriation for the Jay Treaty. As a result, Dallas did not participate in the presidential election of 1796 and had earned the title "trimmer," a derogatory term for someone who is always changing their views to fit with prevailing sentiments, from fellow Republicans.[91] Dallas eventually reentered the political arena, but in 1798 he gave a speech lamenting the degree to which party spirit had infiltrated society. "It has obtruded," he bemoaned, "into every class of society and goes nearly to annihilate the useful as well as the agreeable avocations of life." Good people, he cautioned, no longer want to serve in government, and if something did not change, "no man will accept a situation in the public councils, it will be no longer safe, no longer honorable." At the time, few Pennsylvanians appear to have heeded his warnings, and Republicans seemed much more concerned with the perceived threat posed by Federalists. Dallas's message did, however, foreshadow future problems for the Republicans.[92]

Federalists, for their part, continued to see no need for a formal party organization. As "Unity" explained in an essay entitled "The Philosophy of Politics" printed in the *Gazette of the United States*, "In a republic the public good, determined by the public will, as expressed by the representative government, must be considered the political center of gravity." The existence of a party organization that acted as an intermediary body between the people and their government was therefore both unnecessary and dangerous.[93]

Given their deferential sensibilities and their dislike of many forms of popular politics, Federalists failed to match Republicans' organizational efforts. In Philadelphia, Federalists established committees to oversee electioneering in each ward, but outside the city they continued to approach political mobilization from the top down. Federalists generally seemed uninterested or unwilling to engage in the type of politicking and party-building that Republicans had adopted. Instead, as had been the case throughout the early 1790s, Federalists tended to rely on outward displays of authority and power to mobilize voters.[94] Senator James Ross offered this bleak assessment of Federalists' position in the western parts of the state in a letter to Arthur St. Clair: "You know as well as I do that there is no such thing as a Federal party in Westmoreland county. . . . The Federalist might have secured a number of friends, had there been any permanent, sensible leader, who could have organized and kept them in countenance against [William] Findley. Unfortunately, we have never had anybody there who would undertake and attempt to execute this task."[95]

Without the aid of a party structure, Federalists had to look for other ways to mobilize supporters. One particularly potent weapon was fear of immigrants. Federalists had become convinced that radical foreigners, working through the Republican Party, were plotting to overthrow the regime. Even if immigrants did not actively try to undermine the country, Federalists worried that large numbers of foreigners could make establishing a national culture more difficult. Federalists hammered this theme that immigrants posed a threat to the American people throughout the late 1790s. In the weeks leading up to election day, Federalist writers pleaded with citizens to turn out and vote to protect the country from the invasion of foreigners. An appeal printed in the *Gazette of the United States* shortly before election day in 1797, for example, urged Pennsylvanians to mobilize against the "Jacobins, Democrats, Frenchmen and pretend Republicans" and "[shut] the door against French principles and every thing French."[96] Federalists in the state legislature carried these anti-immigrant attacks further and passed a law requiring all immigrants to provide proof of citizenship in order to cast a ballot. Governor Mifflin vetoed the bill, but Republicans claimed that confusion about the laws led election judges to prevent hundreds of immigrants from voting.[97]

In contrast to the Federalists, Republicans continued to welcome immigrants and worked closely with groups such as the Hibernian Society, a voluntary society for Irish Americans, to mobilize immigrant voters. Republicans embraced the concept of a "hyphenated citizen" and argued that an immigrant could become part of the people in America while still maintaining their ethnic identity.[98] This openness to immigration did not, however, prevent Republicans from using ethnic rivalries to boost turnout. In predominantly German parts of the state, for example, Republican editor Jacob Schneider called on readers to vote for Republicans as a way to prove to the Irish, "who turn up their noses at the Germans," that they were no longer "beasts of burden."[99]

Neither side, however, seemed particularly interested in gaining the support of Black voters. Members of the Pennsylvania Abolition Society (which included both Federalists and Republicans) remained committed to incorporating Black residents into the body politic, and evidence exists that at least one Republican voluntary society welcomed a Black member, but no widespread effort was made to engage people of color in the electoral process. When it came to formal politics, both Republicans and Federalists seem to have accepted that the people meant white men.[100]

Turnout varied throughout the state during the elections of 1797 and 1798. The return of yellow fever in Philadelphia during this time kept voters from the ballot box, a factor historian Richard Miller argued helped give Federalists an advantage. In 1798, for example, only 18 percent of eligible voters cast ballots, and the Federalist candidates won handily. Outside of Philadelphia, however, voter turnout continued to rise. Thanks to the work of the partisan committees, voters flocked to the polls, and turnout soared to above 50 percent in many regions. In another sign of the increasing interest in elections, newspapers across the state began printing detailed election returns. Partisan editors in Philadelphia had been supplying readers with the breakdown of election results, as opposed to just announcing the winners, since the mid-1790s, but it was not until the latter part of the decade that the practice caught on in other parts of the state. A growing number of newspapers also began to include party affiliations when they printed election returns. Greater interest in the election results, it appeared, went hand in hand with the hardening of partisan lines.[101]

The Election of 1799 and the Republican Triumph

The struggle between Republicans and Federalists in Pennsylvania culminated with the gubernatorial election of 1799. With Thomas Mifflin unable to run for reelection due to term limits, the contest would be wide open, and both sides recognized it as a pivotal moment in the battle over the meaning of self-government in Pennsylvania. For Republicans, the campaign would serve as the first real test of their budding statewide organization. Coming on the heels of the XYZ Affair and in the midst of Fries's Rebellion, it would also be an important opportunity for Republicans to demonstrate their faith in elections as the only legitimate expression of the public will. For Federalists, the election offered a chance to capitalize on Republicans' missteps and finally gain complete control over the state.

In a reflection of their divergent views on parties and the role of the people, Federalists and Republicans took markedly different approaches to mobilizing for the elections. Republicans' campaign began in April with a caucus of federal and state representatives who "professed to be anxious to maintain the republican principle." Despite the meeting being closed to the general public, partisans strained to ensure that it appeared representative and at least give the impression that average citizens had a voice in the process. After making sure that there were delegates from each part of the state, the caucus developed a list of potential nominees and appointed a committee of delegates representing each county and the city of Philadelphia to "consider the fitness and enquire into the public standing of the candidates." Over the next few months, the committee "held constant meetings and made numerous enquiries by correspondence and application from all parts of the state." After taking all this information into consideration and allowing "the necessary time for deliberation," a final meeting endorsed Thomas McKean, the state's chief justice, as the party's nominee.[102]

By selecting McKean, Republicans sent a clear message that they had no intention of challenging the existing regime. McKean had been a vocal supporter of independence but had been critical of the 1776 constitution. He then warmly embraced the federal Constitution and helped craft the state's 1790 constitution. At one point during the debates over the new constitution, McKean had even suggested that the state reinstitute property qualifications for voting. During the Washington administration, however, he had slowly drifted from his associations with the Federalists. His transition appeared complete in 1796, when he served as an elector for Thomas Jefferson. (Indeed, one of the reasons Republicans may have selected him was that he received more votes than any other elector.) By 1799, McKean had proved himself a reliable Republican, but he could hardly be considered a threat to the existing constitutions. The party reaffirmed this point by including moderates Alexander James Dallas, who had temporarily set aside his concerns about parties, and former Federalist Tench Coxe on the central committee tasked with overseeing the election.[103]

Although a caucus formally nominated McKean, the party left the actual campaigning to the network of committees that had been formed since 1796. After announcing McKean's nomination, the party issued a circular letter to the Republican committees throughout the state calling on them to hold public meetings to endorse McKean. Such gatherings would help to establish the legitimacy of the nomination by giving the people a chance to ratify the decision of the party caucus. These meetings could also be used to help build and strengthen the party organization. The central committee also urged Republicans residing in areas that did not already have a committee to immediately take steps to form one so they could formally endorse McKean. Beyond that, while the central committee communicated with Republicans throughout the state, the party allowed local committees a significant amount of latitude to select members and craft electioneering strategies. This system ensured that the campaign could adapt to local circumstances and created more opportunities for people to participate in the process.[104]

Federalists took a different approach. On 6 March 1799, after a "Committee of Gentlemen from twenty-one counties" ensured that their chosen candidate would accept the nomination, Federalists announced that they would support James Ross, who had acted as a lead negotiator during the Whiskey Rebellion and served in the U.S. Senate. (The decision appears to have been made before 6 March because the *Gazette of the United States* referred to Ross as the nominee on 5 March.[105]) Similar to what the Republicans had done, Federalists also called for the creation of a network of committees to oversee the campaign in different parts of the state. However, unlike the Republicans, who allowed residents to select who would be on their local committees, Federalists in Philadelphia appointed their members.[106] The difference is a telling sign of both Federalists' lack of a preexisting party structure outside of Philadelphia and their continued commitment to establishing a deferential political culture. As Federalists saw it, electioneering, like governance, should be conducted in a strictly top-down manner.

The most visible part of the campaign took place in print and in a torrent of electioneering articles and broadsides that flooded the state in the months leading up to the election. At no small cost, the local Republican committees usually oversaw the printing and distribution of electioneering propaganda.[107] As had become common practice with Republicans, local editors tailored the messaging specifically for their readers. For example, the *Carlisle Gazette*, printed in an area with a large German population, carried a special plea from General Peter Muhlenberg, one of the most popular Germans in the state, that Germans cast their ballots for McKean.[108] In heavily religious areas, Republicans hammered Ross as a deist and published affidavits from a minister who claimed to have overheard Ross deny a belief in original sin.[109] In more diverse areas,

Republicans relied on familiar tropes about Federalists' plotting to install a monarchy and focused on tying the Ross campaign to the controversial policies of the Adams administration.[110]

Republicans throughout the state went to great lengths to try and allay any concerns that McKean posed a threat to the regime. Journalists portrayed him as "a true friend to the Federal Constitution and Government."[111] Federalists, they claimed, were the ones who had shown a disregard for the rule of law. Republicans simply wanted to apply the Constitution fairly and equally. In this way, journalists tried to establish a clear difference between the Republicans of 1799 and the radicals of the 1780s.[112]

Federalists also used print to promote their candidate, but lacking the Republicans' infrastructure, they relied on the same basic message throughout the state: a McKean victory would result in the breakdown of law and order. Federalists released a barrage of attacks in the weeks before the election and presented Ross as the only candidate who would "suppress the spirit of anarchy and insurrection" and uphold the laws of the nation.[113] Using both the Whiskey and Fries's Rebellions as evidence, Federalist journalists painted Republicans and McKean as bloodthirsty anarchists. No matter what Republicans may say, Federalists warned, McKean "would subvert the liberty, the religion, and the social order of our country."[114] This was the same type of rhetoric that Federalists had used to castigate their opponents for years, a reflection of the fact that fear remained one of their most potent weapons.

The two campaigns also drew on their repertoires of different forms of celebratory politics to energize supporters and boost turnout. Both Republicans and Federalists used the Fourth of July to promote their candidate and link the campaign with the birth of the country. Republicans in Carlisle drank to the United States, the Constitution, and "Thomas McKean the old whig."[115] In Washington County, celebrants toasted "The Constituted Authorities—may Peace be their object; virtue their guide and the happiness of the PEOPLE, their leading principle" and "THOMAS MCKEAN—the first suggester of American Independence—may he succeed our old tried friend *Thomas Mifflin* to the Governmental chair."[116] Federalists, meanwhile, gathered to listen to a series of "animated orations" delivered by students of Dickinson College before raising their glasses to a series of patriot toasts including "The *real* friends of our constitution—the friends of our present government" and "James Ross Esq—All honest hearts and hands united to support his election to the Chief Magistracy of our State."[117]

The intense campaigning brought record numbers of voters to the polls, underscoring not only Pennsylvanians' acceptance of the ballot box as the vehicle for change but also the efficacy of the various mobilization strategies. When the votes were counted, McKean bested Ross by a margin of approximately five thousand votes. Statewide, 56 percent of adult males voted, over 20 percent more than had turned out in any of the previous gubernatorial contests. In some counties, over 80 percent of the eligible voters cast ballots.[118] Although particularly contentious local elections had resulted in similar levels of turnout in previous years, this was the first time that a statewide contest elicited such a response. As Kenneth W. Keller demonstrated in his detailed analysis of the election returns, the counties that voted for McKean had a higher turnout than those that sided with Ross, a reflection of Republicans' superior organization. Additionally, some of the highest turnouts occurred in heavily German-speaking regions where Fries's Rebellion had occurred, which suggests that Republicans had successfully harnessed voters' frustrations with the Federalists.[119]

The election of 1799 marked a turning point in Pennsylvania politics. McKean's victory represented a triumph of party organization and signaled the beginning of the end for Federalists in Pennsylvania. Republicans gained control of the state House of Representatives in the elections of 1799 and the Senate the following year. The focus on elections and party-building had accomplished what direct forms of mobilization did not: a defeat of Federalists' version of deferential republicanism. Reflecting on the political atmosphere, John Ward Fenno Jr., who had assumed editorship of the *Gazette of the United States* following the death of his father, mournfully concluded that "the sun of federalism is fast retiring behind the clouds of turbulence and treason."[120]

As Republicans had been at pains to demonstrate, however, their ascension to power did not amount to a rejection of the regime. Indeed, Republicans succeeded in large part because they had convincingly portrayed themselves as the true defenders of the Constitution. But doing so had come at a cost: Republicans had to sever ties with Revolutionary France and accept that the people spoke exclusively through the ballot box. Defeating the Federalists also required that men like Dallas set aside their fears of polarization and, at least temporarily, join the party organization. On the other end of the spectrum, more radical Republicans had to abandon efforts to engage the people more directly in the deliberative process and rally behind a moderate like Thomas McKean.

Victory presented a new set of challenges for Republicans as well. Opposition to the Federalists had been the incentive for the creation of the party organization. With Federalists out of power, what, if any, purpose would the party serve going forward? Did Pennsylvanians need to remain as engaged and involved, or could they now relax and trust their elected officials? Beyond the uncertainty surrounding the future of the party, Republicans also faced the daunting task of translating their critiques of the Federalists into an actual approach to governing. What would be different now that Republicans ran the state? Would there be structural changes? Would there be any new restrictions on who could be part of the people? Given the party's ideological diversity, would it even be possible to reach a consensus on these questions?

5

Establishing a Democratic Republic

> Pennsylvania seems to have in its' bowels a good deal of volcanic matter, & some explosion may be expected.
>
> —Thomas Jefferson to Robert Smith, 28 August 1804

ON 4 MARCH 1801, Republicans in Philadelphia staged a massive parade to celebrate the inauguration of Thomas Jefferson as president of the United States. Coming on the heels of Thomas McKean's election in 1799, Republicans in Pennsylvania saw Jefferson's narrow victory over incumbent John Adams as the final repudiation of Federalists' version of deferential republicanism. The symbolism of the day suggested that the parade served as a Republican counterpoint to Federalists' Grand Federal Procession. For example, in a nod to the "Federal Ship," one of the most popular floats in the Grand Federal Procession, the Republican parade included a schooner drawn by sixteen white horses. By linking the inaugural parade with the Grand Federal Procession, Republicans sent the message that Jefferson's election represented a turning point in the country's history. Just as supporters of the Constitution believed that the new regime would save the country from ruin, Republicans saw Jefferson's victory as a triumph of liberty over tyranny. In the afternoon, John Beckley delivered an oration that emphasized this point. He proclaimed Jefferson's inauguration as the end of the "reign of terror and political delusion" in America. That evening, Republicans raised their glasses to toasts such as "Our days of triumph—The Fourth of July 1776, Independence declared; the Fourth of March, 1801, Independence preserved!"[1] The political party, it appeared, had emerged as an effective tool for asserting the will of the people. The future belonged to the Republicans.

Even as they feted their success, however, signs of a future rift began to surface. A close reading of Republican toasts from the spring and summer of 1801 point to some underlying tensions. Many Pennsylvania Republicans hoped that Jefferson's election would mark the end of partisanship and hailed him for extending an olive branch to Federalists during his inaugural address by declaring that "we are all republicans, we are all federalists."[2] At a Fourth of July celebration, the militia company the Republican Blues, for example, drank to "Moderation among Republicans—May it differ from the moderation of Tories, and convince them that it is intended to conciliate."[3] Other Republicans, however, tended to see the electoral victories as a mandate from the people to undertake fundamental reforms, and they remained deeply suspicious of Federalists. At a dinner in Northumberland to mark Jefferson's inauguration, celebrants drank to "a speedy revision to our constitution, and a reform to the senatorial branch of our legislature" and condemned Federalists.[4] At least one observer noted the apparent differences: a correspondent in the *Gazette of the United States* remarked that toasts drank by the "decent democrats . . . were in general moderate and such as might be drank by *Americans,*" while those at other gatherings "were truly Jacobinical."[5] Republicans easily overlooked these differences in the midst of the festivities, but as the elation wore off and Republicans turned their attention to the actual process of governance, the conflicting visions for the future of the party could no longer be ignored.

In the years following the election of McKean and Jefferson, the Republican Party in Pennsylvania fractured as simmering disagreements that had been masked behind a shared commitment to defeating the Federalists burst out into the open. For some Republicans, electing new men to office had been the ultimate goal. With leaders like McKean and Jefferson now at the helm, these Republicans believed the public could relax and trust that the country was in good hands. Other members of the Republican coalition, however, viewed the election of like-minded individuals as only the first step toward creating a more participatory form of politics. These men argued that the regime was too insulated from the will of the people, and they demanded structural changes. After a brief honeymoon following the election of 1800, the differences between the two wings became overwhelming, and within a few years the party split into warring factions. Those Republicans who promoted structural changes adopted the name Democrats, while their opponents became known as Quids.[6]

Although a variety of factors contributed to the rupture of the Republican Party in Pennsylvania, this chapter argues that the split between Quids and Democrats stemmed from lingering questions about the proper role of the people in the governing process. Many of the debates revolved around the role and purpose of political parties now that Federalists no longer held power. Quids believed that the Republican Party existed exclusively to defeat the Federalists. Once that had been accomplished, the party organization no longer served a purpose. As a result, Quids hoped to move beyond the bitter partisanship that had characterized the late 1790s. Although they rejected Federalists' deferential republicanism, Quids supported the notion that the public will had to be refined through the selection of representatives and argued that, with Republicans in office, Pennsylvanians could now leave the business of governing to their elected officials. Democrats, in contrast, saw the political party as an agent of the people. With Federalists gone, Democrats hoped to use the party organization to force reforms to the state constitution that would give the people greater control over the governing process. To Democrats, Quids' attempts to move beyond partisanship seemed naive at best and might even be a sign that they harbored Federalist sympathies. Despite their divergent visions for the future, both sides portrayed themselves as the true representatives of the public will and accused their opponents of trying to undermine self-government.

For all their differences, Quids and Democrats did appear to agree on at least one key point: neither faction showed any interest in challenging the norms governing who could participate in electoral politics. If anything, opportunities for women and African Americans to take part in the political process diminished following the "Revolution of 1800." Both Quids and Democrats adhered to the example set by Republicans in the 1790s and welcomed (white) immigrants, but they made no effort to engage Black voters and allowed women to play only a symbolic role in the political process. The struggle between Quids and Democrats was therefore really only about democracy for white men.[7]

To establish their legitimacy and gain control, Quids and Democrats returned to the forms of political mobilization and strategies for marshalling public opinion that Republicans had utilized in the 1790s. Each side staged rallies, developed electioneering committees, employed printed propaganda, organized voluntary societies, and held celebrations. Important differences, however, existed in how the two factions used these tools. Quids preferred more controlled and less direct means of engaging the public, while Democrats favored more direct and popular forms. Ultimately, neither side could declare victory, and facing the threat of a resurgent Federalist Party, the two sides reconciled in 1808. As historian Andrew Shankman has argued, a new version of democracy that was compatible with capitalism emerged from the "crucible of conflict" between the Quids and Democrats. Just as importantly, the end of the schism came with the understanding that parties would remain an integral part of American democracy. Instead of serving as a vehicle for bringing about structural changes, however, the party would focus its efforts on channeling political passions into constitutional channels. The party would, in other words, serve as a check against governmental overreach and against democratic reform.[8]

The State of the State

The dawn of the nineteenth century brought with it important changes to Pennsylvania's political landscape that would help to shape the schism in the Republican Party. According to census records, the state experienced a nearly 35 percent growth rate between 1800 and 1810, and the 1810 census ranked Pennsylvania third in terms of overall population (behind New York and Virginia). The same census showed that Philadelphia continued to be the nation's second largest city, although it appeared to be losing ground to rival Baltimore. The largest growth occurred in the western parts of the state, and the Republican-led assembly voted in 1800 to divide the massive county of Allegheny—located in the northwest corner of the state—into nine smaller counties. The move helped Republicans consolidate their control over the state and increased westerners' influence in the assembly. This shift in power from east to west was further underscored by the move of the state capital from Philadelphia to Lancaster in 1799.[9]

Despite these demographic changes, Philadelphia remained the state's economic center of gravity. Fueled by broader changes in the market economy, the shipping and manufacturing sectors were booming. The port of Philadelphia ranked third in the nation in terms of the value of imports and exports, and Pennsylvanians produced more manufactured goods than any other state. Although the federal government had officially moved to the new capital city along the Potomac River in 1800, Philadelphia remained the banking capital of the country, and many of the country's most important banks—including the first Bank of the United States, the brainchild of Alexander Hamilton—stayed behind.[10]

As had been the pattern in the previous decades, however, some Pennsylvanians benefited more than others from the developing economy. Wealth remained concentrated in the southeast, and while rural areas of the state saw some gain, the disparity between the different regions of the state continued to grow. In the west, land prices continued to rise as high-quality land became scarcer. In the more urban areas, population growth coupled with advances in manufacturing helped lead to a collapse of the apprenticeship system, which effectively severed one of the most important ladders of social mobility. As a result, while some Pennsylvanians reaped record profits, a growing number of others were forced to abandon dreams of economic independence and work for wages.[11]

Pennsylvania continued to boast a vibrant network of newspapers that acted as the state's political arteries. The *Aurora* remained the most influential Republican newspaper, and the paper emerged as the primary organ for Philadelphia Democrats. With the state and national governments meeting elsewhere, however, the paper lost some of its stature. Meanwhile, dozens of new daily and weekly newspapers began circulating during the first decade of the nineteenth century. The most important of these included the *Freeman's Journal,* which would serve as the mouthpiece for the Quids; the Northumberland *Republican Argus;* and the *Democratic Press.* The latter two papers, edited by John Binns, provided space for more moderate Democrats and would play an important role in bringing an end to the schism. A few Federalist papers remained in print, most prominently the *Gazette of the United States,* edited by John Fenno Jr. Federalists did lose one of their most consistent and colorful champions when William Cobbett returned to England in 1800.[12]

Nominations and the Seeds of Discontent

Cracks in the Pennsylvania Republican Party first began appearing in 1802 and 1803 during a debate in Philadelphia County over the public's role in the selection of nominees. Since the late 1790s, the party had effectively controlled the nomination process, and because Philadelphia County was a reliably Republican district, whomever the party nominated would likely be elected. In most parts of the state, a countywide committee composed of representatives from the different townships took charge of developing a slate of candidates for local and regional elections. In Philadelphia County, however, Republicans had generally relied on a single countywide meeting to select nominees.[13] In the larger and more rural parts of the state, Republicans could not reasonably be expected to assemble in one location, so the committee system made sense, but the relative size and population density of Philadelphia County meant that, at least in theory, any interested Republican could participate in the meeting.

By 1802, however, some Republicans had grown frustrated with the use of a countywide meeting. In particular, they took issue with the power Michael Leib wielded over general county meetings. Leib, who had been elected to the U.S. House of Representatives from the Second District, which included Philadelphia County, was a particularly popular figure in the Northern Liberties neighborhood, where the county meeting often occurred. Leib was a skilled organizer and an uncompromising populist. His radical politics and brusque manners appealed to many of the men living in the working-class suburbs outside of Philadelphia. To more moderate Republicans, however, Leib's power epitomized the dangers of an excess of democracy. They saw him as demagogue who appealed to emotion rather than to reason and who cared more about self-aggrandizement than the public good.[14]

The first signs of internal dissension came in September 1802, when a group of disaffected Republicans gathered at the Rising Sun Tavern. The men, who styled themselves "Democratic Republicans," adopted resolutions complaining of "the improper character nominated to represent this county in the congress of the United States."[15] The *Aurora* leapt to Leib's defense and fiercely denounced "the Rising Sun men" as traitors. Under heavy pressure, the group ultimately backed down and acquiesced to the general meeting. Unsurprisingly, the countywide meeting went on to nominate Leib once again.[16]

Relations between the different factions of the Republican Party continued to sour throughout the first part of 1803. Clashes over patronage, judicial reform, and Governor McKean's use of the veto left the party deeply divided. When the issue of nominating procedures in Philadelphia County reemerged in the summer of 1803, therefore, it quickly became wrapped up in the larger struggle between the different factions of the Republican Party. Quids and opponents of Leib demanded that the county be divided into districts while Democrats defended the single countywide meeting.

Although political strategy partially explains this divide over the nomination process—Democrats' superior organizational skills coupled with the fact that the meetings typically occurred in the heavily Democratic neighborhood of Northern Liberties almost guaranteed that any Quid voices would be drowned out during a county meeting—the fight over the nominating process was also a product of ideological differences.[17] Now that Federalists had been defeated, Democrats, led by William Duane, the outspoken editor of the *Aurora*, and Michael Leib, increasingly rejected any intermediaries that stood in the way of the people's right to exercise control over the deliberative process. A general meeting was therefore preferable because it afforded the greatest number of citizens with the opportunity to participate directly in the selection of nominees. Quids, in contrast, favored less direct ways of engaging the public and believed that large gatherings undermined order and reason. A series of smaller meetings that selected delegates to attend a countywide assembly would, they argued, better facilitate debate and allow people who could not travel to a single county meeting to participate in the process. The pyramid structure of the meetings would also work to refine the will of the people and ensure that the final nominee truly represented the will of the people.[18]

In addition to the question of districts versus general county meetings, the two factions also clashed over who should be allowed to participate in the nominating meetings. After an attempt at a joint meeting between Quids and Democrats degenerated into violence in 1803, Democrats passed a resolution stating that henceforward only "known democrats" would be allowed to participate in party meetings. Although political parties had been holding private meetings for years, explicit boundaries on attendance were rare, and Quids reacted with outrage at the restrictions. Accusing Democrats of launching "a political inquisition," Quids and their allies warned that citizens could "soon expect to see the system of Robespierre introduced into the country—and a guillotine erected for the purpose of taking off the heads of those who will not bow at the shrine of Jacobinism."[19] Critics portrayed Leib as a dictator who manipulated the masses. Democrats brushed off these criticisms and argued that Quids were only upset because they had hoped to rely on Federalists to help take control of the meetings.[20]

This debate over who should be allowed to participate in nominating meetings reflected underlying disagreements about the value of political parties now that Republicans controlled the state and national governments. Democrats saw the political party as a positive force that represented the will of the people. From this perspective, critics of the party were enemies of the people. Quids held a different view. As a correspondent in the *Philadelphia Evening Post* explained, Quids accepted parties as necessary to guard against "that state of apathy which precedes despotism" but saw "party carried to the excess" as tyrannical and poisonous to a healthy republic.[21] The time had come, they believed, to start healing the political divide that had defined Pennsylvanian politics for a generation. To that end, Quids began to call for a "union of honest men" that brought together Republicans and reformed Federalists.[22]

At this early stage of the schism, most of the drama centered around what happened in Philadelphia County, but there were signs of tension among Republicans throughout the state. Democrats in Carlisle attacked the policy of having standing committees select candidates as "*Arbitrary* and *Aristocratical*," and called on communities to hold town meetings where the people could participate directly in the process.[23] Similar skirmishes also broke out in Pittsburgh and Bucks County.[24] In each instance, the two sides eventually reconciled, but these clashes underscored the ideological and strategic divide within the Republican Party and foreshadowed some of what would come next.

The Battle Lines: Petitions, Voluntary Societies, and the Future of Self-Government

The percolating disagreements within the Republican Party in Pennsylvania came to a boil in 1805. Democrats had been trying to push through reforms to the state government for years. Their efforts had been consistently blocked by Governor McKean. Frustrated by his repeated use of veto powers, Democrats decided to take their case directly to the people with a petition campaign. The decision to turn to petitions reflected both the reality that Democrats could accomplish little without McKean's support and their commitment to engaging the people in the political process. The subsequent campaign sharply divided the state and laid bare the competing visions for the future of self-government.

On 28 February 1805, the *Aurora* published a long memorial addressed to members of the legislature that outlined the defects of the existing constitution and called on elected officials to take immediate steps toward organizing a new convention. It cast the 1790 state constitution as a counter-revolution that had deprived the people of their right to participate in the governing process. Specifically, the memorial pointed to the fact that state senators served four-year terms, meaning that they could freely operate against the will of their constituents for years before being recalled. "We hold it as a fundamental principle of republican government," the memorial read, "that the agents of the people should feel at all times their responsibility to those who have constituted them." Annual elections were necessary to ensure that senators respected the will of the people. In addition, the memorial demanded drastic cuts to the governor's patronage and veto powers. Investing one man with such extensive powers invited corruption. Finally, it asserted that the judicial branch was too independent and suggested that judges be regularly "bro't to the tribunal of an election" to ensure that they adhered to the public will.[25] The memorial was, in short, a declaration of war against the principles undergirding the existing regime and a call for a return to a more direct form of democracy.

Following the memorial's publication, Democrats mobilized to collect signatures. Nathan Boileau, a prominent member of the legislature, helped to spearhead the effort by sending copies to his allies throughout the state. Notably, however, he tried to keep his involvement secret. The drive for a convention, he explained, "ought to originate with the people." Although the real impetus for a new constitution came from the top down, Democrats understood that, in order to be legitimate, the petition drive needed to at least appear to be a grassroots movement.[26]

As the memorial circulated, Democratic newspapers, led by the *Aurora,* railed against the undemocratic nature of the state constitution. Using populist rhetoric that recalled the fights over the 1776 constitution, Duane and his correspondents portrayed the proponents of the convention as latter-day Patriots fighting to protect the people's right to self-government. Duane urged readers to not be fooled by Quids' "language of *moderation*—it is deceitful as the Syren tongue of an harlot."[27] The men who opposed the new convention only feared that it might restore power to the people.[28] True Republicans, he argued, "know no law superior to the *will of the people.*"[29]

Democrats' calls for a new convention put Quids in a difficult position. Most Quids accepted the idea that the people had the right to alter their form of government but worried that a new constitutional convention would "generate licentiousness and anarchy" and inevitably "agitate, inflame, and may fatally divide the people."[30] As a result, Quids tried to walk a line between acknowledging the legitimacy of the people's right to a new convention and denying that the current situation merited such a drastic measure. "Innovation, in great affairs," explained one writer, "should be adopted with caution" and only after a period of calm deliberation.[31] Furthermore, Quids argued that the existing form of government had been the work of Pennsylvania's "wisest and best Citizens" and "exhibits nothing essentially defective in its theory."[32] In addition to challenging the need for a new convention, Quids rejected the petition as a vehicle for the expression of the public will. The people, they explained, spoke exclusively through "*a vote of citizens at large by printed ballots,* on points properly defined."[33]

Quids did, however, understand that if the Democrats' memorial went unchallenged, it would be very difficult to block the calling of a convention. Even if petitions did not represent a legitimate expression of the public will, the previous decades had clearly demonstrated how a well-organized petition campaign could influence public proceedings. As a result, Quids in Philadelphia responded by forming a new voluntary society, "the Society of Constitutional Republicans," to coordinate their own petition campaign. Members of the society made it clear that they saw the debate over a new convention as a fight over the fundamental meaning of self-government. At its inaugural meeting in March 1805, the members of the new society, which included high-profile political veterans Alexander James Dallas and George Logan, pledged "to preserve and perpetuate the principles of A DEMOCRACY which recognizes the PEOPLE, as the legitimate sources of all the powers of Government." The best way to accomplish this, they argued, was to maintain and defend "THE CONSTITUTION of the Union, and of the State which THE PEOPLE have deliberately established, as the foundations of civil liberty, public order, and national prosperity."[34] In other words, protecting the will of the people meant protecting the constitution and vice-versa.

Following the meeting in Philadelphia, the society distributed circulars throughout the state calling on like-minded men to begin collecting signatures on petitions opposing the calling of a convention. Aware that Democrats would likely accuse them of betraying the spirit of the Republican Party, the authors compared the current debate over the state constitution to the struggle with the Federalists. "The avowed motive, *the only avowed motive,* of our political warfare, from the year 1790, to the year 1801, was to preserve and perpetuate the free, Republican institutions," the circular explained. "The same motive still actuates the Citizens in Philadelphia who form the 'Society of Constitutional Republicans.'" Just as its members had come together to defeat "federalism, artfully employed to disguise monarchy," so to would they work to guard against "democracy unworthily employed as a cover for anarchy."[35]

Democrats in Philadelphia responded to the Quids' new voluntary societies by staging a large public meeting to adopt a series of resolutions creating the "Society of Friends of the People." Explaining that the society became necessary when "it is insinuated that the people are incompetent to manage their own affairs or to be trusted with their own welfare," members portrayed the organization as a necessary countermeasure designed to defend the people's right to exercise their sovereignty. Like the Quid organization, the Society of Friends of the People agreed to meet on a regular basis and called on allies throughout the state to form local sister societies.[36]

Over the next month the two voluntary societies competed for support and signatures. In the process, both Quids and Democrats began to more clearly articulate their views on the nature of democracy and the proper role of citizens. Democratic writers became more vehement in their commitment to the principle of majority rule and passionately defended the people's right to assert their will over the governing process. The people, according to Democrats, might make occasional mistakes, but they would always be the best guardians of liberty. As "Cato," a correspondent in the *Aurora*, wrote, "It is a correct maxim, that the will of the people ought to rule, and that the will of a majority is the will of the people. Therefore, every part of a constitution, which prevents the will of the people, from becoming supreme law . . . is unjust, and dangerous and ought to be abolished."[37] Anyone who disagreed must either be deluded or an opponent of self-government. Indeed, every true patriot had a responsibility to "aid in correcting the aristocratic tendencies of the constitution."[38]

Quids countered in the press with their own version of popular sovereignty. While they agreed with Democrats that all power flowed from the people, Quids argued that history showed that the people could behave rashly. As one correspondent explained, "Despots deprive the people of liberty, under the doctrine that man is a restless violent animal, always inclined to subvert order. Jacobins destroy regular government by avowing, that the people are always actuated by the true knowledge of their own interest—and that their own delegated authorities are secret enemies. Republicans know that human nature is intrinsically good, but liable to error and passion." In order for self-government to succeed, therefore, it must include safeguards like a strong executive and an independent judiciary that could serve as a check on the will of the people. It also required that voters trust their elected officials. These buffers were, Quids asserted, what prevented the country from slipping into anarchy.[39]

Between late February and mid-April 1805, the legislature received a total of 169 petitions with 10,893 signatures addressing the matter of calling a convention. Of that total, Democrats and proponents of the convention delivered 79 petitions with 4,944 names, and opponents of the convention produced 90 with 5,949 signatures.[40] Although Quids had managed to collect more signatures, they could hardly take comfort from the number of people who supported changes to the constitution. Additionally, many of the petitions opposing the convention had come from traditionally Federalist areas, while Republican regions were more likely to support changes to the constitution.

Democrats in the legislature also made it clear that they were not ready to give up their campaign for reform. Although they agreed to at least temporarily set aside their demands for changes to the constitution, Democrats forced through a resolution that called the 1790 constitution defective and proclaimed that "no man, or generation of men, is authorised to say to their successors, that we have arrived at the *acme* of perfection in any human institution, beyond which it is impossible for you to pass."[41] Democrats, in short, remained committed to structural changes.

Clodhoppers versus the "Union of Honest Men"

With the question of a new convention on hold, Democrats set their sights on the upcoming gubernatorial campaign. Thomas McKean had won reelection in 1803 by a landslide, but his veto of various reform measures and his well-known aristocratic temperament had left him deeply unpopular with Democrats. His reputation suffered further damage in early 1805 when the *Aurora* reported that, during a meeting with two Democratic members of the state legislature, the governor had lost his temper and referred to those who supported the convention as a "set of clodpoles [clodhoppers], and ignoramuses."[42] The outburst fit the narrative that McKean was aloof and condescending toward common people and served as the final straw for Democrats. Embracing the label "clodhopper," a term that means rustic and uncouth, as a sign of their humble roots and commitment to populism, Democrats resolved to oppose McKean's reelection.[43]

The election pitted two different versions for the future of the Republican Party against each other. Democrats saw the contest as an opportunity to demonstrate that, despite what had happened with the petition campaign, a majority of Pennsylvanians supported their reforms. Even if they could not force a new convention, with McKean gone Democrats could force through structural changes that would give the people greater control over the deliberative process. For Quids and their allies, McKean's reelection became about protecting the constitution and showing that the "union of honest men" spoke for the people.

The campaign began on 1 April 1805 when Democrats nominated Speaker of the State House of Representatives Simon Snyder as their candidate for governor. Snyder's background stood in stark contrast to McKean's privileged upbringing. The Democratic candidate came from modest beginnings and had worked his way up to become one of the most influential political figures in the state. Originally from Lancaster, he had established himself as key figure in the assembly and had served as Speaker of the House three times. He was also of German descent, an important factor given the large number of Pennsylvanian voters with German heritage.[44] Two days after Democrats endorsed Snyder, Quids in the legislature responded by joining with a few Federalists and formally nominating McKean for a second term.[45]

In the coming months, although both Quids and Democrats drew on their experience mobilizing in the 1790s, their underlying disagreement about the role of the people led the two groups to adopt different approaches to electioneering. For example, although neither faction had sought public input before selecting their candidate, Quids and Democrats organized meetings throughout the state to give the public an opportunity to endorse their selections. But as part of their efforts to move beyond partisanship, Quids actively recruited Federalists to attend these meetings.[46] In contrast, Democrats, who portrayed their opponents as enemies of the people, established committees of "vigilance" tasked with enforcing party discipline.[47] These differences, in turn, helped to drive the two factions even further apart as Democrats saw the alliance with Federalists as an unforgivable political sin and Quids saw Democrats' committees as a step toward autocracy.

The two campaigns also clashed over the use of celebratory politics. Democrats, under the leadership of Duane and Leib, controlled most of the longstanding Republican voluntary societies including the Tammany Society and militia companies tasked with organizing fetes. In the summer of 1805, Democrats started to purge Quids and anyone who had opposed a new convention or supported McKean. With the moderates gone, Democrats began using celebrations as an opportunity to promote their vision for society. At a dinner in honor of the Louisiana Purchase in May 1805, for example, Democratic voluntary societies drank toasts to "The people, the source of government—May they never suffer their servants to become their masters" and "Execration to political hypocrisy—the worst enemies of the people are those who pretend to save them from themselves." Glaringly absent from the list of toasts was the customary acknowledgment of the governor.[48] The celebratory snubbing of McKean continued during the annual Independence Day celebrations. Breaking tradition, Democratic militia companies refused to salute the governor during their exercises. Such rituals of deference had no place in the society Democrats envisioned. Instead, celebrants mocked McKean with toasts such as, "Clodhoppers, stumbling blocks in the way of his *excellency*—May they teach him good manners and decorum at the next election."[49]

Quids responded by challenging the value of celebratory politics. Writers attacked the Tammany Society and other Democratic groups as a "scourge of the people" that existed only for the purpose of "individual aggrandizement." Such organizations, they argued, might have served a purpose in the 1790s during the struggle with Federalists, but with Jefferson and McKean in office they were no longer necessary.[50] Some Quids went further than just attacking the voluntary societies and condemned the entire practice of celebrating holidays as counterproductive and wasteful. "A Philadelphian" pointed out that "the labor of a whole day is in the first place lost, were this all, it would be soon gotten over; but citizens form themselves into large companies, dine at some tavern, spend from two to six dollars, and many of their families are the worse for weeks by celebrating one grand holiday." This type of feting served no purpose, and the author suggested a more appropriate way to celebrate the nation would be to partake in an orderly procession and attend an oration on the blessing of being an American instead of attending "costly dinners and swallowing down bottles of wine." Honoring holidays in this manner would teach citizens to love their country and respect the rule of law, rather than encourage licentiousness.[51]

The growing chasm between Quids and Democrats came into stark relief in print as both sides blanketed the state with electioneering literature in the final weeks of the campaign. The *Freeman's Journal*, edited by William McCorkle, emerged as the most prominent Quid newspaper. McCorkle presented himself as the antithesis of the vitriolic William Duane. Although he printed a fair number of attacks on prominent Democrats, McCorkle claimed to be disgusted with the politics of character assassination. A successful republic, he asserted, required calm deliberation and the free flow of ideas, the very things that Democrats sought to stifle with fearmongering and demagoguery. According to McCorkle, "honest Republicans" could no longer stand by while these men tore at the social fabric of the country.[52] The election, he argued, represented a "struggle, in which the very character and principles of a republican government are implicated."[53]

Alexander James Dallas elaborated on what Quids thought was at stake in one of the most widely distributed Quid electioneering pieces.[54] Dallas began by tracing the rise of the Republican Party in Pennsylvania, arguing that it had been "a principle of concert and conciliation" that led to a triumph over Federalists. Republicans, he suggested, had only succeeded because they accepted the limits of the existing regime and had adopted a more moderate stance. Now that Republicans held power, however, Dallas warned that the country faced a new threat from "a small but active COMBINATION OF MALCONTENTS" who clamored for more power. While the majority of citizens recognized "that their position did not afford a view of the whole of the political ground," Dallas claimed these agitators had become "deranged by Utopian theories" and now promoted reckless changes that would destabilize the state and throw it into chaos by removing any checks on the public will. Responsible citizens, he suggested, understood that they did not have the capacity to govern directly. The pamphlet concluded by asking readers to trust in the wisdom of experience and "to evince to the world, that a Democratic Republic, can enjoy energy without tyranny, and Liberty without anarchy" by standing up for the constitution and reelecting Governor McKean.[55]

Democrats responded to the Quids' defense of the existing regime by doubling down on their calls for reforms. The campaign had the effect of amplifying Democrats' commitment to giving the people greater control over the governing process. Rejecting the existing regime as a poorly disguised aristocracy characterized by "British checks and balances," Democrats began calling for a breakdown of all barriers between the people and the deliberative process.[56] Some correspondents to the *Aurora* even started questioning whether "the voice of the people" could ever truly be known "through the medium of representation."[57] Other contributors challenged the entire premise of a written constitution as it placed boundaries on the will of the people.[58]

The radicalism of some Democrats might help explain the decision by Quid leaders in Philadelphia to announce that they "had disregarded what may *now* be called but shades of difference in political opinion" and endorsed a slate of candidates for local offices that included a few well-known Federalists.[59] Although Quids and Federalists had been working together against the Democrats for months, this act represented the first formal union. The fact that some Republicans would not only agree to vote for Federalists but also dismiss the political battles of the 1790s as a mere disagreement between "shades of difference in political opinion" is further evidence of Quids' determination to both protect the regime and move beyond the partisanship of the 1790s. Quids and Federalists across the state followed this example and aligned in support of McKean. According to one correspondent, by the time of the election Federalists and Quids became "so completely amalgamated" that they could no longer be separated.[60]

Democrats pounced on the public union as further proof of Quids' political heresy and warned voters that McKean's reelection would result in a return to the terrors of the Adams administration. On election day, Duane implored allies to turn out in defense of the people's liberties. "TODAY," he cried, "you are to meet your old and uniform political opponents, the *federalists* who are supported by a mongrel faction destitute of all principle."[61] The combined efforts of Quids and Federalists, however, proved too much to overcome.

The mobilization efforts underlying the heated contest between Quids/Federalists and Democrats drove a total of 82,866 Pennsylvanians, or nearly 55 percent of the state's eligible voters, to cast ballots on election day. McKean received 43,674 votes (53 percent) while Snyder garnered 38,924 (47 percent). McKean won in every county that tended to vote for Federalists and in most of the counties where the two parties split evenly, while Snyder took the areas that usually sided with Republican candidates. With a few exceptions, both candidates did well across the state, an indication of how divided Pennsylvanians had become.[62]

The Federalist/Quid coalition had prevailed, and the regime remained intact. This did not, however, mean that all of the questions about the role of the people had been answered. If anything, the success of the "union of honest men" added further uncertainty. Despite what Democrats might have claimed, Quids had not simply embraced Federalists' views. They might have opposed structural reforms, but they had no interest in reconstructing the Republican Court or promoting deferential republicanism. Still, Federalists had been integral to McKean's victory, and it was reasonable to assume that they would exert some influence going forward. Democrats faced their own problems as well. Coming on the heels of the failed convention movement, McKean's victory suggested that Democrats might need to rethink their approach to political mobilization. The increasingly radical rhetoric coming from the *Aurora*, along with the heavy-handedness of leaders Duane and Leib, had left some Democrats feeling alienated. As a result, the future of political parties in Pennsylvania remained opaque.

Factional Breakdown

Both Democrats and Quids in Pennsylvania struggled to find their footing following the election of 1805. Neither faction seemed capable of realizing their vision for the state. Having bested Democrats twice in 1805, Quids initially held out hope that they could bring about an end to the political bickering. As a sign of their willingness to bury the hatchet, the Philadelphia Society of the Constitutional Republicans adopted an address less than a month after McKean's reelection stating that the society had succeeded in its mission of protecting the constitution and as a result would soon dissolve. The address concluded by urging anyone who might have been led astray by a "faction" during the last election, or who might have fallen under the spell of Democrats' siren song, to set aside their differences and work in support of Republican principles.[63]

Democrats, however, showed little interest in working with Quids. Duane laughed at the "extraordinary and ludicrous" idea that they could simply set aside their differences. Why, he wondered, would he want to cooperate with men who derided Democrats as "jacobins" and aligned themselves with enemies of the people?[64] A handful of correspondents in the *Aurora* hinted that there might be room in the party for some repentant Quids, but most Democrats appeared to agree with Duane. Quids, explained one writer, had been exposed as "naked *federalists*" and could never be forgiven.[65]

At the same time that Democrats rejected detente, Quids found their alliance with Federalists increasingly difficult to maintain. With the prospect of a war with Great Britain looming and the passage of the controversial Embargo Act in 1807, Federalists experienced something of a resurgence nationally. In Pennsylvania, Federalists who had remained on the sidelines for years resurfaced and began attacking the Jefferson administration. The public criticism of Jefferson put Quids in an awkward position. As long as Federalists remained quiet, Quids had been happy to put aside past difficulties and work with their former adversaries. The Federalist revival changed the equation and left Quids with a difficult choice: they could continue to cooperate with Federalists, and in the process implicitly work against Jefferson, or they could abandon the Federalists and try again to rejoin the Democrats. Neither option looked appealing because each would require the sacrifice of principle—either the rebuke of the leader of the Republican Party or a likely acceptance of Democrats' demands for reform.[66]

While Quids foundered, Democrats suffered from their own internal squabbles. Although the party initially remained united in the wake of the election of 1805, fissures surfaced as members began debating how to move forward. Some Democrats, most prominently William Duane and Michael Leib, continued to demand changes to give the people greater control over the deliberative process and began calling for the impeachment of Governor Thomas McKean. Other members disagreed. With Federalism on the rise, a segment of the party led by John Binns, the editor of the *Northumberland Gazette* and *Democratic Press*, and Nathan Boileau, a leader in the state legislature, seemed ready to make peace with the constitution. Binns and Boileau believed that Democrats should shift their attention away from pushing structural reforms and instead focus on making government more accountable within the existing framework.[67]

The clashing views for the future of the Democratic Party erupted into the open in June 1807 when a pamphlet entitled *Narrative of Facts Relative to the Conduct of Some of the Members of the Legislature* began to circulate. Purportedly written by a committee of Democratic members of the legislature, the pamphlet seemed to confirm some of what the Quids had been saying about Leib since 1802. It accused him of behaving like an autocrat and detailed numerous instances in which his penchant for bombast had worked against the party's interests. For example, it portrayed Leib's efforts to impeach McKean as nothing but a publicity stunt and an attempt "to re-establish his popularity." Ultimately, the pamphlet depicted the party organization as the great bulwark against tyranny and warned that if Leib went unchecked, the future appeared grim. "The affairs of our party are at a crisis," it concluded. "We must either get rid of this man or the party will fall."[68]

The gulf between different wings of the Democrats widened a few months later when John Binns began printing articles in the *Democratic Press* that called for districts, as opposed to a single countywide meeting, to nominate candidates for the upcoming elections in Philadelphia County. Echoing some of the arguments Quids had made in their earlier campaign against the countywide meeting, a series of articles signed by "A Citizen of the Northern Liberties" defended districts as the most effective, organized, and practical method of conducting county business. The articles asserted that the size of the county made it impractical for all interested citizens to attend a single meeting. Perhaps more importantly, the author suggested that the current practice of gathering in Northern Liberties, the epicenter of Leib's and Duane's popularity, invited chicanery. In a clear shot at Leib and Duane, the author claimed that a countywide meeting enabled a small group of men to hijack the nomination process. Allowing such a flawed process to continue, the writer warned, would delegitimize the entire party structure. Open and fair nominations were crucial to the party's future. "THE POWER OF NOMINATION IS THE POLITICAL LEVER UPON WHICH DEPENDS THE RISE OR FALL OF PARTIES," he exclaimed. It was imperative that the legitimacy of the nomination process be unimpeachable. Only by dividing the county into districts would Democrats ensure that the party's ticket actually represented the will of the people.[69]

Although the authors of the anti-Leib pamphlet and the articles promoting district nominations adopted some of the same positions as the Quids, important differences exist between the two. Whereas Quids promoted districts and attacked Leib as part of an effort to move beyond parties, these authors saw dividing the county into districts and ousting Leib from power as necessary steps to save the party. Unlike the Quids, who saw political parties as a cancer that had to be removed because they created unnecessary divisions within society, these Democrats saw the party as an expression of the public will that had to be protected at all costs.

This distinction did not, however, appear to matter to Leib and his allies, who saw the pamphlet and the articles as part of a plot to prevent the people from having a real voice in their government. Duane denounced the authors as "Quadroons" who "are only the successors in *fact* and *form* of the *third party* or quids."[70] Leib organized a series of Democratic meetings where participants adopted resolutions condemning the effort to use districts as an obvious ploy to "distract and disorganize the democratic interest, or to gratify personal hatred and malice, or to favor the ambitious views of a certain set of individuals."[71] Real Democrats, another group declared, believed that "whenever the people can deliberate for themselves, they ought never to delegate their authority."[72] Districts, they claimed, were designed to dilute the voice of the people. In addition to denouncing the district movement, the Democratic assemblies adopted resolutions defending Leib as a champion of the people and praising him for all he had done to protect the Democratic interest.[73]

The public rift within the Democratic Party signaled a new phase in the debate over the role of the people in the political process. An increasingly vocal segment of the Democratic Party led by Binns and Boileau began arguing that the best way to protect the people's rights and liberties was to focus on strengthening the party rather than trying to change the constitution. The party, in their minds, functioned best as a tool for keeping citizens informed and engaged rather than as an instrument for regime change. With that in mind, these Democrats concluded that Duane's and Leib's radicalism and uncompromising attitudes had cost Snyder the election in 1805. To prevent a similar outcome in the future, they thought that the party had to focus more on organization and work to bring Quids back into the fold. This approach might mean abandoning hopes for structural reforms, but such concessions were necessary to build a broad coalition. Democrats aligned with Leib and Duane, in contrast, remained firmly committed to engaging the people directly in the deliberative process and saw any deviation from this position as a sign of weakness and/or corruption. With Quids and Federalists on their own collision course, Pennsylvanians found themselves at another crossroads.

The End of the Schism

The election of 1808 proved to be a pivotal moment in the struggle to define the nature of democracy in Pennsylvania. Given that McKean would be barred from running for a fourth term, Pennsylvanians from across the ideological spectrum eagerly anticipated the election of 1808. Democrats aligned with Leib and Duane saw it as their opportunity to finally elect an ally in their quest for reforms. Other Democrats, however, worried that a campaign focused on changes to the constitution would alienate moderates and potentially deliver the state to the Federalists. Quids, meanwhile, hoped to repeat their success from 1805 and select a candidate who could serve as a check on the Democratic-controlled legislature. For their part, Federalists saw the election as a chance to reclaim power and steer the state back toward their version of deferential republicanism. Each group had a different approach to mobilizing voters, and the intense electioneering served as a magnifying glass that clarified the larger debate over the future of popular government in Pennsylvania. In the process, the campaign became a political furnace that would ultimately fuse the factions of the Republican Party and distill the party's views on the role of citizens, political mobilization, and the meaning of democracy.

The Democrats' campaign opened with a public fight over nomination practices that pitted the more radical Duane and Leib against the more moderate wing. In 1805, the party had used a legislative caucus to nominate Simon Snyder for governor. In late August 1807, a gathering of Delaware County Democrats adopted resolutions calling for a statewide convention of delegates. Attendees of that same meeting also accused Binns and the *Democratic Press* of trying to "create a division of the democratic republicans of Pennsylvania," an indication that the participants aligned with Leib and Duane.[74] Shortly thereafter, at a meeting organized by Leib, Philadelphia Democrats assembled and adopted resolutions which denounced the legislative caucus as an "assumption of power" that deprived the people of their right to select their own candidates. This process, they argued, left the door open to corruption and abuse. In keeping with the larger commitment to giving the people as much control over the deliberative process as possible, these Democrats argued that the convention method would "keep the successful candidate within the controul of the people" and provide a greater number of voters with an opportunity to have their voices heard.[75]

Although framed as an effort to make the nomination process more democratic, the call for a statewide convention also represented an attempt by the Duane/Leib wing to control the nominating process. As Speaker of the House, Snyder had a deep well of support among Democrats in office, and leaving the decision to a legislative caucus would almost guarantee that he would receive the nomination again. While Leib and Duane had acquiesced to Snyder's candidacy in 1805, they had never fully embraced him as the leader of the party. A convention, therefore, presented Leib and Duane with their best chance to convince Democrats to nominate an alternative to Snyder in 1808.

Snyder's allies recognized the threat posed by the calls for a convention and immediately mobilized in defense of the caucus. Pro-Snyder meetings adopted resolutions criticizing the call for a convention as an "unnecessary, useless, and dangerous innovation." The legislative caucus was, they argued, the best possible strategy "to prevent schism, discord, and disunion among the people." Engaging the public too directly in the nomination process would do nothing but inflame passions and create unnecessary divisions. In short, average citizens should trust that party officials would make the best possible choice.[76]

In the end, the party reached something of a compromise and agreed that parts of the state with no Democratic elected officials could select delegates to attend the legislative caucus. In another concession to the Duane-Leib faction, the caucus suggested that local meetings provide instructions to their representatives. The people could thus have a more direct voice in the process.[77] At least superficially, this hybrid approach placated the Duane and Leib wing, and in early March 1808 the Democratic Party unanimously endorsed Snyder for governor. Leib served as secretary of the gathering while his close friend Thomas Leiper acted as chair. Duane, meanwhile, was selected to be on the state committee to oversee the campaign. Such displays of unity, however, would not last long.[78]

With Democrats lining up behind Snyder, Federalists and Quids tried to work through their differences. Coming into the election, Quids backed John Spayd, a prominent judge who had served as a Republican in the state assembly in the 1790s. Having supported McKean in 1805, however, Federalists "resolved not to be under the direction of the Quids" anymore and threw their support behind James Ross, who had run as a Federalist against McKean in 1799 and 1802. According to the Federalists, the state needed a man like Ross at the helm to protect the constitution and help restore order by reinstituting some form of social hierarchy. Quids and Federalists met twice in an attempt to resolve their differences, but neither group would abandon their preferred candidate. As a result, the two groups nominated separate candidates, setting up a three-way race.[79]

The collapse of the Quid/Federalist "union of honest men" and nomination of Ross raised the stakes for Democrats. While deeply unpopular with Democrats, McKean had at least been a Republican. He might have opposed changes to the constitution but he did not support Federalists' deferential republicanism. Ross, in contrast, was the epitome of Federalism, and his election would imperil all the progress that had been made since 1800. At the same time, the Quids' split from the Federalists left the door open for a potential reunification of the two factions. But doing so would require Democrats to adopt a more moderate stance.

To help direct Snyder's campaign away from the radicalism of the Duane/Leib wing of the party, Democrats aligned with Binns and Boileau decided to form two new voluntary societies: the "Society of Independent Democrats" and the "Associated Friends of Democracy and Simon Snyder." With Duane and Leib in charge of the official Democratic committees, these new organizations provided a home for those Democrats who opposed continued efforts to change the constitution and who worried that Duane's and Leib's uncompromising views might alienate voters. Just as importantly, the societies could potentially serve as a bridge for Quids to return to the party.[80]

The formation of the Society of Independent Democrats and the Associated Friends of Democracy and Simon Snyder shattered Democrats' facade of unity. Although both sides continued to support Snyder, the strategic and ideological differences between the two wings of the party became apparent when comparing the pages of the *Democratic Press* and the *Aurora*. Articles in the *Democratic Press* portrayed Snyder as a defender of the constitution. He was, explained one author, "a lover of our political institutions . . . [and] an open and firm friend to the constitution of this state."[81] Binns also published pieces that specifically targeted Quids. "A Constitutional Republican" wrote a series of open letters to the Quids, urging them to support Snyder. Professing to be "a zealous friend of Mr. *Madison and the administration of* Mr. *Jefferson*," the author claimed to be a firm defender of the state constitution and to have voted for McKean in the previous election. He concluded, however, that while Spayd was a good man, Snyder offered the only real hope for defeating Ross and the Federalists. The writer also assured any likeminded readers that the question of a change to the constitution "has been totally abandoned" by Snyder and his friends. Quids could therefore feel safe casting their ballot for Snyder.[82] Other writers assured Quids that real Republicans had "never approved of this system of driving men from their party" because of minor disagreements.[83]

While the *Democratic Press* courted the Quid vote, the *Aurora* depicted the upcoming election as a referendum on the existing regime. In June, the paper printed an address from the Democratic Committee that claimed the constitution violated the first principle of a republican government that "*the will of the majority ought to govern.*" The most egregious example, it asserted, was the office of the governor. "Though not actually a monarch, he has qualified monarchical powers, such as are dangerous to our rights," the text exclaimed. "If we are competent to govern ourselves, then ought no constitutional power to exist in any one man, which implies an incapacity in the people for self government?" In other words, while it was important that voters support Snyder, the real goal should be fundamental reform.[84]

This divide between radical and moderate Democrats also spilled into the realm of celebratory politics. Both sides gathered on the Fourth of July in an effort to establish themselves as the real inheritors of the Revolution. The Society of Independent Democrats in Philadelphia began their festivities by listening to an oration by Walter Franklin that extolled the virtues of the constitution. In the speech, which was reprinted in the *Democratic Press,* Franklin responded specifically to the efforts to engage the people more directly in the deliberative process. He claimed that the success of the country since the adoption of the new federal and state constitutions served as proof of the genius of "the principles of *Representative Democracy*. . . . For although the sovereignty of the people be inherent and indefeasible and all legitimate power be founded on their will, yet it is impossible that in an extended or populous country it can be exercised by them in their proper persons. They must delegate it to others in whom they can place confidence." At the conclusion of the speech, celebrants took shots at the Duane/Leib wing with toasts such as "*The Printers of America*—not *above* the people, but *of* them," and praised "the democratic committee of Berks County," which had managed to reunite Quids and Democrats.[85] In contrast, more radical groups of Democrats, such as the Carlisle Republican Pike Company, used the Fourth of July as an opportunity to demand change with toasts including "The ensuing Election—May it shew the apostates of republicans their own insignificance," "Lukewarm Republicans—May their attachment to the Feds be followed by their subversion instead of their aggrandizement," and "May we never have another M'Kean refrain the will of the people."[86] Along the same lines, Philadelphia Democrats raised their glasses to "the constitution and the laws, the perfection of which consists in the facility wherewith they may be amended."[87]

With some Democrats openly courting their vote and others still emphasizing the need for constitutional reforms, Quids struggled to find a path forward. They had originally hoped to rely on a revamped Society of Constitutional Republicans to publish addresses and coordinate electioneering efforts on behalf of Spayd. The organization, however, lacked the same vigor it had shown in 1805, and by midsummer Spayd's candidacy had all but collapsed.[88] As a result, Quids could either hold their noses and vote for Ross, a Federalist whom many of them had campaigned against in 1799 and 1802, or cast their ballots for Snyder, whom they had rejected as a dangerous radical in 1805.

The journey of the *Freeman's Journal* illustrates some of the challenges facing Quids. Founded as the primary mouthpiece for the growing Quid opposition, the paper welcomed news of Spayd's nomination as a way to prevent the election of Snyder. Confidence in Spayd, however, proved short-lived. With the Spayd campaign lagging, the paper announced in May that Quids should support someone else. Then in August, William McCorkle, the paper's editor, announced that Quids should cast their ballots for Ross. Completing its transformation into a Federalist paper, the *Freeman's Journal* also began criticizing Jefferson's foreign policy and the Embargo.[89]

McCorkle faced an immediate backlash for his decision to embrace Federalism. In August, a meeting of Philadelphia Quids declared that they "view with concern and decided disapprobation" the endorsement of Ross by the *Freeman's Journal*, and they resolved that they would "not support JAMES ROSS for governor, because we believe him hostile to the Constitution of the United States, and to the equal rights of the people."[90] McCorkle responded with a tirade of abuse and accused the meeting of trying to deprive him of his freedom of speech. The Quid coalition had disintegrated.[91]

McCorkle's apostacy opened the door for moderate Democrats to make a play for Quids' support. With the main Quid newspaper firmly in the Federalist camp, Binns offered to start publishing the accounts of Quid meetings in the *Democratic Press*. Stating that Quids and Democrats agreed on "nineteen out of twenty" issues, Binns called on all Pennsylvania Republicans to unite. If they hoped to defeat Ross, Democrats and Quids had to put the interest of the party ahead of personalities. "As individuals we may observe our personal likings and disliking but as members of a political party they must be sacrificed to the general will."[92] The party had to come first. In other words, the time had come for Quids to accept the realities of parties, just as it was time for Democrats to accept the realities of the constitution.

Binns's efforts to reach Quids paid off. In late August, Philadelphia Quids adopted resolutions endorsing Snyder and acknowledging that a vote for Spayd would in effect be a vote for Ross.[93] While some Quids in other parts of the state stayed loyal to Spayd, and, at least according to the Federalist press, a few Quid meetings endorsed Ross, the majority of Quids appeared to have followed the Philadelphians and decided to return to the Republican-Democratic fold. Even Tench Coxe, one of the most outspoken Quid critics of the Democrats, made peace with his former adversaries and agreed to support Snyder.[94] By replacing Duane's and Leib's uncompromising focus on structural reforms and unforgiving attitude with an approach that focused on elections, coalition-building, and party unity, Democrats had created a path toward reconciliation.

The election, however, was far from over. Federalists were energized and better organized than ever. In fact, during the election of 1808, Federalists in Pennsylvania employed many of the same strategies for mobilizing voters that Republicans had pioneered in the late 1790s. Although they had long embraced popular politics as a way of rallying support for the federal government and promoting their version of deferential republicanism, Federalists had never taken any real steps toward building a party structure. In 1799, they had attempted to create a statewide network, but the emphasis on centralization and top-down organization hampered its development, and the movement collapsed following the elections of McKean and Jefferson. By 1808, however, Federalists' qualms regarding grassroots organizing had vanished.

Following their split with the Quids, Federalists in some parts of the state seized control of the local chapters of the Society of Constitutional Republicans and used the organization to oversee the Ross campaign. Like their Democratic counterparts, Ross's supporters used the voluntary society to create committees of correspondence and committees of vigilance. Federalists also appropriated some of Republicans' rhetoric and painted Snyder as an aristocrat who "hated . . . the poor people of the country."[95] Perhaps the clearest evidence of the shift in Federalists' approach to mobilization is that Ross appears to have personally undertaken a campaign tour in the early stages of the contest.[96] Together, these changes in their use of mobilization techniques suggest that even Federalists had come to recognize the value of party organization.[97]

The stiff competition led to a record number of Pennsylvanians voting in 1808. A total of 111,482 citizens, or approximately 70 percent of those eligible to vote, cast ballots. Of those who turned out, 67,829 (61%) sided with Snyder, 39,647 (35%) with Ross, and 4,006 (4%) with Spayd. Snyder and the Democrats had trounced their opponents. Despite Federalists' attempts at organization, Ross only managed to carry six counties. Spayd, who in the final days of the campaign had to fight off rumors that he had dropped out of the race, got nearly 25 percent of the vote in Northumberland and Berks Counties but did poorly in most areas.[98]

The election results highlight two important points. First, the state had reverted to the traditional Federalist/Republican dichotomy. Snyder won in Philadelphia County and western and central counties that had traditionally leaned Republican, while Ross won in Federalist strongholds such as Luzerne and Delaware Counties. Quids had been effectively reabsorbed into the two parties. Second, the election illustrates the importance of parties and political organization. The network of partisan committees and voluntary societies, along with nearly nonstop election coverage in the newspapers, proved remarkably successful at mobilizing voters. Similar turnout levels would not be seen in Pennsylvania again until the Jacksonian era, a testament to both the sophistication of the parties in 1808 and to the public's commitment to having a voice in the political process.

More broadly, the election of 1808 reaffirmed the political consensus that had been forged during the 1790s. Leib's and Duane's vision for the state had proved too radical for most Pennsylvanians. The regime remained in place, and citizens would only exercise their sovereignty through the ballot box. Although this outcome pleased Quids, their reunification with the Democrats came at a cost. By siding with Snyder, Quids had implicitly accepted the existence of a permanent party structure that would act as an intermediary between the people and their government. The party would serve as the engine of mobilization on election day and ensure that citizens remained active and involved in the political process throughout the year. The Ross campaign suggests that even Federalists had begun to accept this fact. The state and nation still faced contentious questions about who could be counted as part of "the people," but by 1808 the basic outlines of American democracy had taken shape.

Conclusion

Race, the People, and the Legacy of 1808

On 31 December 1808, the Associated Friends of Democracy and Simon Snyder gathered to ring in the new year and reflect on their recent success at the polls. In an adopted address, the group declared that Snyder's victory had demonstrated once and for all "that true democracy is not a system of disorder, but of peace, patriotism, and public tranquility." With Snyder in office, Pennsylvanians could now place their trust "in the well-proved probity and fidelity of our rulers, the men of our choice." The address went on to stress the importance of unity and to assert that "no measure seems better calculated to make firm our independence, and secure our freedom, than a union of parties."[1] The New Year's Eve address neatly encapsulated the legacy of the election of 1808. In Pennsylvania, "true democracy" would mean that the people would exercise their sovereignty by electing their "rulers" and participating in a political party.

This is not the version of democracy Pennsylvanians had first conceived of when they declared their independence. With the Colonial Assembly dragging its feet, Patriots had been forced to rely on popular forms of mobilization to establish their legitimacy. Radicals then channeled this energy into the creation of the state's 1776 constitution, which established that instead of being rulers, "all officers of government, whether legislative or executive" would be the people's "trustees and servants, and at all times accountable to them."[2] Under this regime, Pennsylvanians might delegate some responsibilities to their elected officials, but average citizens always retained the right to exercise their sovereignty. While highly participatory, this version of self-government faced problems from the outset. Underlying divisions, exacerbated by the ongoing war and debates about the constitution, created a combustible atmosphere that made the state nearly impossible to govern. As a result, Pennsylvanians repeatedly took matters into their own hands and used town meetings, committees, and violence to assert their will. While these forms of mobilization gave residents the opportunity to participate directly in the political process, the frequent appeals to the people bred resentment, and when coupled with anger at the treatment of moderates, opened the door to attacks on the regime's legitimacy.

In the mid-1780s, political moderates capitalized off the regime's failures by using populist rhetoric, petitions, and town meetings to position themselves as the true champions of the people's rights and liberties. These moderates' campaign culminated with the adoption of new federal and state constitutions in 1788 and 1790; these constitutions redefined the meaning of self-government in Pennsylvania and established that the people could exercise their sovereignty exclusively through the ballot box. While this approach represented a retreat from the more participatory form of politics associated with the previous regime, Pennsylvanians voted overwhelmingly in support of the new constitutions. The people, it seemed, were content to surrender some of their authority in exchange for a stronger government.

The new constitutions did not, however, end the debate over the meaning of self-government in Pennsylvania. According to Federalists, in order for the country to succeed, citizens had to be taught to respect the power of the federal government and learn to follow the dictates of the "natural aristocracy" composed of men of wealth, talent, and education. To promote these changes, Federalists began focusing on developing practices designed to cultivate a deferential version of republicanism. This strategy helped Federalists maintain a grip on the reins of power throughout the early 1790s, but efforts to reshape the political culture also gave rise to an opposition movement. Inspired by events in France and convinced that Federalists were plotting to destroy self-government, members of the opposition responded by turning to forms of mobilization designed to give the people more control over the deliberative process. The Whiskey Rebellion, the collapse of Democratic and Republican Societies, and the failed campaign to use popular pressure to block adoption of the Jay Treaty, however, clearly demonstrated the limits of these forms of mobilization under the new regime.

In the wake of these defeats, the opposition began to move away from attempts to engage the people directly in the governing process and instead focused on winning elections. This change laid the foundation for the creation of the Republican Party. Between 1796 and 1799, Republicans in Pennsylvania constructed a multilayer party organization that incorporated existing forms of mobilization to turn out voters on election day. In so doing, Republicans tacitly accepted the limits of citizenship under the constitutions. Instead of participating in the deliberative process by attending a town meeting to instruct representatives or serving on a committee to oversee price regulations, members of the party attended rallies to promote a particular candidate and worked on committees tasked with coordinating electioneering activities. A focus on coalition-building and electability also required Republicans to moderate some of their views and select candidates, like Thomas McKean, who could appeal to a large swath of voters. Federalists fought back by trying to silence their opponents using targeted legislation and acts of violence, but their efforts were not enough to stem the Republican tide. Thanks to an unprecedented get-out-the-vote effort, Republicans seized control of the state in 1799.

While Republicans' victory clearly represented a repudiation of the Federalists' brand of deferential republicanism, what it meant beyond that remained unclear. A schism in the Republican Party demonstrated that questions about the role the people would play in the governing process did not end following the so-called Revolution of 1800. Quids hoped to move beyond the partisanship that characterized the late 1790s and argued that Pennsylvanians no longer needed to remain as active. The party organization might have been a necessary evil to defeat the Federalists, but with Republicans in power, Quids believed that parties no longer served a purpose. In contrast, Democrats—led by William Duane and Michael Leib—saw the party as a critical tool for ensuring that government remained accountable to the people. These men hoped to use the party to force structural reforms that would give the people greater control over the deliberative process. Ultimately, after years of battling for control, neither side could claim victory. In reconciling, Quids and Democrats agreed to a basic framework for American democracy in which the people exercised their sovereignty through casting ballots and participating in political parties.

The type of democracy forged in Pennsylvania was therefore the product of conflict and compromise: opponents of the 1776 constitution had to become willing to engage in popular politics, Republicans had to accept the boundaries of the new regime, Quids had to recognize that parties had become a permanent fixture, and Democrats had to drop their demands for structural changes. No single factor drove these changes. Rather, political strategy, ideology, economics, and international events all played a role. This was not a strictly top-down or bottom-up process either. A relatively small group of men may have been the ones who wielded political power, but they could only do so with the support of the broader public. Ultimately, parties emerged out of the interplay among elites, commoners, and middling Pennsylvanians.

This does not mean that the struggle to define the meaning of self-government did not result in "winners" and "losers," or that the birth of parties amounted to a pure triumph for democracy. The reliance on elections and the growth of political parties undoubtedly benefited some residents (particularly those with money) more than others. It created a system where a relatively small group of party leaders could wield a significant amount of power over the governing process. This version of democracy also privileged the status quo and made structural change difficult to accomplish. By definition, a political party is more concerned with winning elections than with any democratic reforms. Establishing voting as the primary expression of sovereignty also had the effect of silencing those like women and Black people who did not have access to the franchise.

Scholars have, however, overstated the extent to which popular politics declined in Pennsylvania following the adoption of the new federal and state constitutions. Parties incorporated many of the forms of mobilization associated with the Revolution, and voter turnout skyrocketed following the rise of parties, a sign that more people were taking part in the political process. In fact, as Jeffrey Pasley put it, "Early partisan political culture—which developed during the 1790s, fully emerged after Jefferson was elected in 1800, and faded only after the parties became better organized in the 1830s—was one of the most participatory and transformative that the United States has ever experienced."[3]

In the end, democracy in America both expanded and contracted in the decades following the Revolution. Focusing on only one aspect of this dynamic obscures the fact that Americans were still trying to figure out what self-government meant. By following the evolution of different forms of mobilization in the decades following independence, this book demonstrates that Pennsylvanians embraced parties because other forms of mobilization proved unwieldy and ineffective. Doing so, however, came at a cost. Accepting elections as the primary vehicles for the expression of the public will meant that residents accepted a more limited form of citizenship than what existed in the 1770s and 1780s. What they got in exchange was a more stable, and arguably more effective, way of translating the theory of popular sovereignty into a functioning government that balanced liberty with order.

Of course, the emergence of political parties did not mean that Pennsylvanians ceased engaging in other forms of mobilization. A vibrant civil society took shape alongside the growth of parties. For example, having been beaten at the polls, Federalists took refuge in a host of new voluntary societies. By establishing subscription libraries and forming professional associations, Federalists sought to promote their version of deferential republicanism outside the realm of electoral politics. Unlike a political party, however, these civic organizations made no pretensions about representing the will of the people. Private groups and individual citizens were free to associate and take part in civic life in a variety of ways. Only elected officials could speak for the people as a whole.[4]

The central role of parties did not go unchallenged either. As historian Daniel Peart demonstrates, some Pennsylvanians began to question the effectiveness of political parties following the Panic of 1819. A debate over the possibility of new tariffs scrambled the existing divisions and drove both protectionists and free traders to launch campaigns to sway public opinion through lobbying and petitioning. While these efforts took place outside the party structure, neither group sought structural changes to the regime. In fact, far from leading to a decline in the role of political parties, the split over tariffs helped lay the foundation for the emergence of the Second Party System—a period when parties exerted even more influence over the deliberative process.[5]

The rise of parties did not, however, settle every question about the nature of democracy in Pennsylvania. Indeed, as residents came to an agreement that the people exercised their sovereignty through parties and elections, attention increasingly shifted to the debate about who was considered part of the people. This question had hovered above the debates about democracy and influenced the ways in which Pennsylvanians approached mobilization. In the early days of the Revolution, radicals had used the Test Laws to effectively define the people as only those who supported the new regime. Although the move was designed to buttress the fiction that the government represented the will of the people, the disenfranchisement of large numbers of voters created resentment and fueled an eventual backlash against the radicals. Federalists faced a similar fate in the 1790s when they sought to define the people as only native-born Americans who supported the federal government. Democrats also sought to impose restrictions on who could be considered part of the people by arguing that anyone who opposed the party represented a threat to the people. In the end, the version of the people that triumphed was not tied to political allegiance. This definition did not, of course, mean that there were no boundaries on who could be considered part of the people. In fact, as the people became less bound by political views, race took on even greater importance.

Although skin color had always been a factor in how Pennsylvanians thought about "the people," in the 1780s and 1790s some Pennsylvanians—both Black and white—held out hope for a truly biracial society. The gradual emancipation process, they believed, would provide the races with a chance to get used to living together as equals. The delay would also give newly freed men and women an opportunity to acquire the skills necessary to succeed in the republic. This dream began to fade in the early nineteenth century. Rather than leading to improvements, the growing numbers of free people of color that accompanied the ending of slavery caused race relations to worsen. Many white residents, especially those from the middling and working classes, resented the success of the Black community. With racial lines hardening, even abolitionists abandoned their hopes for a biracial society. Instead of working toward integration, critics of slavery began advancing farfetched colonization schemes that would send all people of color "back" to Africa.[6]

As Pennsylvanians gave up on a mixed-race version of the people, white residents began taking steps to enforce an all-white version of the people by excluding people of color from various forms of political mobilization. Independence Day celebrations, which had traditionally attracted a racially diverse crowd, became racially segregated. In 1813, James Forten, a wealthy Black man, reported that it was "a well known fact" that on the Fourth of July, Black people "dare not be seen after twelve o'clock in the day, upon the field to enjoy the times; for no sooner do the fumes of that potent devil, Liquor, mount into the brain, than the poor black is assailed like the destroying Hyena or the avaricious Wolf!"[7] Because these rituals helped to define the symbolic boundaries of the people, white residents could no longer tolerate the presence of people of color.[8]

White Pennsylvanians also sought to police the color line by preventing Black men from casting ballots on election day. Under both the 1776 and 1790 constitutions, adult Black men who paid taxes were entitled to cast ballots. How many Black men took advantage of this right remains unclear, but as elections came to represent the sole determining voice of the people, white Pennsylvanians began systematically working to exclude people of color. In 1822, Representative Samuel Breck noted that "owing to custom, prejudice, or design [Black voters] never presume to approach the husting."[9] Similarly, Alexis de Tocqueville described a conversation in Philadelphia in which he asked a Mr. Smith if "Blacks had citizen's rights." Smith responded, "Yes, in law, but they cannot present themselves at the poll." When Tocqueville enquired why that was the case, Smith answered, "They would be ill-treated." "The Law," Smith continued, "is nothing when it is not supported by public opinion." Legally, Black men might have been part of the people, but in practice the term really only included white men.[10]

As white Pennsylvanians increasingly defined people of color as outside the boundaries of the people, racial violence became commonplace, particularly in Philadelphia where working-class whites often competed with people of color for jobs. Because Black men and women were not really viewed as part of the people, violence could be more easily justified. A steady influx of white immigrants and economic changes associated with the market revolution created a particularly combustible environment. The situation came to a head in 1834 when a white mob terrorized Black residents over a three-day period.[11]

Efforts to establish an all-white understanding of the people in Pennsylvania culminated with the adoption of a new state constitution in 1838. Despite impassioned pleas from Black citizens and their white allies, the new constitution officially restricted the franchise to "white freemen." At the same time, the constitution made it easier for poor white men to vote and lowered the residency requirement in an effort to entice (white) immigrants to settle in the state. In Pennsylvania, "the people" now officially meant white men.[12]

Black Pennsylvanians did not passively accept disenfranchisement. Deprived of the right to vote, they turned to other forms of mobilization to try and assert their rights. On 14 March 1838, "a very numerous and respectable meeting of the colored citizens of Pennsylvania" adopted resolutions condemning the changes in suffrage laws and appointed a committee to prepare an address to the public. The subsequent *Appeal of Forty Thousand Citizens, Threatened with Disenfranchisement* laid out the moral, legal, and economic reasons why African Americans deserved the right to vote. Other Black residents sent petitions and organized voluntary societies to protest their status.[13]

The debate over slavery and the rights of freed African Americans also helped to inspire women to start challenging their status as a voiceless part of the people. In the 1840s, activists utilized many of the same tools as Black men to build support for women's suffrage. Women gave public speeches, organized rallies, circulated petitions, and lobbied law makers. In 1852, Pennsylvania's Lucretia Mott, who had signed the Seneca Falls Declaration of Sentiments, helped organize a women's rights convention in West Chester, Pennsylvania. The gathering adopted resolutions that condemned sexual inequality and demanded that women have the right to vote.[14]

Although supporters of suffrage for women and Black men succeeded in building grassroots organizations in the 1840s and 1850s, this type of direct mobilization failed to bring about a change. Under the existing regime, the people spoke through elections and parties, and voters (white men) in Pennsylvania showed no interest in revisiting the suffrage laws.

A Civil War was required for the meaning of "the people" to change. Standing on the blood-soaked ground of Gettysburg, President Abraham Lincoln declared "that this nation, under God, shall have a new birth of freedom—and that government of the people, by the people, for the people, shall not perish from the earth." The Fifteenth Amendment, which states that "the right of citizens of the United States to vote shall not be denied or abridged by the United States or any State on account of race, color, or previous condition of servitude," established that the people would, at least in theory, once again include people of color.[15]

The war, however, did not settle the debate about the meaning of the people. Despite the language of the Civil War amendments, people of color continued to suffer from a variety of legal, social, and economic forms of discrimination. As had been the case in the early 1800s, Blacks who attempted to vote faced the threat of violence. Octavius Catto, a Black civil rights leader, was murdered during a race riot on election day in Philadelphia in 1871. White Pennsylvanians also instituted poll taxes and literacy tests designed to make it difficult for African Americans (and recent immigrants) to vote. Long after the adoption of the Fifteenth Amendment was ratified in 1870, the color line continued to divide the races and prevent African Americans from fully integrating into the people. Systematically disenfranchised, Black Americans again turned to grassroots mobilization to fight for their rights. Often with at least tacit support from elected officials, white Americans responded with coordinated campaigns of terror and violence. A full century passed before the federal government began to take meaningful steps to ensure that government "by the people, for the people" included African Americans by passing the Civil Rights Act in 1964 and the Voting Rights Act in 1965.[16]

Women faced a different challenge following the Civil War. Many women had expected to see their rights expand. Instead, the amendments adopted in the aftermath of the Civil War made women's fight for equality more difficult. The Fourteenth Amendment specifically guaranteed the right to vote to "male inhabitants"—the first time the Constitution mentioned gender. The Fifteenth Amendment barred discrimination based on "race, color, or previous condition of servitude" but said nothing about sex. Disheartened but not defeated, women's rights advocates continued to wage a nationwide campaign to gain suffrage.

It took decades of activism and the pressures of a world war before women in Pennsylvania finally gained access to the vote. As late as 1915, a majority of Pennsylvania voters opposed a referendum that would have given women the franchise. In 1919, however, the state legislature agreed to ratify the Nineteenth Amendment, which established that "the right of citizens of the United States to vote shall not be denied or abridged by the United States or by any State on account of sex." The amendment was formally ratified the following year, thereby ensuring that women in Pennsylvania finally had their own voice in the deliberative process.[17]

This brief overview of the struggle to establish a more inclusive version of the people illustrates the complex legacy of the version of democracy forged in the years following the Revolution. On the one hand, the system has proven flexible enough to accommodate changing views on race and sex. The incorporation of women and African Americans into the people did not alter the basic framework for American democracy. The meaning of the people may have changed, but the people still speak through elections and political parties. On the other hand, the fight to include African Americans and women as part of the people is a reminder that exclusion has been a part of American democracy since its inception. The silencing of dissent is part of what made it possible to imagine that the government represented the will of the people. A system that privileges parties and elections also makes substantive reform painfully difficult to accomplish. Because they lacked the franchise, women and African Americans were forced to use other forms of mobilization to have their voices heard. Both groups turned to public rallies, parades, and acts of civil disobedience in efforts to draw attention to their cause. Critics could, however, easily dismiss these forms of mobilization as dangerous and unrepresentative of the true will of the people. Opponents of change could also strike back and claim their violence was justified. The movements' success ultimately depended on women's and African Americans' ability to win over people who already had the vote. It is also important to note that access to the franchise is not a panacea. Being able to vote may entitle someone to be part of the people, but it does not guarantee equal treatment under the law.

The struggle to define "the people" is also far from over. Millions of American citizens cannot vote because they have been convicted of felonies (a disproportionate number of whom are Black). The Supreme Court's decision to strike down a key provision of the Voting Rights Act in 2013 has opened the door to a new era of voter suppression. Systematic purges of voter rolls, strict voter ID laws, inconvenient polling locations, and coordinated campaigns of disinformation work to silence an ever-increasing segment of the people (again, a disproportionate number of whom are Black). At the same time, the Supreme Court has gutted campaign finance laws, which opened the door for corporations and the ultrawealthy to pour enormous sums of money into campaigns. Lies and misinformation have also caused many Americans to lose faith in the results of their elections. What these developments mean for the future of the people in America remains unclear. If history is a guide, the answer will likely depend on what happens on election day.

NOTES

Abbreviations

DCM William Duane, ed., *Extracts from the Diary of Christopher Marshall: Kept in Philadelphia and Lancaster during the American Revolution, 1774–1781* (Cambridge, MA: Harvard University Press, 1877)

DED Elaine Forman Crane, ed., *The Diary of Elizabeth Drinker*, 3 vols. (Boston: Northeastern University Press, 1991)

DHFFE Merrill Jensen et al., eds., *The Documentary History of the First Federal Elections*, 4 vols. (Madison: University of Wisconsin Press, 1976–89)

DHRC Merrill Jensen et al., eds., *The Documentary History of the Ratification of the Constitution*, 37 vols. to date (Madison: Wisconsin Historical Society, 1976–)

LBR L. H. Butterfield, ed., *Letters of Benjamin Rush*, 2 vols. (Princeton, NJ: Princeton University Press, 1951)

PA Samuel Hazard et al., eds., *Pennsylvania Archives*, 119 vols. (Philadelphia and Harrisburg: Pennsylvania Historical and Museum Commission, 1852–1933)

PTJ Julian P. Boyd et al., eds., *The Papers of Thomas Jefferson*, 45 vols. to date (Princeton, NJ: Princeton University Press, 1950–)

Introduction

1. John Adams to Abigail Adams, 18–19 June 1795, in Butterfield et al., *Adams Family Correspondence*, 10:455–58. Adams believed that Ross had taken ill because he "drank too freely of cold Water."
2. Stewart, *Redemption from Tyranny*; Jones, "Herman Husband." See also Fennell, "From Rebelliousness to Insurrection," 192–226.
3. U.S. Congress, *Annals of Congress*, 1st Cong., 2nd sess., 13 August 1789, 732.
4. By "governing process," I mean the actual process of developing and enforcing policies and laws that will govern the behavior of others. Participating in a town meeting that will issue binding instructions, for instance, is an example of individuals playing a role directly in the governing process. Voting, by extension, is an indirect way of participating in the governing process. Similarly, I use the term "deliberative process" to refer to the

actual process of debating and creating laws and policies. My thinking on this subject is informed by the scholarship on deliberative democracy. For a good overview, see Gustafson, *Imagining Deliberative Democracy in the Early American Republic,* chap. 1. See also Bohman and Rehg, *Deliberative Democracy,* and Monroe, *The Democratic Wish.*

5. There has been an ongoing debate about when the first "real" political parties formed. Pennsylvania had a long history with factions, but before the 1790s these groups tended to be fluid and lacked any real internal organization. As a result, using labels risks imparting a degree of cohesion or permanence that may not have existed. To make matters more complicated (and much to the chagrin of contemporary students), early Americans often recycled names. Thus, a "Republican" in 1786 meant something very different than a "Republican" in 1796 (which, of course, is different from what being a Republican means today). To avoid confusion, the group that supported the 1776 constitution is referred to here as "radicals" and those who opposed it as "moderates" rather than "Anti-Constitutionalists" or "Republicans." Although these terms are far from ideal, they delineate the differences between the two. Additionally, I use the lowercase "federalists" to describe the people who supported the federal Constitution and uppercase "Federalists" for those who promoted a more deferential form of republicanism in the 1790s. There is obvious overlap between the "federalists" and the "Federalists," but important differences in ideology and approaches to political mobilization existed. The only group in this book that I refer to as a political party is the Republicans post-1796. In using this term, I am not suggesting that Republicans had all the same trappings as a modern political party. Instead, the term is meant to highlight the fact that, following the Whiskey Rebellion and Jay Treaty, Republicans began to focus on building an organization that could mobilize voters on election day. My use of the term "party" is informed by Pasley, *The First Presidential Contest,* 8–15. See also R. P. Formisano, "Federalists and Republicans: Parties, Yes—System, No," in Kleppner et al., *The Evolution of American Electoral Systems,* 33–76.
6. Conway, "Political Parties and Political Mobilization."
7. Anderson, *Imagined Communities.* On the absence of a national identity, see Waldstreicher, *In the Midst of Perpetual Fetes;* John Murrin, "A Roof without Walls: The Dilemma of American National Identity," in Beeman, Botein, and Carter, *Beyond Confederation,* 333–49; and Loughran, *The Republic in Print.* On voting patterns, see Dinkin, *Voting in Provincial America.*
8. Bradburn, *Citizenship Revolution;* Irvin, *Clothed in Robes of Sovereignty.* See also Adams, *The First American Constitutions,* 36.
9. On the importance of Pennsylvania in the struggle to define the nature of democracy in the post-revolutionary period, see Shankman, *Crucible of*

American Democracy, and Wood, *Creation of the American Republic*, 88–90. For an insightful analysis of Philadelphia's history as the "Cradle of Liberty," see Nash, "Philadelphia or Boston."

10. Ryerson, *The Revolution Is Now Begun*. See also Hawke, *In the Midst of a Revolution;* Olton, *Artisans for Independence;* Ireland, *Religion, Ethnicity, and Politics;* Rappaport, *Stability and Change in Revolutionary Pennsylvania;* Frantz and Pencak, *Beyond Philadelphia;* Moyer, *Wild Yankees;* and Pencak, *Pennsylvania's Revolution*. For examples of this periodization outside of Pennsylvania, see Maier, *From Resistance to Revolution*, and Breen, *American Insurgents, American Patriots*. More generally on the question of periodization, see the articles in the joint issue of the *William and Mary Quarterly*, 3rd series, 74, no. 4 (2017), and the *Journal of the Early Republic*, 37, no. 4 (Winter 2017), "Writing to and from the Revolution."
11. See, e.g., Koschnik, *Let a Common Interest Bind Us Together;* Carpenter, *Democracy by Petition;* Waldstreicher, *In the Midst of Perpetual Fetes;* Gilje, *Rioting in America;* Coleman, *Harnessing Harmony;* and Lohman, *Hail Columbia!*
12. The classic example of the declension model in Pennsylvania is Brunhouse, *The Counter-Revolution in Pennsylvania*. See also Bouton, *Taming Democracy*, and Rosswurm, *Arms, Country and Class*. For scholars looking beyond Pennsylvania, see Holton, *Unruly Americans;* McDonnel, *The Politics of War;* Klarman, *The Framers' Coup;* Nelson, *Commons Democracy;* and Smith, *The Freedoms We Lost*. On parties forcing moderation at the expense of progressive change, see Cotlar, *Tom Paine's America*. For examples of scholars who generally see the era of the American Revolution as a period when the rights and freedoms of average Americans increased, see Wilentz, *The Rise of American Democracy*, and Wood, *The Radicalism of the American Revolution*.
13. Supporters of the federal Constitution outnumbered their opponents forty-six to twenty-three at the state's ratification convention. Although voters did not get a chance to ratify the 1790 state constitution, candidates who promised to revise the 1776 constitution dominated the convention. On Federalists' popularity, see Ireland, "The People's Triumph."
14. On this point, see Fischer, *The Revolution in American Conservatism;* Banner, *To the Hartford Convention;* Elkins and McKitrick, *The Age of Federalism;* Ben-Atar and Oberg, *Federalists Reconsidered;* Potter, *The Federalist's Vision of Popular Sovereignty;* and Andrew W. Robertson, "Voting Rights and Voting Acts: Electioneering Ritual, 1790–1820," in Pasley, Robertson, and Waldstreicher, *Beyond the Founders*, 57–78.
15. Otto von Bismarck, "Die Politik ist die Lehre vom Möglichen," in *Fürst Bismarck: Neue Tischgespräche und Interviews*, ed. Heinrich Ritter von Poschinger (Stuttgart: Deutsche Verlags-Anstalt, 1895), 1:248.

16. Roney, *Governed by a Spirit of Opposition;* Smith, *The Freedoms We Lost;* Owen, *Political Community in Revolutionary Pennsylvania.*
17. Pearl, *Conceived in Crisis;* Spero, *Frontier Country.* See also Griffin, *American Leviathan;* Edling, *Perfecting the Union;* Edling, *A Revolution in Favour of Government;* and Novak, "The Myth of the Weak American State." For a general overview of the literature, see Ron and Rao, "Taking Stock of the State in Nineteenth-Century America."
18. Brunhouse, *The Counter-Revolution in Pennsylvania;* Tinkcom, *Republicans and Federalists in Pennsylvania;* Higginbotham, *Keystone in the Democratic Arch.*
19. See, e.g., Baumann, "The Democratic-Republicans of Philadelphia"; Ireland, "The Ethnic-Religious Dimension of Politics"; Brockelman and Ireland, "The Internal Revolution in Pennsylvania"; and Miller, *Philadelphia—The Federalist City.*
20. Robertson, *The Language of Democracy;* Waldstreicher, *In the Midst of Perpetual Fetes;* Newman, *Parades and the Politics of the Street;* Travers, *Celebrating the Fourth;* Branson, *These Fiery Frenchified Dames;* Zagarri, *Revolutionary Backlash.*
21. For a helpful discussion of the different approaches, see David Waldstreicher, Jeffrey L. Pasley, and Andrew W. Robertson, "Introduction: Beyond the Founders," in Pasley, Robertson, and Waldstreicher, *Beyond the Founders,* 1–18. On Pennsylvania, see Shade, "'Corrupt and Contented.'"
22. For a discussion of the use of the term "democracy" in revolutionary America, see Seth Cotlar, "Languages of Democracy in America from the Revolution to 1800," in Innes and Philip, *Re-Imagining Democracy in the Age of Revolutions,* 15–21. On the 1776 constitution as a "radical manifesto," see Owen, *Political Community in Revolutionary Pennsylvania,* 19–50. On the blurred lines between democracy and republicanism, see Adams, *The First American Constitutions,* 99–117.
23. Nash and Soderlund, *Freedom by Degrees.*
24. Hofstadter, *The Idea of a Party System;* Martin, *Government by Dissent;* Young, *Dissent.*
25. The classic exploration of the ambiguities of "the people" is Morgan, *Inventing the People.* See also Neem, *Creating a Nation of Joiners;* Frank, *Constituent Moments;* Parkinson, *The Common Cause;* and Pearl, "Becoming Patriots."
26. Branson, *These Fiery Frenchified Dames,* 4–20; Zagarri, *Revolutionary Backlash,* 68–75; Waldstreicher, *In the Midst of Perpetual Fetes,* 82–84, 166–72.
27. On this hope for a biracial future, see Polgar, *Standard-Bearers of Equality.*
28. This is a point that is explored more completely in the conclusion.
29. On the role of newspaper editors, see Pasley, *"The Tyranny of Printers,"* and Adelman, *Revolutionary Networks.*
30. Quoted in Jones, "Herman Husband," 341.

1. "The Mobility Triumphant"

1. 15 May 1776, Allen, "Diary of James Allen," 187.
2. Smith, *The Freedoms We Lost,* 17–46.
3. Ryerson, *The Revolution Is Now Begun,* 25–88; Adams, *The First American Constitutions,* 38. For a thoughtful overview of Quakers' views on the Revolution, see Calvert, *Quaker Constitutionalism,* 207–45.
4. Pearl, *Conceived in Crisis,* 39–69; Spero, *Frontier Country,* 127–48; Beeman, *The Varieties of Political Experience,* 224–36. See also Moyer, *Wild Yankees,* 13–37, and Holton, *Liberty Is Sweet,* 19–38.
5. Kenny, *Peaceable Kingdom Lost;* Pearl, *Conceived in Crisis,* 101–27; Griffin, *American Leviathan,* 46–49, 64–67, 74–77; Nathan Kozuskanich, "'Falling under the Domination of Presbyterians': The Paxton Riots and the Coming of the American Revolution in Pennsylvania," in Pencak, *Pennsylvania's Revolution,* 7–30.
6. Seymour, *The Pennsylvania Associators;* Spero, *Frontier Country,* 223–27. The Intolerable Acts in particular were what drove many Pennsylvanians to begin organizing. See the essays in Frantz and Pencak, *Beyond Philadelphia.*
7. Ryerson, *The Revolution Is Now Begun,* 180–202; Ryerson, "Political Mobilization and the American Revolution." See also Selsam, *The Pennsylvania Constitution of 1776,* 49–100; Brunhouse, *The Counter-Revolution in Pennsylvania,* 6–12; and Roney, *Governed by a Spirit of Opposition,* 158–88.
8. Ryerson, *The Revolution Is Now Begun,* 149–75.
9. Caesar Rodney to Thomas Rodney, 1 May 1776, in Ryden, *Letters to and from Caesar Rodney,* 74. For a lively account of the election, see Hawke, *In the Midst of a Revolution,* 13–31.
10. Two semi-stable factions, the Quaker party and the Proprietary party, had emerged in Pennsylvania in the mid-eighteenth century, and during particularly close elections the two sides battled for every vote. For more on politics and elections in colonial Pennsylvania, see Dinkin, *Voting in Provincial America,* 33–34, 38–39, 44, 81–83, 155–61. For a general discussion of the political divisions in colonial Pennsylvania, see Thayer, *Pennsylvania Politics,* and Brewin, "The History of Election Day in Philadelphia," 35–71.
11. *Pennsylvania Gazette,* 13 March 1776. Cato, thought to be Reverend Dr. William Smith, an Anglican clergyman and provost of the College of Pennsylvania, also undertook a lengthy rebuttal to the arguments laid out in *Common Sense. Pennsylvania Evening Post,* 30 April 1776.
12. *Pennsylvania Journal,* 24 April 1776. See also *Pennsylvania Journal,* 3, 10 April, 8 May 1776. On Tom Paine's role in the events surrounding the Revolution in Pennsylvania, see Foner, *Tom Paine and Revolutionary America.*

13. Bouton, *Taming Democracy*,14–27; Lemon, *The Best Poor Man's Country*.
14. On populist movements during the Revolution, see Formisano, *For the People*, 19–42. On the rhetoric of populist movements more generally, see Kazin, *The Populist Persuasion*, 1–7.
15. *Pennsylvania Packet*, 18 March 1776.
16. *Pennsylvania Packet*, 8 April 1776.
17. Old Trusty, *To the Tories*.
18. Dinkin, *Voting in Provincial America*, 33–34.
19. *Pennsylvania Packet*, 28 April 1776. See also *Pennsylvania Journal*, 3, 10, 24 April 1776.
20. See, for instance, *Pennsylvania Gazette*, 1 May 1776.
21. 6 March 1776, Allen, "Diary of James Allen," 186.
22. For an overview of this type of thinking, see Calvert, "Liberty without Tumult."
23. For a discussion of whether the election should be viewed as an accurate reflection of Pennsylvanians' views on independence, see Rosswurm, *Arms, Country, and Class*, 92–93.
24. 1 May 1776, *DCM*, 67–68; Hawke, *In the Midst of a Revolution*, 29–30; Ryerson, *The Revolution Is Now Begun*, 173. In addition to complaints that the sheriff's attempt to close the polls early skewed the vote, Tom Paine, writing as "Forrester," blamed the loss on the fact that a number of Germans were prevented from casting ballots and many would-be supporters of independence were serving in the army. See *Pennsylvania Journal*, 8 May 1776. For other charges of irregularities, see *Pennsylvania Gazette*, 15 May 1776.
25. Hawke, *In the Midst of a Revolution*, 117–27; Ryerson, *The Revolution Is Now Begun*, 211–12.
26. On Patriots' use of Hessians to build support for independence, see Parkinson, *The Common Cause*, 216–33.
27. Hawke, *In the Midst of a Revolution*, 92–94, 116–17, 123–24.
28. 16 May 1776, *DCM*, 71; Hawke, *In the Midst of a Revolution*, 133.
29. Carp, *Rebels Rising*, 172–201.
30. Smith, *The Freedoms We Lost*, 1–43. On the relationship between elected officials and voters more generally, see Squire, *The Rise of the Representative*, 158–89.
31. *The Alarm; or, An Address to the People of Pennsylvania*.
32. John Adams to James Warren, 20 May 1776, in Butterfield et al., *Adams Family Correspondence*, 2:4, 195–97; Clitherall, "Extracts from the Diary of Dr. James Clitherall"; *Pennsylvania Gazette*, 22 May 1776.
33. *Pennsylvania Packet*, 18 June 1776.
34. For records relative to the calling of the state constitutional convention, see *PA*, series 2, 3:640–65.
35. *Pennsylvania Gazette*, 26 June 1776.

36. Wood, *Creation of the American Republic*, 232–33, 333–35; Adams, *The First American Constitutions*, 274–78; Hawke, *In the Midst of a Revolution*, 181–200; Brunhouse, *The Counter-Revolution in Pennsylvania*, 13–16; Selsam, *The Pennsylvania Constitution of 1776*, 177–83; Calvert, *Quaker Constitutionalism*, 253–55; Pearl, *Conceived in Crisis*, 170; Kruman, *Between Authority and Liberty*, 24–28, 37–49, 76–87; Foster, *In Pursuit of Equal Liberty*, 78–79; Gary Nash, "Philadelphia's Radical Caucus That Propelled Pennsylvania to Independence and Democracy," in Young, Nash, and Raphael, *Revolutionary Founders*, 67–85.
37. For a copy of the constitution of Pennsylvania (1776), see *Proceedings Relative to Calling the Conventions*, 55–65.
38. Selsam, *The Pennsylvania Constitution of 1776*, 183–94.
39. *Pennsylvania Packet*, 26 November 1776.
40. "Constitution of Pennsylvania," section 47.
41. *Pennsylvania Packet*, 26 November 1776.
42. Shaeffer, "Public Consideration of the 1776 Pennsylvania Constitution"; Owen S. Ireland, "Bucks County," in Franz and Pencak, *Beyond Philadelphia*, 36.
43. Ireland, "The Ethnic-Religious Dimension of Politics"; Scharff and Westcott, *History of Philadelphia*, 435.
44. For a discussion of the Test Laws and the importance of consent in the new regime, see Sullivan, *The Disaffected*, 25–32. See also Pearl, *Conceived in Crisis*, 164–65; Calvert, *Quaker Constitutionalism*, 261–73; Ousterhout, "Controlling the Opposition in Pennsylvania"; and Brunhouse, *The Counter-Revolution in Pennsylvania*, 16–17, 40–41.
45. Benjamin Rush to Anthony Wayne, 19 May 1777, in *LBR*, 1:148.
46. John Adams to Abigail Adams, 4 October 1776, in Butterfield et al., *Adams Family Correspondence*, 2:137–38.
47. *Pennsylvania Journal*, 23 April 1777; *Pennsylvania Packet*, 18, 25 March, 20 May 1777; Brunhouse, *The Counter-Revolution in Pennsylvania*, 16–21; Wood, *Creation of the American Republic*, 233–35; Calvert, *Quaker Constitutionalism*, 257–58; Cutterham, *Gentlemen Revolutionaries*, 60–65.
48. Brunhouse, *The Counter-Revolution in Pennsylvania*, 28–29.
49. *Pennsylvania Journal*, 16 October 1776.
50. *Pennsylvania Gazette*, 23 October 1776; *Pennsylvania Journal*, 23 October 1776; *Pennsylvania Packet*, 22 October, 5 November 1776; Brunhouse, *The Counter-Revolution in Pennsylvania*, 18–19.
51. Quoted in Robert G. Crist, "Cumberland County," in Frantz and Pencak, *Beyond Philadelphia*, 126.
52. Brunhouse, *The Counter-Revolution in Pennsylvania*, 21–22, 33–35; *Pennsylvania Journal*, 12, 19 March 1777. On Bedford County, see Tim H. Blessing, "The Upper Juniata Valley," in Frantz and Pencak, *Beyond Philadelphia*, 159.

53. *In General Assembly of the State of Pennsylvania.*
54. Brunhouse, *The Counter-Revolution in Pennsylvania,* 44–45. For an overview of the British occupation of Philadelphia, see Sullivan, *The Disaffected,* 102–31. See also Johnson, *Occupied America.*
55. For an overview of anti-constitutionalists' reasons for demanding the convention, see "A Serious Address to the People of Pennsylvania," *Pennsylvania Gazette,* 5, 10 December 1778.
56. *Pennsylvania Gazette,* 3 February 1779.
57. Petition for the Establishment of Lancaster County, Records of the Proprietary Government, Executive Correspondence, Pennsylvania State Archives; Tully, *Forming American Politics,* 257–309; Beeman, *The Varieties of Political Experience,* 212–14.
58. *Pennsylvania Chronicle,* 22 August 1768, cited in Olton, *Artisans for Independence,* 54–55; Mark, "The Vestigial Constitution"; Carpenter, *Democracy by Petition,* 60–69; Pearl, *Conceived in Crisis,* 46–63, 144–46. For more on the role of town meetings and instructions in the lead-up to 1776, see Ray Raphael, "The Democratic Moment: The Revolution and Popular Politics," in Gray and Kamensky. *The Oxford Handbook of the American Revolution,* 121–32, and Maier, *American Scripture,* 217–23.
59. Radicals had mounted a petition campaign following the assembly's first resolution on a convention before Howe's occupation of Philadelphia put the debate over the constitution on hold. *Pennsylvania Gazette,* 19 January, 21, 26 May 1777; Brunhouse, *The Counter-Revolution in Pennsylvania,* 28–29.
60. *Pennsylvania Evening Post,* 1 April; 16 February; 30 March 1779. On the Whig Society, see, *Pennsylvania Evening Post,* 20 March 1777, and *Pennsylvania Gazette,* 26 January 1777. On the Republican Society, see *Pennsylvania Packet,* 25 March 1779; Koschnik, *Let a Common Interest Bind Us Together,* 13–19; and Rosswurm, *Arms, Country, and Class,* 176. On voluntary societies in colonial Pennsylvania, see Roney, *Governed by a Sprit of Opposition,* 59–79.
61. For copies of some of the petitions, see "Memorials against the Calling of a Convention, 1779," in *PA,* series 2, 3:343–79.
62. "General Assembly Petitions and Miscellaneous Records," roll 257, General Assembly Petitions and Miscellaneous Records, Pennsylvania State Archives.
63. "Remonstrance of the Inhabitants of Berks County," in *PA,* series 2, 3:368; "Remonstrances of the Inhabitants of Lancaster County," in *PA,* series 2, 3:353.
64. See *Minutes of the Third General Assembly,* 51–69. In fact, as historian Terry Bouton has pointed out, more people appear to have signed petitions in opposition to the convention than would vote during the debates over the ratification of the federal Constitution. Bouton, *Taming Democracy,* 57.

65. *Pennsylvania Packet*, 11 March 1779.
66. *Minutes of the Third General Assembly*, 68; Brunhouse, *The Counter-Revolution in Pennsylvania*, 58–60.
67. *Minutes of the Third General Assembly*, 55. On the wartime economy, see Rosswurn, *Arms, Country, and Class*, 166–71; Brunhouse, *The Counter-Revolution in Pennsylvania*, 51–52, 68; and Foner, *Tom Paine and Revolutionary America*, 145–78.
68. "Proclamation against the Forestalling of Markets," in *PA*, series 4, 3:709–13.
69. 22, 25 May 1779, *DCM*, 217.
70. 22, 24 May 1779, *DED*, 1:605.
71. Rosswurn, *Arms, Country, and Class*, 166–78, 178 (quotation).
72. *Pennsylvania Packet*, 27 May 1779; *Pennsylvania Gazette*, 2 June 1779; Rosswurm, *Arms, Country, and Class*, 166–79, 181.
73. *York, 18th June 1779*; Paul E. Doutrich, "York County," in Frantz and Pencak, *Beyond Philadelphia*, 102–3.
74. 14, 16, 19 June 1779, *DCM*, 220–21; Brunhouse, *The Counter-Revolution in Pennsylvania*, 73.
75. *Pennsylvania Evening Post*, 29 June 1779; Owen, *Political Community in Revolutionary Pennsylvania*, 54–78.
76. *Pennsylvania Packet*, 8 June 1779; Breen, *The Will of the People*, 133, 177–79.
77. *Pennsylvania Packet*, 1 July 1779; Rosswurm, *Arms, Country, and Class*, 181–84.
78. 25 May 1779, *DED*, 1:606.
79. James Read to George Read, 7 August 1779, in Read, *The Life and Correspondence of George Read*, 351.
80. *Pennsylvania Packet*, 15 July 1779; Foner, *Tom Paine and Revolutionary America*, 172–73; Olton, *Artisans for Independence*, 83–86.
81. *Proceedings of the General Town-Meeting, July 26–27, 1779*; Foner, *Tom Paine and Revolutionary America*, 173–74; Brunhouse, *The Counter-Revolution in Pennsylvania*, 74, 82.
82. *Pennsylvania Packet*, 10 September 1779.
83. *Pennsylvania Packet*, 18 September 1779; Rosswurm, *Arms, Country, and Class*, 192–93. On 21 and 22 September, the assembly took up a bill entitled "An Act for the More Effectually Preventing Engrossing and Forestalling, for the Encouragement of Commerce and Fair Trade, and for Other Purposes Therein Mentioned," which was published for public consideration. The assembly had postponed discussion of a similar measure in February. See *Minutes of the Third General Assembly*, 58, 131–33.
84. Rosswurm, *Arms, Country, and Class*, 181–83, 188–89; Brunhouse, *The Counter-Revolution in Pennsylvania*, 60–68, 71. On frontier violence during

the Revolution, see Moyer, *Wild Yankees*, 37–70, and Spero, *Frontier Country*, 223–46.

85. 30 August 1779, *DED*, 1:622.
86. "Statement of Charles Willson Peale," in Reed, *Life and Correspondence of Joseph Reed*, 1:423. The most complete account of the events that occurred between 27 September and 4 October 1779, what would become known as Fort Wilson's Riot, can be found in Rosswurm, *Arms, Country, and Class*, 209–17. See also Alexander, "The Fort Wilson Incident."
87. "Statement of Charles Willson Peale," 423–24.
88. 4 October 1779, *DED*, 1:627.
89. Gibson, "The Attack on Ft. Fisher, Oct. 4, 1779."
90. "Allen McLane's Narrative," in Reed, *Life and Correspondence of Joseph Reed*, 2:151; "Philip Hagner's Narrative," in Reed, *Life and Correspondence of Joseph Reed*, 2:426.
91. "Allen McLane's Narrative," 2:151.
92. "Philip Hagner's Narrative," 2:426–27.
93. "The Reminiscences of David Hayfield Conyngham," *Proceedings and Collections of the Wyoming Genealogical Society* 8 (1904): 214–15.
94. Rosswurm, *Arms, Country, and Class*, 217.
95. Foster, *In Pursuit of Equal Liberty*, 104–5; Foner, *Tom Paine and Revolutionary America*, 178–80.
96. *Pennsylvania Packet*, 16, 21, 26 October 1779. Kenneth Owen suggests that the violence at Fort Wilson "effectively pushed the General Assembly" to take action to address the concerns of lower and middling residents. While intriguing, it is also important to recognize the change in membership in the assembly that occurred following the 4 October elections. Moderates lost nearly a dozen seats, giving the radicals complete control over the reins of power. Owen, "Violence and the Limits of the Political Community," in Griffin et al., *Between Sovereignty and Anarchy*, 169.
97. Foster, *In Pursuit of Equal Liberty*, 106–8; Brunhouse, *The Counter-Revolution in Pennsylvania*, 76–80.
98. Nash and Soderlund, *Freedom by Degrees*.
99. Polgar, *Standard-Bearers of Equality*; Nash, *Forging Freedom*, 60–63; Brunhouse, *The Counter-Revolution in Pennsylvania*, 80–82.
100. Michell et al., *The Statutes at Large of Pennsylvania*, 9:49–51, 86, 110–11, 147–49. On the use of racially charged propaganda, see Parkinson, *The Common Cause*. The term the "color line" was first used by Frederick Douglass in "The Color Line," *North American Review*, 1 June 1881, 567, and was later popularized by W. E. B. Du Bois. See Du Bois, *The Philadelphia Negro: A Social Study*, reprint ed. (Philadelphia: University of Pennsylvania Press, 1996), 325.

101. *Pennsylvania Packet,* 12 October 1779; Rosswurm, *Arms, Country, and Class,* 238–46; Brunhouse, *The Counter-Revolution in Pennsylvania,* 86–87.
102. *Pennsylvania Packet,* 10 October 1779.
103. Unless otherwise stated, information on the makeup of the assembly is taken from the Pennsylvania Election Statistics Project, Wilkes University.

2. Mobilizing the Moderates

1. *Pennsylvania Packet,* 20 January 1784; Scharff and Westcott, *History of Philadelphia,* 432–33.
2. *Pennsylvania Packet,* 24 January 1784. Eventually, enough money was raised to rebuild the arch near the State House and it opened (without the lamps) on 10 May 1784 to a crowd of thousands. *Pennsylvania Packet,* 12 May 1784.
3. Quoted in Brunhouse, *The Counter-Revolution in Pennsylvania,* 143.
4. Foster, *In Pursuit of Equal Liberty,* 106–8. On the broader shift from laudatory to hortatory rhetoric, see Robertson, *The Language of Democracy,* 20–36.
5. Arnold, *A Republican Revolution,* 152–73.
6. *Independent Gazetteer,* 11, 4 October 1783; Foster, *In Pursuit of Equal Liberty,* 123–28.
7. *Independent Gazetteer,* 11 October 1783.
8. *Independent Gazetteer,* 11 October 1783.
9. *Independent Gazetteer,* 27 September 1783.
10. *Independent Gazetteer,* 8 October 1783.
11. *Independent Gazetteer,* 11 October 1783.
12. Minutes from the Council of Censors, 19 January 1784, in *Proceedings Relative to Calling the Conventions,* 69–77.
13. Dissent of the Minority, in *Proceedings Relative to Calling the Conventions,* 77–80.
14. Minutes from the Council of Censors, 21 January 1784, in *Proceedings Relative to Calling the Conventions,* 80–82.
15. *Freeman's Journal,* 18, 25 February, 3 March 1784.
16. Stephen Chambers to John Rose, 5 April 1784, *Pennsylvania Magazine of History and Biography* 12, no. 4 (1898): 500–501.
17. Benjamin Rush to Reverend William Linn, 4 May 1784, in *LBR,* 1:333–34; see note 4 for Linn's response; Brunhouse, *The Counter-Revolution in Pennsylvania,* 160.
18. For additional information on what occurred between sessions of the Council of Censors, see Brunhouse, *The Counter-Revolution in Pennsylvania,* 161–63. The scandal involved accusations that Samuel Miles, a censor from Philadelphia, improperly spent state money. The assembly

ultimately cleared Miles of any wrongdoing, but the scandal damaged his reputation.

19. *Freeman's Journal*, 30 July 1783. For a response to this letter, see *Independent Gazetteer*, 2 August 1783, and Smith, *The Freedoms We Lost*, 182.
20. *Independent Gazetteer*, 26 February 1785.
21. *Independent Gazetteer*, 22 March 1785.
22. *Independent Gazetteer*, 4 June 1785. For other examples, see *Pennsylvania Packet*, 10 February 1785, and *Independent Gazetteer*, 5, 26 March 1785.
23. Brunhouse, *The Counter-Revolution in Pennsylvania*, 172–73. On the economy in the 1780s, see Ferguson, "The Nationalists of 1781–1783." On merchants and their role, see Doerflinger, *A Vigorous Spirit of Enterprise*. On artisans' shift in support of a strong national government, see Olton, *Artisans for Independence*, 109–20. See also Ireland, *Religion, Ethnicity, and Politics*, 147–217.
24. For a good overview of the challenges facing the country under the Articles of Confederation, see Van Cleve, *We Have Not a Government*.
25. *Pennsylvania Packet*, 15 June 1785.
26. *Freeman's Journal*, 22 June 1785. See also *Pennsylvania Packet*, 6 September 1785, and *Pennsylvania Evening Herald*, 14 September 1785.
27. In the summer of 1783, defenders of the Test Laws organized a series of public meetings to try and prevent their repeal. See *Pennsylvania Packet*, 17 June, 8, 31 July, 7 August 1783, and *Pennsylvania Evening Post*, 17 June 1783. For an overview of the Test Laws, see Westcott, *Names of Persons Who Took the Oath*, vi–xli. For an exploration of moderates' campaign against the Test Laws, see Arnold, *A Republican Revolution*, 173–86.
28. *Independent Gazetteer*, 26 March 1785.
29. *Independent Gazetteer*, 7 May 1785. See also *Pennsylvania Evening Herald*, 11 March 1786.
30. *Pennsylvania Evening Herald*, 8 October 1785; 4 October 1786.
31. Benjamin Rush to Unknown, 10 November 1784, in *LBR*, 1:339–40.
32. George Lux to Benjamin Rush, 18 February 1785, quoted in Brunhouse, *The Counter-Revolution in Pennsylvania*, 168.
33. *Independent Gazetteer*, 8 October 1785.
34. *Independent Gazetteer*, 23 September 1786.
35. Brunhouse, *The Counter-Revolution in Pennsylvania*, 88; Arnold, *A Republican Revolution*, 194–232.
36. Bouton, *Taming Democracy*, 142–44. As evidence of this, Terry Bouton cites low turnout rates in 1786 in counties including Philadelphia, Bucks, Northampton, Dauphin, Lancaster, and York. This analysis, however, overlooks the fact that turnout was up in some regions, such as Philadelphia City. Additionally, although low, turnout in Philadelphia and Bucks Counties was actually higher than in previous years. Turnout was also heavily

dependent on local elections. Cumberland County, for example, saw record turnout due to competitive local elections for sheriff and coroner. For election results, see *PA*, series 6, volume 11, and Brunhouse, *The Counter-Revolution in Pennsylvania*, 328–45. Turnout was calculated by using the most recent census data to calculate the approximate number of adult males in each county. For 1786, I relied on the "List of Taxable" found in the *Pennsylvania Evening Herald*, 27 September 1786. As voters cast ballots for multiple candidates, I added up the total number of votes cast and divided it by the number of open seats.

37. Ireland, "The Crux of Politics."
38. Foster, *In Pursuit of Equal Liberty*, 138–39.
39. Ireland, *Religion, Ethnicity, and Politics*, 220–29; Rosemary S. Warden, "Chester County," in Frantz and Pencak, *Beyond Philadelphia*, 19–20; Brunhouse, *The Counter-Revolution in Pennsylvania*, 191–94.
40. Bouton, *Taming Democracy*, 88–104; Slaughter, *The Whiskey Rebellion*, 46–89; Moyer, *Wild Yankees*, 8–10, 54–55.
41. Caldwell, *William Findley from West of the Mountains;* Everett, "John Smilie, Forgotten Champion of Early Western Pennsylvania," 77–89.
42. The best discussion of the economic situation in Pennsylvania following the Revolution is Harper, *The Transformation of Western Pennsylvania*. See also Fennell, "From Rebelliousness to Insurrection." On efforts to work within the political structure, see Bouton, *Taming Democracy*, 105–44. On the movements to create a new state, see Slaughter, *The Whiskey Rebellion*, 26–45.
43. Bouton, *Taming Democracy*, 145–67; Fennell, "From Rebelliousness to Insurrection," 5–43; Moyer, *Wild Yankees*, 65–68. As Anthony M. Joseph points out, however, that for all the focus on opposition to the excise, most Pennsylvanians paid their taxes. See Joseph, "The Decline of the Cheerful Taxpayer in Pennsylvania, c. 1776–1815," in Pencak, *Pennsylvania's Revolution*, 282–304.
44. There exists a vast literature on violence and popular uprisings in England and America. For English crowds, see Thompson, "The Moral Economy of the English Crowd," and Thompson, "Patrician Society, Plebian Culture." On the American tradition, see Wood, "A Note on the Mobs in the American Revolution"; Howe, "Republican Thought and the Political Violence of the 1790s"; Maier, *From Resistance to Revolution;* Young, *The American Revolution;* Gilje, *The Road to Mobocracy;* Slaughter, "Crowds in Eighteenth-Century America"; Pencak, Dennis, and Newman, *Riot and Revelry in Early America;* Young, *Liberty Tree;* and Frank, *Constituent Moments*. On the use of ritual and participation of the militia, see Martin, *Government by Dissent*, 23–25.
45. On the tradition of blackened faces, see Moyer, *Wild Yankees*, 139, and Martin, *Government by Dissent*, 23–24.

46. "Deposition of James Bell, 1784," and "Deposition of Philip Jenkins, 1786," in *PA*, series 1, 10:594–95; Dorsey Penticost to Supreme Executive Council, 16 April 1786, in *PA*, series 1, 10:757; Bouton, *Taming Democracy*, 159–63; Fennell, "From Rebelliousness to Insurrection," 5–43.
47. Irvin, *Clothed in Robes of Sovereignty*, 9–14; Waldstreicher, *In the Midst of Perpetual Fetes*, 17–52. On colonial celebratory culture as a way to establish loyalty to the monarch, see McConville, *The King's Three Faces*, 49–80, and Bushman, *King and People in Provincial Massachusetts*.
48. Travers, *Celebrating the Fourth*, 6–7; Newman, *Parades and the Politics of the Street*, 3–10; Waldstreicher, *In the Midst of Perpetual Fetes*, 53–62; Irvin, *Clothed in Robes of Sovereignty*, 133–64.
49. *Pennsylvania Evening Post*, 5 July 1777; *Pennsylvania Packet*, 8 July 1777. John Adams's description of the naval display differed slightly from the account printed in the newspapers. According to Adams, the vessels displayed the "colours of all nations." John Adams to Abigail Adams 2d, 5 July 1777, in Butterfield et al., *Adams Family Correspondence*, 2:274–75. On the symbolic importance of the Fourth of July, see Travers, *Celebrating the Fourth*, 3–13. See also Irvin, *Clothed in Robes of Sovereignty*, 142–50.
50. *Pennsylvania Journal*, 12 July 1780; Irvin, *Clothed in Robes of Sovereignty*, 164; Travers, *Celebrating the Fourth*, 25–26.
51. *Pennsylvania Evening Post*, 5 July 1783; Scharff and Westcott, *History of Philadelphia*, 432.
52. *Freeman's Journal*, 30 July 1783.
53. *Freeman's Journal*, 7 July 1784; *Independent Gazetteer*, 10 July 1784. On 4 July 1784, residents also gathered to watch a hot air balloon demonstration. After the balloon rose about fifteen feet, however, the basket holding the passengers hit a wall, knocking them out. This turned out to be quite fortunate because the balloon caught fire shortly thereafter. Scharff and Westcott, *History of Philadelphia*, 436–37.
54. The group had gathered on the Fourth of July in other cities before 1785, but there is no evidence that the group met in Pennsylvania. On the Society of the Cincinnati, see Myers, *Liberty without Anarchy*. For a discussion of the Society of the Cincinnati and symbolism, see Koschnik, *Let a Common Interest Bind Us Together*, 101–5. See also Travers, *Celebrating the Fourth*, 61.
55. *Pennsylvania Evening Herald*, 9 July 1785; *Pennsylvania Mercury and Universal Advertiser*, 9 July 1785.
56. Travers, *Celebrating the Fourth*, 61.
57. *Pennsylvania Packet*, 8, 13 July 1786. The same trend of giving more space to Fourth of July descriptions occurred in the *Carlisle Gazette*. See *Carlisle Gazette*, 5, 19 July 1786.
58. Jackson, *An Oration to Commemorate the Independence of the United States*; *Pennsylvania Packet*, 6 July 1786.

59. With the exception of the aged Benjamin Franklin, Pennsylvania's delegates to the Constitutional Convention were all associated with the moderates, and during the ratification debate, virtually every prominent moderate supported the adoption of the new Constitution. On the federal Constitution as a rejection of the 1776 Pennsylvania constitution, see Ireland, *Religion, Ethnicity, and Politics*, 11–12, 28–32.
60. Rush, "Address to the People of the United States," *American Museum I*, January 1787, in *DHRC*, 13:46; Kramer, *The People Themselves*, 129–30; Leonard and Cornell, *The Partisan Republic*, 1–2; Adams, *The First American Constitutions*, 133–35; Wood, *Creation of the American Republic*, 344–89 and *passim*. See also Elizabeth Lewis Pardoe, "Constructing Community and the Diversity Dilemma: Ratification in Pennsylvania," in Pencak, *Pennsylvania's Revolution*, 258–78.
61. Woody Holton convincingly argues that "the people" influenced the Constitutional Convention indirectly because delegates understood that they would need to secure the people's consent. See Holton, *Unruly Americans*.
62. Fritz, *American Sovereigns*, 119–52; Laura F. Edwards, "The Contradictions of Democracy in American Institutions and Practices," in Innes and Philip, *Re-Imaging Democracy in the Age of Revolutions*, 48–51; Miller, "The Ghostly Body Politic." See also Wilf, *Imagined Republic*.
63. Klarman, *The Framers' Coup*, 411–17. Despite the requirement that each state either vote for or against the Constitution, some states proceeded to ratify but also submit amendments. See Maier, *Ratification*, for an overview of the ratification process across the country.
64. Pennsylvania Assembly: Saturday, 29 September 1787, in *DHRC*, 2:110–14; Ireland, *Religion, Ethnicity, and Politics*, 24–27. See also Maier, *Ratification*, 97–124.
65. Ezekiel Forman to Alexander Hamilton, 24 September 1787, quoted in Ireland, *Religion, Ethnicity, and Politics*, 5–6.
66. Assembly Proceedings, in *DHRC*, 2:62–65.
67. *Independent Gazetteer*, 10 October 1787; Ireland, "The People's Triumph," 98.
68. Philadelphia City and County Nomination Tickets, in *DHRC*, 2:225–27.
69. Northampton County Nominations, in *DHRC*, 2:229–30.
70. Carlisle Meeting, 3 October 1787, in *DHRC*, 2:173–74.
71. Philadelphia Meeting, 6 October 1787, in, *DHRC*, 2:174–75.
72. James Wilson's Speech at the State House Yard, *Pennsylvania Herald*, 9 October 1787, in *DHRC*, 2:167–72.
73. *Pennsylvania Packet*, 10 October 1787.
74. *Pennsylvania Gazette*, 3 October 1787. In preparation for the ratification debate in 1787, leading Pennsylvania federalists including Thomas Fitzsimons and Benjamin Rush recruited some of the most talented writers in

the nation to defend the Constitution. Brunhouse, *The Counter Revolution in Pennsylvania,* 204.

75. *Independent Gazetteer,* 15 January 1788; *Pennsylvania Gazette,* 5 November 1788, in *DHFFE,* 1:330–31; Ireland, *Religion, Ethnicity, and Politics,* 54–55.
76. *Carlisle Gazette,* 3 October 1787; *Independent Gazetteer,* 29 September, 9, 13, 20, 23 October 1787; *Pennsylvania Evening Herald,* 4 October 1787.
77. *Independent Gazetteer,* 23 January 1788; Cornell, *The Other Founders,* 121–28.
78. *Independent Gazetteer,* 23 January 1788; Maier, *Ratification,* 75, 101, 145.
79. *Independent Gazetteer,* 26 January, 12 March 1788; Martin, *Government by Dissent,* 66–67.
80. *Independent Gazetteer,* 11, 12 March 1788; *Carlisle Gazette,* 1 November 1787. For a discussion of the importance of anonymity in print during the debates over the Constitution, see Cornell, *The Other Founders,* 37–38, 105–6. The debate over anonymity led to a libel case when Eleazer Oswald refused to reveal the authors of articles that attacked Andrew Brown, editor of the *Federal Gazette.* A federalist judge who overheard the trial found Oswald guilty. Anti-federalists believed the whole trial had been an attempt to further scare anti-federalists. See Cornell, *The Other Founders,* 128–36.
81. *Independent Gazetteer,* 10 October, 22 November 1787. See also *Pennsylvania Gazette,* 23 January, 17 October 1787, and *Independent Gazetteer,* 22 November 1787.
82. Ireland, *Religion, Ethnicity, and Politics,* 75–107; Ridner, *The Scotch Irish of Early Pennsylvania,* 90–92; Ireland, "The Invention of American Democracy."
83. For a discussion of the Carlisle Riot in the context of the broader anti-federalist movement, see Cornell, *The Other Founders,* 109–20, and Cornell, "Aristocracy Assailed." See also Waldstreicher, *In the Midst of Perpetual Fetes,* 93–97. On the context of politics in Carlisle, see Ridner, *A Town In-Between,* 150–76.
84. *Carlisle Gazette,* 2, 9 January 1788, in *DHRC,* 2:604–10, 670–78; Maier, *Ratification,* 159.
85. *Carlisle Gazette,* 2, 9 January 1788, in *DHRC,* 2:604–10.
86. Pennsylvania Supreme Court to Sheriff Charles Leeper, 23 January 1788, in *DHRC,* 2:684–85.
87. *Carlisle Gazette,* 27 February 1788, in *DHRC,* 2:646–47; William Petrikin to John Nicholson, 24 February 1788, in *DHRC,* 2:695–96. For an example of one of these associations, see "An Address to the Minority of the Convention," *Carlisle Gazette,* 2 January 1788, in *DHRC,* 2:651–53.
88. John Montgomery to James Wilson, 2 March 1788, in *DHRC,* 2:701–6.
89. John Montgomery to James Wilson, 2 March 1788, in *DHRC,* 2:701–6; *Carlisle Gazette,* 5 March 1788, in *DHRC,* 2:699–701; John Shippen to Joseph Shippen, 3 March 1788, in *DHRC,* 2:706–7.

90. Frank, *Constituent Moments*, 93–97.
91. *Pennsylvania Mercury and Universal Advertiser*, 1 January 1789.
92. "Resolution of Assembly—Calling a Convention, 1789," in *PA*, series 1, 11:564–65; Adams, *The First American Constitutions*, 137–44.
93. *Federal Gazette*, 25 March 1789.
94. *Federal Gazette*, 18 March 1789.
95. *Federal Gazette*, 14 April 1789.
96. *Federal Gazette*, 18 March 1789.
97. Rogers, *An Oration, Delivered July 4, 1789*.
98. *Pennsylvania Mercury and Universal Advertiser*, 11 July 1789.
99. The first petitions began arriving on 1 September 1789. *Minutes of the Third Session of the Thirteenth General Assembly*, 224–37; Brunhouse, *The Counter Revolution in Pennsylvania*, 223–24.
100. *Minutes of the Third Session of the Thirteenth General Assembly*, 250–51.
101. Kruman, *Between Authority and Liberty*, 37–49.
102. For the text of the two constitutions, see *Proceedings Relative to Calling the Conventions*, 55–65, 296–308.
103. Foster, "The Politics of Ideology"; Tinkcom, *Republicans and Federalists in Pennsylvania*, 9–16.

3. Choppy Beginnings

1. *Federal Gazette*, 24 November 1789.
2. Hopkinson, *An Account of the Grand Federal Procession*.
3. Kenneth R. Bowling, "The Federal Government and the Republican Court Move to Philadelphia," in Bowling and Kennon, *Neither Separate nor Equal*, 3–33. See also Anna Coxe Toogood, "Philadelphia as the Nation's Capital, 1790–1800," in Bowling and Kennon, *Neither Separate nor Equal*, 34–57. Congress originally left Philadelphia in 1783 following a mutiny by the Pennsylvania Line. See Bowling, "New Light on the Philadelphia Mutiny of 1783."
4. Ireland, "The Invention of American Democracy."
5. See documents listed under "Proceedings of the Lancaster Conference," in *DHFFE*, 1:323–29. The Lancaster Conference was organized in response to an anti-federalist meeting at Harrisburg. Although the anti-federalists would eventually produce a "Harrisburg Ticket," the gathering was primarily an opportunity to discuss potential amendments to the Constitution. "Proceedings of the Harrisburg Convention, September 3–6, 1788," in *DHFFE*, 1:258–59.
6. On the "Philadelphia junto," see Miller, *Philadelphia—The Federalist City*, 22–25, 29–30.
7. *Gentlemen, Permit Us to Congratulate You*. Interestingly, while some newspapers printed the broadside in its entirety, the *Federal Gazette* did not

include the names of the signers. As a result, the notice in the *Federal Gazette* seemed to express a more generalized sentiment as opposed to the opinions of seven men. See *Independent Gazetteer*, 18 September 1790, and *Federal Gazette*, 13 September 1790.

8. James Hutchinson to Albert Gallatin, 11 June 1790, as quoted in Tinkcom, *Republicans and Federalists in Pennsylvania*, 35.
9. *Pennsylvania Packet*, 7 October 1790; *Independent Gazetteer*, 9 October 1790.
10. *Independent Gazetteer*, 18 September 1790; *Pennsylvania Gazette*, 22 September 1790.
11. *Independent Gazetteer*, 25 September 1790.
12. *Independent Gazetteer*, 18, 25 September 1790
13. Unless otherwise noted, all votes are from "A New Nation Votes Database."
14. Arthur St. Clair to Thomas Fitzsimons, 12 October 1790, quoted in Tinkcom, *Republicans and Federalists in Pennsylvania*, 39.
15. Waldstreicher, *In the Midst of Perpetual Fetes*, 85–126; Bradburn, *Citizenship Revolution*, 143–49; Smith, *Civic Ideals*, 137–49; Fritz, *American Sovereigns*, 156–57. For an insightful interpretation of the myriad ways Federalists sought to create a national culture, see Hattem, *Past and Prologue*, 141–82. See also Boonshoft, *Aristocratic Education and the Making of the American Republic*, 79–88.
16. James Wilson, "Oration of the Fourth of July," *Pennsylvania Gazette*, 9 July 1788.
17. Waldstreicher, *In the Midst of Perpetual Fetes*, 53–107, and *passim*; Newman, "Principles or Men?"; Koschnik, "Political Conflict and Public Contest"; Frank, *Constituent Moments*.
18. *Dunlap's American Daily Advertiser*, 30 June 1792. For an overview of Federalists' use of the Fourth of July, see Travers, *Celebrating the Fourth*, 88–106, and Lohman, *Hail Columbia!* 42–54.
19. *Carlisle Gazette*, 14 July 1790.
20. *Gazette of the United States*, 25 July 1792. For similar sentiments, see Porter, *An Oration to Commemorate the Independence of the United States*.
21. *Mail; or Claypoole's American Daily Advertiser*, 14 July 1792.
22. *Carlisle Gazette*, 7 July 1790.
23. *Pennsylvania Packet*, 5 July 1790.
24. *Federal Gazette*, 13 July 1792; *Dunlap's American Daily Advertiser*, 12 July 1791.
25. On women's roles in Federalist celebratory culture, see Waldstreicher, *In the Midst of Perpetual Fetes*, 82–84, 167–69, 236–38; Zagarri, *Revolutionary Backlash*, 70–75; and Newman, *Parades and the Politics of the Street*, 87, 95.
26. *Federal Gazette*, 1 July 1790. See also *Dunlap's American Daily Advertiser*, 28 June 1791; 3 July 1792.
27. *Independent Gazetteer*, 2 July 1791. At least some revelers did not seem to take this message to heart. Elizabeth Drinker noted in her diary that

"riotous doings" and broken windows marred Fourth of July celebrations at Gray's Garden in 1791. See 4 July 1791, *DED*, 1:841.

28. *Federal Gazette*, 3 July 1793.
29. On Washington as a Federalist symbol, see Newman, "Principles or Men?"; Newman, *Parades and the Politics of the Street*, 44–82; Waldstreicher, *In the Midst of Perpetual Fetes*, 117–26; Estes, *The Jay Treaty Debate*, 209–11; Schwartz, *George Washington*; Longmore, *The Invention of George Washington*; and Furstenberg, *In the Name of the Father*.
30. *Federal Gazette*, 12 February 1790; *Gazette of the United States*, 23 February 1791; *Pennsylvania Packet*, 12 February 1789, 15 February 1790; Koschnik, *Let a Common Interest Bind Us Together*, 82–87; Newman, *Parades and the Politics of the Street*, 60. Washington helped to reenforce this type of reverence for the president by carefully scripting every public performance. See Chervinsky, *The Cabinet*, 142–49.
31. *Federal Gazette*, 24 February 1791; *Dunlap's American Daily Advertiser*, 23 February 1791.
32. *Federal Gazette*, 23 February 1792.
33. For a discussion of the Republican Court, see the articles in the special issue on "Re-Introducing the Republican Court," *Journal of the Early Republic*, 35, no. 2 (Summer 2015). See also Henderson, "Furnishing the Republican Court"; Rasumussen, "Capital on the Delaware"; Robert J. Gouge, "The Philadelphia Economic Elite at the End of the Eighteenth Century," in Hutchins, *Shaping a National Culture*, 15–43; Bowling, "The Federal Government and the Republican Court Move to Philadelphia"; and Furstenberg, *When the United States Spoke French*, 126–28. On Washington's style as president, see Moats, *Celebrating the Republic*, 35–67.
34. *General Advertiser*, 22 February 1792. A member of the militia in Philadelphia went so far as to write an angry letter condemning the city council for ordering his company to escort Washington through the city because it implied that the company was not already planning to do so. *Federal Gazette*, 19 March 1789.
35. For a discussion of the French Revolution's impact on American politics, see Sharp, *American Politics in the Early Republic*, 69–92. For the impact on American political culture, see Newman, *Parades and the Politics of the Street*, 120–51, and Waldstreicher, *In the Midst of Perpetual Fetes*, 112–16, 131–40.
36. Hale, "Neither Britons nor Frenchmen."
37. Estes, *The Jay Treaty Debate*, 36–53. On Washington's decision-making process, see Chervinsky, *The Cabinet*, 264–307.
38. *General Advertiser*, 26, 23 January 1793. See also Bowling and Veit, *The Diary of William Maclay*, 29, 70, 74, 182. For an analysis of Maclay's diary and his critique of the Republican Court, see Freeman, *Affairs of Honor*, 11–61.
39. *National Gazette*, 26 December 1792.

40. *General Advertiser*, 2 January 1793; Newman, *Parades and the Politics of the Street*, 50–68; Pasley, "*The Tyranny of Printers*," 79–94; Daniel, *Scandal and Civility*, 109–47.
41. *National Gazette*, 4 July 1792.
42. *General Advertiser*, 19, 28 August 1794; Newman, *Parades and the Politics of the Street*, 145–47; Scharff and Westcott, *History of Philadelphia*, 418. On French influence on the political culture more generally, see Furstenberg, *When the United States Spoke French*, 47–50.
43. Waldstreicher, *In the Midst of Perpetual Fetes*, 126–45; Travers, *Celebrating the Fourth*, 88–106; Koschnik, "Political Conflict and Public Contest," 226–27; Frank, *Constituent Moments*, 144. For an insightful look at how the opposition used music to support this process, see Lohman, *Hail Columbia!* 63–85.
44. *General Advertiser*, 2 August 1794.
45. Branson, *These Fiery Frenchified Dames*, 56–81.
46. Cobbett, *History of American Jacobins*, 13–15.
47. *Gazette of the United States*, 13 July 1793. See also *Gazette of the United States*, 17 August 1793, and Wood, *Creation of the American Republic*, 372–76.
48. *National Gazette*, 15 June 1793; Carter, "Denouncing Secrecy and Defining Democracy."
49. *National Gazette*, 30 January 1792. Madison was speaking directly to the question of the Post Office Act of 1792, which allowed for newspapers to travel through the mail at a heavily reduced cost. See John, *Spreading the News*, 37–45, 60–63. See also Denver Brunsman, "James Madison and the National Gazette Essays," in Leibiger, *A Companion to James Madison and James Monroe*, 143–58, and Sheehan, "The Politics of Public Opinion."
50. *National Gazette*, 4 July 1792. For further discussion of the ideology of the Democratic Societies, see Link, *Democratic-Republican Societies*, 100–125; Koschnik, *Let a Common Interest Bind Us Together*, 22–40; Wilentz, *The Rise of American Democracy*, 53–71; Schoenbachler, "Republicanism in the Age of Democratic Revolution"; Sioli, "The Democratic Republican Societies at the End of the Eighteenth Century"; and Seth Cotlar, "Languages of Democracy in America from the Revolution to the Election of 1800," in Innes and Philip, *Re-Imagining Democracy in the Age of Revolutions*, 23–24.
51. Koschnik, *Let a Common Interest Bind Us Together*, 23–27.
52. *Gazette of the United States*, 10 March 1794.
53. *General Advertiser*, 4 August 1794.
54. *Greenleaf's New York Journal*, 19 February 1794.
55. "Principles, Articles, and Resolutions," 30 May 1793, in Foner, *The Democratic-Republican Societies*, 64–66.
56. Cobbett claimed that at least one member of the club resigned in protest. Cobbett, *History of American Jacobins*, 29–30; Philip Foner, "The

Democratic-Republican Societies: An Introduction," in Foner, *The Democratic-Republican Societies*, 12–13. The well-known cartoon "A Peep into the Anti-Federal Club," a caricature of the Pennsylvania Democratic Society, did include a Black man. Instead of being representative of actual Black members, however, the figure was likely included as another way of signifying the perceived moral depravity of the club. "A Peep into the Anti-Federal Club," 1793, Library Company of Philadelphia.

57. On the political roles of women, see Zagarri, *Revolutionary Backlash*, 4–10, 68–88, and Branson, *These Fiery Frenchified Dames*, 76–81.
58. Civic Festival, 1 May 1794, in Foner, *The Democratic-Republican Societies*, 103; Link, *Democratic-Republican Societies*, 84–90; Bradburn, *Citizenship Revolution*, 108–9. On the hope that national distinctions would fade, see Cotlar, *Tom Paine's America*, 49–81.
59. *Gazette of the United States*, 4 February 1794. For a similar explanation of how Federalists understood the relationship between the people and their government, see *Gazette of the United States*, 21, 26 July 1794.
60. *Gazette of the United States*, 8 September 1796. On the differences between the Democratic and Republican Societies and the Federalists, see Koschnik, "The Democratic Societies of Philadelphia." See also John L. Brooke, "Ancient Lodges and Self-Created Societies," in Hoffman and Albert, *Launching the Extended Republic*, 273–377; Neem, "Freedom of Association in the Early Republic"; and Leonard and Cornell, *The Partisan Republic*, 55–57.
61. *Philadelphia Gazette*, 13 August 1794; Bradburn, *Citizenship Revolution*, 130–38.
62. See, e.g., *Gazette of the United States*, 20 February 1794.
63. Bouton, *Taming Democracy*, 88–124. The best overview of the events surrounding the Whiskey Rebellion remains Slaughter, *The Whiskey Rebellion*.
64. *To the Independent Electors of Pennsylvania*; "Minutes of the Meeting at Pittsburgh," in *PA*, series 2, 4:29–31; Alexander Hamilton to George Washington, 5 August 1794, in Boyd, *The Whiskey Rebellion*, 31–47.
65. *United States v. Insurgents of Pennsylvania*, 2 U.S. 335 (1795); Alexander Hamilton to George Washington, 5 August 1794, in Boyd, *The Whiskey Rebellion*, 31–47; Findley, *History of the Insurrection*, 58–67; Myrsidaes, "A Tale of a Whiskey Rebellion Judge"; Davis, "Guarding the Republican Interest."
66. William Faulkner of Washington County initially agreed to rent to Neville but quickly changed his mind after a group of men showed up to his house and threatened to scalp him if he did not recant the offer. *United States v. Insurgents*, 6–7; Findley, *History of the Insurrection*, 58–59.
67. Alexander Hamilton to George Washington, 1 September 1792, in Syrett et al., *Papers of Alexander Hamilton*, 7:336–40.
68. Proclamation of the President, 15 September 1792, in *PA*, series 2, 4:32–33.

69. Thomas Mifflin to Judges of the Supreme Court, 21 March 1794, in *PA*, series 2, 4:58.
70. Alexander Addison to Thomas Mifflin, 31 March 1794, in *PA*, series 2, 4:60. On Addison's views on the insurrection more generally, see Myrsidaes, "A Tale of a Whiskey Rebellion Judge," 141–45.
71. William Findley to Thomas Mifflin, 21 November 1792, in *PA*, series 2, 4:48–50. On Findley's role more broadly, see Terry Bouton, "William Findley, David Bradford, and the Pennsylvania Regulation of 1794," in Young, Nash, and Raphael, *Revolutionary Founders*, 233–51.
72. *United States v. Insurgents*, 8–9; Findley, *History of the Insurrection;* Alexander Hamilton to George Washington, 5 August 1794, in Boyd, *The Whiskey Rebellion*, 40–43.
73. *United States v. Insurgents*, 10; Alexander Hamilton to George Washington, 5 August 1794, in Boyd, *The Whiskey Rebellion*, 43; Findley, *History of the Insurrection*, 74; William Irvine to Alexander James Dallas, 20 August 1794, in *PA*, series 2, 4:180–81.
74. Testimony of John Baldwin, quoted in Bouton, *Taming Democracy*, 233; *United States v. Insurgents*, 11–12; John Gibson to Thomas Mifflin, 18 July 1794, in *PA*, series 2, 4:69–70; Thomas Butler to Henry Knox, 18 July 1794, in *PA*, series 2, 4:74–75. On Washington's reaction to the brewing crisis more generally, see Chervinsky, *The Cabinet*, 236–59.
75. Brackenridge, *Incidents of the Insurrection*, 1:47–50; "Circular of the Western Insurgents to the Militia Officers," 28 July 1794, in *PA*, series 2, 4:79. For an overview of the meeting and a discussion of those involved, see Slaughter, *The Whiskey Rebellion*, 183–86.
76. Brackenridge, *Incidents of the Insurrection*, 1:85–86; Findley, *History of the Insurrection*, 98. For an overview of the meeting, see Slaughter, *The Whiskey Rebellion*, 186–89.
77. Brackenridge, *Incidents of the Insurrection*, 1:87–100; "Meeting at Parkinson's Ferry," 14 August 1794, in *PA*, series 2, 4:159–61; U.S. Commissioners to Edmund Randolph, 17 August 1794, in *PA*, series 2, 4:164–65; *United States v. Insurgents*, 18–19.
78. For a discussion of the army's march, see Slaughter, *The Whiskey Rebellion*, 205–21. For an example of the interactions between civilians and troops, see Jonathan Forman, "Journal of the March to Pittsburgh," Jonathan Forman Papers, box 1, folder 2, Darlington Collection, University of Pittsburgh.
79. *Dunlap and Claypoole's American Daily Advertiser*, 5 July 1794. Opposition to Federalist fiscal policies grew following the Revenue Act of 1794, which placed duties on certain manufactured items. For an excellent overview of the Republican opposition to the tax, see Roland M. Baumann, "Philadelphia's Manufacturers and the Excise Tax of 1794," in Boyd, *The Whiskey Rebellion*, 140–63.

80. *Independent Gazetteer,* 14 June 1794.
81. George Washington to John Jay, 1 November 1794, George Washington Papers, 1741–1799, series 4, General Correspondence, Library of Congress.
82. *Gazette of the United States,* 3 September 1794.
83. *Gazette of the United States,* 2 August 1794. See also *Gazette of the United States,* 25 July 1794.
84. *Dunlap and Claypoole's American Daily Advertiser,* 23 August 1794.
85. *Aurora,* 26 July, 25 September 1794.
86. *Aurora,* 12 August 1794.
87. *Aurora,* 12 August 1794; Jeffery L. Pasley, "Whiskey Chaser: Democracy and Violence in the Debate over the Democratic-Republican Societies and the Whiskey Rebellion," in Griffin et al., *Between Sovereignty and Anarchy,* 187–215; Leonard and Cornell, *The Partisan Republic,* 57–60.
88. *Aurora,* 12 August 1794. This is a point that would later be echoed in the published accounts of the uprisings written by William Findley and Hugh Henry Brackenridge. See Findley, *History of the Insurrection,* and Brackenridge, *Incidents of the Insurrection.* On how these accounts reflected a changing interpretation of democracy, see Nelson, *Commons Democracy,* 60–67. For a discussion of how these debates played out in Massachusetts, see Neem, *Creating a Nation of Joiners,* 47–50.
89. *Aurora,* 16 September 1794.
90. Address from the German Republican Society, in Foner, *The Democratic-Republican Societies,* 98–102; Pasley, "Whiskey Chaser," 208.
91. On the underlying ideological divisions within the Democratic Society of Philadelphia, see Pasley, "Whiskey Chaser," 199–211. The Democratic and Republican Societies in the western parts of the state, particularly those linked to the uprisings, ceased meeting immediately following the rebellion. Those in Philadelphia, however, continued to meet regularly, and historian Sean Wilentz argues that Federalists' attacks actually emboldened the societies. He contends that the Philadelphia societies did not disband until after the Jay Treaty debates. While there is no question that many former members of the Philadelphia Democratic and Republican Societies participated in the protests surrounding the Jay Treaty, there is no evidence that either the Democratic or Republican Societies had any part. Albrecht Koschnik, for instance, concludes that the groups ceased meeting in December 1794. "If the Democratic Society existed beyond 1794," he finds, "it did so in a radically different manner: as a private association, without publications, not as a[n] openly political organization." The New York Democratic Society did, however, continue to function. See Wilentz, *The Rise of American Democracy,* 62–71, and Koschnik, *Let a Common Interest Bind Us Together,* 23–38, 262n96.

92. The most thorough account of this election is Baumann, "John Swanwick." See also Miller, *Philadelphia—The Federalist City*, 62–69, and Tinkcom, *Republicans and Federalists in Pennsylvania*, 141–42.
93. Baumann, "John Swanwick."
94. For Federalist attacks on Swanwick, see *Gazette of the United States*, 27 September, 6, 13 October 1794.
95. *Dunlap and Claypoole's American Daily Advertiser*, 11, 13 September 1794; *Independent Gazetteer*, 13 September 1794. Swanwick also published a letter to a representative from Washington County that outlined his position. *General Advertiser*, 16 September 1794.
96. *Gazette of the United States*, 8 October 1794; *Philadelphia Gazette*, 14 October 1794; Schweitzer, "The Spatial Organization of Federalist Philadelphia," 31–57; Miller, *Philadelphia—The Federalist City*, 5–15, 63–64.
97. Edmund Randolph to George Washington, 16 October 1794, in Twohig et al., *Papers of George Washington: Presidential Series*, 17:75; Parsons, *Extracts from the Diary of Jacob Hiltzheimer*, 208; Carey, *He Wou'd be a Poet*, 25–28. For a good description of Oeller's Hotel, see Furstenberg, *When the United States Spoke French*, 105–6.
98. "T.T.," *Gazette of the United States*, 11 October 1794.
99. For an overview of electioneering practices in Philadelphia, see Brewin, "The History of Election Day in Philadelphia." Federalists actually petitioned the House of Representatives alleging that Republicans had stolen the election. After investigating the complaint, the House Committee on Elections concluded that the allegations had no basis. U.S. Congress, *Journal of the House of Representatives of the United States*, 4th Cong., 1st sess., 17 December 1795, 382; 15 March 1796, 472; 18 March 1796, 475.
100. *Gazette of the United States*, 11 October 1794; *General Advertiser*, 11, 14 October 1794. On Federalists' general aversion to engaging in electioneering, see Fischer, *The Revolution in American Conservatism*, 91–97.
101. According to Bache, Swanwick received at least another one hundred votes, but a Federalist captain of the militia burned the returns. For the controversy surrounding the militia returns, see *General Advertiser*, 1, 5, 6 November 1794.
102. For an overview of the debates surrounding the Jay Treaty, see Estes, *The Jay Treaty Debate*, and Elkins and McKitrick, *The Age of Federalism*, 388–415.
103. *Independent Gazetteer*, 11 March 1795.
104. *Aurora*, 22 June 1795.
105. The treaty was ratified on the condition that article 12, which dealt with trade between America and the Caribbean, be amended.
106. Ironically, the Federalists had already decided to release the treaty and had planned to do so the very same day.

107. Southern Republicans were also upset that Jay did not secure compensation for enslaved people carried off at the end of the Revolutionary War. Todd Estes does an excellent job analyzing the provisions of the treaty and outlining the various positions taken by historians. Estes, *The Jay Treaty Debate*, 29–31. For a more positive portrayal of the Jay Treaty, see Dawson, *"Stop the Wheels of Government,"* 14–18.
108. *Aurora*, 3 July 1795.
109. *Independent Gazetteer*, 6 July 1795. Federalists offered a different account of the events. The *Gazette of the United States* claimed that the procession did not begin until "a very late, and silent hour of the night, when the *sober* citizen had retired to rest" and consisted of no more than "a few idle and ill-intentioned persons." *Gazette of the United States*, 9 July 1795. See also Oliver Wolcott to Laura Collins Wolcott, 8 July 1795, in Gibbs, *Memoirs of the Administrations of Washington and John Adams*, 1:209.
110. *Aurora*, 17 July 1795.
111. U.S. Congress, *Annals of Congress*, 1st Cong., 2nd sess., 13, 15 August 1789, 733–34, 763; Berkin, *The Bill of Rights*, 88–89; Ray Raphael, "The Democratic Moment: The Revolution and Popular Politics," in Gray and Kamensky, *The Oxford Handbook of the American Revolution*, 133–35. For a discussion of the ambiguity of petitioning under the Constitution, see Carpenter, *Democracy by Petition*, 30–32, 62–63, and *passim*; Bogin, "Petitioning and the New Moral Economy of Post-Revolutionary America"; and Krotoszynski, *Reclaiming the Petition Clause*, 109–11. See also Morgan, *Inventing the People*, 224–30, 283–84; Higginson, "A Short History of the Right to Petition Government"; and Smith, "The Right to Petition for Redress of Grievances."
112. *Gazette of the United States* 15, 23, 29 July 1795.
113. *Gazette of the United States*, 24 July 1795.
114. *Aurora*, 17 July 1795.
115. For a good overview of how the different interpretations of the relationship between the people and the Constitution shaped the Jay Treaty debate, see Gienapp, *The Second Creation*, 248–324.
116. Timothy Pickering to Stephen Higginson, 27 July 1795, in Pickering and Upham, *The Life of Timothy Pickering*, 3:184.
117. *Aurora*, 24 July 1795. The committee consisted of the prominent Republicans Thomas McKean, Charles Pettit, Thomas Lee Shippen, Stephen Girard, Jared Ingersoll, Blair McClenachan, William Shippen, Abraham Coats, Alexander James Dallas, John Hanna, John Swanwick, Moses Levy, John Barker, and William Coats.
118. *Aurora*, 27 July 1795. For a copy of the memorial, see *Dunlap and Claypoole's American Daily Advertiser*, 28 July 1795. The committee delivered the memorial to Washington on 14 August. See *Gazette of the United States*, 15 August 1795.

119. *Aurora,* 27 July 1795; *Gazette of the United States,* 27 July 1795; Oliver Wolcott to George Washington, 26 July 1795; Oliver Wolcott to Laura Collins Wolcott, 26 July 1795, in Gibbs, *Memoirs of the Administrations of Washington and John Adams,* 217–18; Timothy Pickering to George Washington, 27 July 1795; Pickering to Stephen Higginson, 27 July 1795, in Pickering and Upham, *The Life of Timothy Pickering,* 3:182–84.
120. Oliver Wolcott to George Washington, 26 July 1795; Oliver Wolcott to Laura Collins Wolcott, 26 July 1795, in Gibbs, *Memoirs of the Administrations of Washington and John Adams,* 1:217–18.
121. Timothy Pickering to George Washington, 27 July 1795; Pickering to Stephen Higginson, 27 July 1795, in Pickering and Upham, *The Life of Timothy Pickering,* 3:182–84.
122. *Gazette of the United States,* 27 July 1795.
123. For the debate over the number of people who attended, see *Gazette of the United States,* 27, 30, 31 July 1795, and *Aurora,* 29, 31 July, 3 August 1795.
124. *Aurora,* 1 August 1795.
125. *Gazette of the United States,* 29 July 1795.
126. *Gazette of the United States,* 31 July 1795.
127. *Aurora,* 1, 4 August 1795. Washington might have signed the treaty regardless of what happened at the meetings, but the uproar did at least confirm some of his conclusions about the opposition in general. In a letter to Alexander Hamilton written shortly after the town meetings, Washington commented that "the difference of conduct between the friends, and foes of order, and good government is in noth[in]g more striking than that, the latter are always working, like bees, to distil their poison; whilst the former, depending, often times, *too much,* and *too long* upon the sense, and good dispositions of the people to work conviction, neglect the means of effecting it." Washington to Hamilton, 29 July 1795, in Syrett et al., *Papers of Alexander Hamilton,* 18:524–26. For a discussion of Washington's decision to sign the treaty, see Estes, *The Jay Treaty Debate,* 96–98.
128. *Aurora,* 8 September 1795; *Gazette of the United States,* 10 September 1795.
129. *Aurora,* 29 April 1796; Kurtz, *The Presidency of John Adams,* 66–69; Estes, "Shaping the Politics of Public Opinion," 416–21.
130. *Western Telegraphe, and Washington Advertiser,* 15 March 1796.
131. *Claypoole's American Daily Advertiser,* 16 April 1796. Some communities organized public meetings to adopt the petitions. Because these gatherings formed to express support for an established government position, they were, by their very nature, different than those held by Republicans or those in the 1780s.
132. Data on petitions found in the *Journal of the House of Representatives* supplemented with reports found in the *Gazette of the United States.* Numbers given are approximations because the official records do not indicate the number of

signatures on a petition or whether the House received more than one petition relating to the treaty on the same day from the same locality. The *Gazette of the United States* is likewise incomplete. For more on the counter-petition drive, see *Aurora*, 29 April 1796, and Gawalt, *Justifying Jefferson*, 96–97, 117.

133. *Aurora*, 19 April 1796.
134. *Aurora*, 20, 26 April 1796. Federalists in western Pennsylvania also helped spread a rumor that Pinckney's Treaty, an agreement that would have secured Americans' navigation rights on the Mississippi River, was somehow tied to the Jay Treaty and that refusing to fund the Jay Treaty would also prevent Pinckney's Treaty from going into effect. Access to the Mississippi was a major issue for westerners, and the rumor appears to have led to at least some people signing a petition calling on Congress to fund the treaty. See *Claypoole's American Daily Advertiser*, 26 March 1796.
135. Findley would later make the dubious claim that his absence was an accident and that the vote had come as a surprise. Elkins and McKitrick, *The Age of Federalism*, 446–47; Estes, *The Jay Treaty Debate*, 181–87; Kurtz, *The Presidency of John Adams*, 71–73. Frederick Muhlenberg was also stabbed by his brother-in-law for voting in favor of the treaty. See 5 May 1796, *DED*, 2:41.

4. From Opposition to Party

1. *Claypoole's American Daily Advertiser*, 19 September 1796; Neem, *Creating a Nation of Joiners*, 33–34.
2. List, "The Role of William Cobbett in Philadelphia's Party Press."
3. On the immigration of Irish and French radicals, see Durey, *Transatlantic Radicals*, 4–11, 228–33, and *passim*; Bric, *Ireland, Philadelphia, and the Re-Invention of America*; and Cotlar, *Tom Paine's America*, 49–82.
4. Tinkcom, *Republicans and Federalists in Pennsylvania*, 20, 272; Pasley, "The Tyranny of Printers," 407–9; Ferguson, *Early Western Pennsylvania Politics*, 161–64.
5. Shankman, *The Crucible of American Democracy*, 56–60, 65; Bouton, *Taming Democracy*, 245–47; Ridner, *A Town In-Between*, 179–81.
6. Pasley, *The First Presidential Contest*.
7. On Jefferson's and Hamilton's relationship in the cabinet, see Chervinsky, *The Cabinet*. Less clarity existed when it came to the choice for vice president, but Aaron Burr of New York and Thomas Pinckney of South Carolina appeared the most likely candidates for the opposition and Federalists, respectively. Alexander Hamilton and other Federalists who did not trust John Adams worked quietly behind the scenes in an attempt to get Pinckney elected president and Adams vice president. The plan was never very feasible, but it did attract the support of a number of influential Pennsylvania Federalists and contributed to the eventual breakdown of the

Federalist coalition. See David W. Houpt, "John Adams and the Elections of 1796 and 1800," in Waldstreicher, *A Companion to John Adams and John Quincy Adams*, 142–65.

8. Cunningham, *Jeffersonian Republicans*, 94.
9. Tinkcom, *Republicans and Federalists in Pennsylvania*, 163; Pasley, *The First Presidential Contest*, 351. This same debate over whether to divide the state into districts or conduct at-large elections occurred during the state's first four congressional elections. See Houpt, "Contested Election Laws."
10. The one notable exception to the rule that Pennsylvanian politicians did not organize statewide occurred in 1792 when Federalists successfully pushed through a bill that called for at-large, as opposed to district, elections for the state's federal representatives. In response, leaders of the opposition in Philadelphia distributed a circular letter throughout the state soliciting suggestions for possible nominees. The resulting "Rights of Man" ticket, however, included more than half of the same candidates Federalists would endorse, suggesting that party lines had not yet formed. See Houpt, "Contested Election Laws."
11. Bowers, "From Caucus to Convention in Pennsylvania Politics," 282; Walton, "Nominating Conventions in Pennsylvania," 270; *Aurora*, 24 October 1796.
12. The full list of Republican electors included Thomas McKean, James Boyd, William Brown, John Whitehill, Peter Muhlenberg, Abraham Smith, Jacob Morgan, James Hanna, John Smilie, Joseph Heister, John Piper, William Irvine, William Maclay, Jonas Hartzell, and James Edgar.
13. Although the slate selected to serve as electors in 1792 included prominent men such as Thomas McKean and Joseph Heister, the majority were relatively obscure politicians whose primary qualification appeared to be that they supported ratification of the federal Constitution.
14. *Gazette of the United States*, 4 November 1796. The men Federalists nominated in 1796 were Robert Coleman, Samuel Miles, Samuel Postlethwaite, William Wilson, Israel Whelen, John Carson, Henry Wynkoop, Thomas Bull, Jacob Hay, Benjamin Elliott, John Woods, Valentine Eckhart, Ephraim Douglas, John Arndt, and Thomas Stokely.
15. *Republican State Committee Circular*, 25 September 1796. See also *Western Telegraphe, and Washington Advertiser*, 25 October 1796.
16. John Beckley to William Irvine, 17 October 1796, in Gawalt, *Justifying Jefferson*, 128; Pasley, "'A Journeyman, Either in Law or Politics.'"
17. Fisher Ames to Oliver Wolcott, 26 September 1796, in Gibbs, *Memoirs of the Administrations of Washington and John Adams*, 1:384. Ames went on the write that he expected "a great deal of noise, whipping, and spurring; money, it is very probably will be spent, some virtue and more tranquility lost; but I hope public order will be saved."
18. *Philadelphia Gazette*, 29 October 1796.

19. Pasley, *The First Presidential Contest*, 358–59; Tinkcom, *Republicans and Federalists in Pennsylvania*, 168.
20. Quoted in Ferling, *Adams v. Jefferson*, 90.
21. Pasley, *The First Presidential Contest*, 358–59.
22. The parade was not without incident. Rumors circulated that the sailors planned to prevent voters from casting ballots. When an alderman tried to stop the parade, a fight ensued that resulted in the jailing of sixty participants. The entire episode served as a stern reminder of the dangers associated with popular politics. Baumann, "The Democratic-Republicans of Philadelphia," 566; *North Carolina Gazette*, 14 November 1796.
23. *Claypoole's American Daily Advertiser*, 7 November 1797; Chauncey Goodrich to Oliver Wolcott, 15 November 1796, in Gibbs, *Memoirs of the Administrations of Washington and John Adams*, 1:394; Dawson, *"Stop the Wheels of Government,"* 38–39.
24. Had the returns from Greene County, which were not received in time to be certified, been included, Jefferson would have received all fifteen electoral votes. Tinkcom, *Republicans and Federalists in Pennsylvania*, 168–72; Pasley, *The First Presidential Contest*, 351.
25. On the XYZ Affair and deterioration of relations between France and the United States, see Elkins and McKitrick, *The Age of Federalism*, 537–90, and DeConde, *The Quasi-War*, 3–108.
26. Abigail Adams to Mary Cranch, 13 April 1798, in Mitchell, *New Letters of Abigail Adams*, 333–35.
27. Seth Cotlar, "The Federalists' Transatlantic Cultural Offensive of 1798," in Pasley, Robertson, and Waldstreicher, *Beyond the Founders*, 274–99.
28. *Porcupine's Gazette*, 13, 14 April 1798.
29. *Gazette of the United States*, 25 August 1798.
30. Ray, "'Not One Cent for Tribute,'" 401, 402. Ray argued that the meetings were "indigenous and impulsive in nature" and "not contrived demonstrations carefully orchestrated by good Federalists." This might be correct for many of the meetings, but the meetings in Philadelphia had clearly been organized. Even if there were an element of spontaneity, Federalists certainly used the meetings to help establish a popular backing for their agenda in Congress. See also Bradburn, *Citizenship Revolution*, 153–58.
31. *Gazette of the United States*, 1, 7 May 1798; Ray, "'Not One Cent for Tribute,'" 404–9.
32. Koschnik, *Let a Common Interest Bind Us Together*, 118–20.
33. *Porcupine's Gazette*, 4 May 1798. See also *Porcupine's Gazette*, 2, 5, 7, 8, 17 May 1798; Newman, *Parades and the Politics of the Street*, 154–63; and Koschnik, *Let a Common Interest Bind Us Together*, 115–16.
34. *Porcupine's Gazette*, 31 July 1798; Newman, *Parades and the Politics of the Street*, 181–82.

35. Lohman, *Hail Columbia!* 112–22, 122 (quotation). See also Coleman, *Harnessing Harmony*, 32–39.
36. *Porcupine's Gazette*, 7 May 1798.
37. Waldstreicher, *In the Midst of Perpetual Fetes*, 157; Zagarri, *Revolutionary Backlash*, 91–92; Branson, *These Fiery Frenchified Dames*, 82–86.
38. *Gazette of the United States*, 18, 17 February 1798. See also *Gazette of the United States*, 2 May 1798.
39. *Aurora*, 14 May 1798.
40. *Gazette of the United States*, 7 May 1798.
41. There is some evidence that specific militia companies supported "Republican" causes in the early 1790s. See, for instance, *General Advertiser*, 8 July 1794. They did not, however, openly identify themselves as Republicans.
42. Quoted in Koschnik, *Let a Common Interest Bind Us Together*, 122; Scharff and Westcott, *History of Philadelphia*, 494.
43. Scharff and Westcott, *History of Philadelphia*, 494; *Aurora*, 3 May 1798.
44. Koschnik, *Let a Common Interest Bind Us Together*, 130–40.
45. Cotlar, "The Federalists' Transatlantic Cultural Offensive."
46. DeConde, *The Quasi-War*, 101–3; Newman, *Fries's Rebellion*, 69–78.
47. An Act in Addition to the Act, Entitled "An Act for the Punishment of Certain Crimes against the United States."
48. Newman, *Fries's Rebellion*, 71–78.
49. On reactionary populism, see Formisano, *For the People*, 1–17.
50. Michael Durey argues that radical immigrants fueled the growth of the Republican Party because they saw political parties as natural. Many immigrants also arrived as experienced mobilizers. Durey, *Transatlantic Radicals*, 235–36.
51. See U.S. Congress, *Annals of Congress*, 5th Cong., 3rd sess., 2785–3001. The number of signatures for each county were Montgomery—1,940; York—1,800; Washington—1,544; Franklin—1,487; Berks—1,400; Philadelphia County—1,210; Northampton—1,100; Lancaster—950; Chester—755 and 692; Philadelphia City—587; Dauphin—504; Cumberland—320 and 270; and Mifflin—314 and 270. Petitions were also received from Bedford and Northumberland but the exact numbers of signatures were not specified.
52. *Herald of Liberty*, 26 November 1798.
53. *Farmers Register*, 26 December 1798.
54. *Aurora*, 12 February 1799; *Farmers Register*, 9 January 1799.
55. U.S. Congress, *Annals of Congress*, 5th Cong., 3rd sess., 9 January, 25 February 1799, 2597–99, 2985–3017. Federalists voting in favor of the resolutions included Robert Waln, Richard Thomas, John Chapman, and Thomas Hartley. Republicans voting against the resolutions were Joseph Heister, John Hanna, Andrew Gregg, William Findley, Albert Gallatin, and Robert Brown. Federalist John Kittera did not vote.

56. Deposition of James Jackson, 23 October 1799, Rawle Family Papers, 2:31, Historical Society of Pennsylvania (quotations). See also *Oracle of Dauphin*, 9, 16, 23 January, 6 February, 6, 20 March 1799; Newman, *Fries's Rebellion*, 87–94, 99–100, 13–47. For an excellent overview of the forms of resistance, see Lurie, "Liberty Poles and the Fight for Popular Politics."
57. Hamilton, "Federalist No. 78," in Shapiro, *The Federalist Papers*, 391–97.
58. Churchill, "Popular Nullification, Fries' Rebellion, and the Waning of Radical Republicanism," 105–40. On the origins of the uprising, see Bouton, "'No Wonder the Times Were Troublesome'"; Ridgway, "Fries in the Federalist Imagination"; Newman, "The Federalists' Cold War," 63–104; Bouton, *Taming Democracy*, 245–49; Newman, *Fries's Rebellion*, 1–111; and Leonard and Cornell, *The Partisan Republic*, 75–77.
59. Newman, *Fries's Rebellion*, 112–21; Deposition of John Jameson, n.d., Rawle Family Papers, 2:92; Deposition of George Mitchell, n.d., Rawle Family Papers, 2:95.
60. Newman, *Fries's Rebellion*, 123–25.
61. Newman, *Fries's Rebellion*, 131–41.
62. As quoted in Newman, *Fries's Rebellion*, 140.
63. *Porcupine's Gazette*, 12 March 1799.
64. *Gazette of the United States*, 11 March 1799.
65. *Philadelphia Gazette*, 16 March 1799.
66. Newman, *Fries's Rebellion*, 143–44.
67. Deposition of Henry Ohl, 27 April 1799, Rawle Family Papers, 2:91.
68. Deposition of John Fogel, 13 April 1799, Rawle Family Papers, 2:69.
69. *Reading Adler*, 20 March 1799; Newman, *Fries's Rebellion*, 149–51; Churchill, "Popular Nullification, Fries' Rebellion, and the Waning of Radical Republicanism," 126–33; Martin, *Government by Dissent*, 44–52.
70. *Aurora*, 16, 22, 25 March; 5, 30 April; 15 July 1799
71. Thomas Jefferson to James Madison, 30 January 1787, in *PTJ*, 11:92–93; Jefferson to Edmund Pendleton, 14 February 1799, in *PTJ*, 31:36–39.
72. *Farmers Register*, 3 April 1799; *Aurora*, 16 March 1799.
73. Other scholars have suggested that young Federalists may have been more likely to turn to violence as a way to assert their masculinity. While undoubtedly a factor for some, this explanation does not explain why the political violence was so one-sided. See, for instance, Koschnik, *Let a Common Interest Bind Us Together*, 113–16, and Waldstreicher, *In the Midst of Perpetual Fetes*, 159.
74. DeConde, *The Quasi-War*, 74–108, 82–83 (quotation).
75. Smith, *Freedom's Fetters*, 192–93; *Aurora*, 9 August 1798; *Porcupine's Gazette*, 1 February 1799. For another instance of violence against an editor, see *Farmers Register*, 20 February 1799. As Andrew W. Robertson has pointed out, changes in political rhetoric might have also factored into the growing

number of attacks on newspaper editors. See Robertson, *The Language of Democracy*, 1–35.

76. MacPherson, *William MacPherson, Brigadier General.*
77. Carpenter, *The Two Trials of John Fries*, 112.
78. William MacPherson to Mahlon Ford, 27 March, 15 April 1799, quoted in Lurie, "Liberty Poles and the Fight for Popular Politics," 686; Newman, *Fries's Rebellion*, 143–44, 154–64.
79. *Aurora*, 13 May 1799 (translated from *Reading Adler*, 9 April 1799).
80. *Aurora*, 24 May 1799; Lurie, "Liberty Poles and the Fight for Popular Politics," 688.
81. *Aurora*, 13 May 1799 (translated from *Reading Adler*, 9 April 1799).
82. *Aurora*, 13 May 1799; *Oracle of Dauphin*, 8 May 1799; Newman, *Fries's Rebellion*, 162–63.
83. *Aurora*, 10, 13, 24 May 1799.
84. *Aurora*, 16, 17, 21 May 1799; *Gazette of the United States*, 15, 16 May 1799.
85. *Aurora*, 16 May 1799.
86. *Aurora*, 17 May 1799.
87. *Aurora*, 17 May 1799.
88. Keller, "Rural Politics and the Collapse of Pennsylvania Federalism," 6–8.
89. Pasley, "*The Tyranny of Printers*," 105–31; Fischer, *The Revolution in American Conservatism*, 131.
90. Keller, "Diversity and Democracy," 214–15.
91. As quoted in Tinkcom, *Republicans and Federalists in Pennsylvania*, 168. See also Walters, *Alexander James Dallas*, 73.
92. *Aurora*, 31 January 1798; Tinkcom, *Republicans and Federalists in Pennsylvania*, 193–94.
93. *Gazette of the United States*, 20 February 1798.
94. Keller, "Diversity and Democracy," 192; Keller, "Rural Politics and the Collapse of Pennsylvania Federalism," 7–8; Fischer, *The Revolution in American Conservatism*, 1–27, 95–97.
95. James Ross to Arthur St. Clair, 6 July 1798, in Smith, *The Life and Public Services of Arthur St. Clair*, 2:422–25.
96. *Gazette of the United States*, 2 October 1797.
97. *Aurora*, 20 April 1797; Keller, "Diversity and Democracy," 184–85; Carter, "A 'Wild Irishman' under Every Federalist's Bed," 178–89; Durey, *Transatlantic Radicals*, 148–251.
98. Bradburn, *Citizenship Revolution*, 210–32; Cotlar, *Tom Paine's America*, 82–111.
99. As quoted in Keller, "Rural Politics and the Collapse of Pennsylvania Federalism," 20.
100. On the efforts to integrate free African Americans into the political community, see Polgar, *Standard-Bearers of Equality*, 122–210. See also Bradburn,

Citizenship Revolution, 235–62. The True Republican Society noted that "Citizen Sambo," or Cyrus Bustill, a prominent member of the Black community in Philadelphia, attended a meeting. Foner, *The Democratic-Republican Societies*, 13.

101. Miller, *Philadelphia—The Federalist City*, 94, 108; Tinkcom, *Republicans and Federalists in Pennsylvania*, 154, 161–62, 175–80.
102. For a summary of this process, see *Herald of Liberty*, 13 May 1799. See also *Aurora*, 16 April 1799, and Miller, *Philadelphia—The Federalist City*, 113.
103. Tinkcom, *Republicans and Federalists in Pennsylvania*, 221–23.
104. *Aurora*, 16 April 1799.
105. *Gazette of the United States*, 5 March 1799.
106. "Federalist Circular," *Aurora*, 11 April 1799; *Philadelphia Gazette*, 11 April 1799; *Porcupine's Gazette*, 12 April 1799.
107. *Herald of Liberty*, 18 November 1799. In fact, individual Philadelphia Republicans spent so much of their own money that a special committee had to be appointed following the election to raise money to reimburse donors.
108. *Kline's Carlisle Gazette*, 2 October 1799.
109. *Declaration of the Reverend Mr. David Jones*. The accusations concerned Federalists enough to publish a statement from members of a Presbyterian congregation in Washington County that Ross regularly attended church. *To the Electors of Pennsylvania*.
110. *Herald of Liberty*, 26 August 1799.
111. *Kline's Carlisle Gazette*, 25 September 1799.
112. *Aurora*, 11 September 1799.
113. *Philadelphia, May 27th. Sir, Deeply Interested in the Approaching Election*.
114. *Gazette of the United States*, 14 August 1799; Dallas, *To the Citizens of the County of Philadelphia*.
115. *Kline's Carlisle Gazette*, 10 July 1799.
116. *Herald of Liberty*, 8 July 1799.
117. *Kline's Carlisle Gazette*, 10 July 1799. See also *Gazette of the United States*, 18 July 1799, and *Philadelphia Gazette*, 26 July 1799.
118. Keller, "Rural Politics and the Collapse of Pennsylvania Federalism," 41; Jeffrey L. Pasley, "The Cheese and the Words: Popular Political Culture and Participatory Democracy in the Early American Republic," in Pasley, Robertson, and Waldstreicher, *Beyond the Founders*, 46–47.
119. Keller, "Rural Politics and the Collapse of Pennsylvania Federalism," 40–41.
120. *Aurora*, 5 March 1799.

5. Establishing a Democratic Republic

1. *Aurora*, 6 March 1801.
2. First Inaugural Address, 4 March 1801, in *PTJ*, 33:148–52.

3. *Herald of Liberty*, 13 July 1801.
4. *Aurora*, 6 March 1801.
5. *Gazette of the United States*, 9 March 1801.
6. The term "Quid," derived from the Latin phrase *tetrium quid*, meaning "third way," was first used by Democrats as a way of mocking the moderate wing of the party. Quids, however, embraced the name and it stuck. Higginbotham, *Keystone in the Democratic Arch*, 58–59.
7. This is a topic that is explored more fully in the conclusion.
8. Shankman, *The Crucible of American Democracy*; Phillips, "William Duane, Philadelphia's Democratic Republicans, and the Origins of Modern Politics," 365–87.
9. Ferguson, *Early Western Pennsylvania Politics*, 158–59.
10. Doerflinger, *A Vigorous Spirit of Enterprise*, 335–44.
11. Shankman, *The Crucible of American Democracy*, 160–72.
12. On Binns, see Durey, *Transatlantic Radicals*, 37–38, 261, and Shankman, *The Crucible of American Democracy*, 92–93. On the newspapers in the west, see Ferguson, *Early Western Pennsylvania Politics*, 161–63.
13. In 1801, a general county meeting agreed to appoint a committee of twenty-three delegates from the different election districts. Higginbotham, *Keystone in the Democratic Arch*, 36–37.
14. Shankman, *The Crucible of American Democracy*, 98–99; Higginbotham, *Keystone in the Democratic Arch*, 44–45.
15. *Aurora*, 17 September 1802.
16. *Aurora*, 17, 18, 20 September 1802; *Philadelphia Gazette*, 23 September 1802; Higginbotham, *Keystone in the Democratic Arch*, 44.
17. *Philadelphia Gazette*, 23 September 1802; *Carlisle Gazette*, 6 October 1802; *Poulson's American Daily Advertiser*, 12 October 1802; Higginbotham, *Keystone in the Democratic Arch*, 42, 61–63, 70–72.
18. *Freeman's Journal*, 21 June 1804.
19. *Poulson's American Daily Advertiser*, 16, 23 July 1803.
20. On charges that Quids relied on Federalists, see *Aurora*, 13, 14, 16, 28, 29, 30 July 1803.
21. *Philadelphia Evening Post*, 17 May 1804.
22. *Freeman's Journal*, 25 March, 28 June, 5 July 1805. The term "union of honest men" came from a toast delivered by Vice President Aaron Burr during a dinner with Federalists. See Cheetham, *A View of the Political Conduct of Aaron Burr*.
23. *Kline's Carlisle Gazette*, 6 October 1802. See also *Kline's Carlisle Gazette*, 15, 22 October 1802.
24. Higginbotham, *Keystone in the Democratic Arch*, 37–39.
25. *Aurora*, 28 February 1805.

26. Nathan Boileau to Jonathan Roberts Jr., 1 March 1805, as quoted in Higginbotham, *Keystone in the Democratic Arch*, 82.
27. *Aurora*, 14 March 1805.
28. *Aurora*, 21 March 1805.
29. *Aurora*, 25 March 1805.
30. *Freeman's Journal*, 18 March 1805.
31. *Freeman's Journal*, 23 March 1805.
32. *Freeman's Journal*, 18 March 1805.
33. *Freeman's Journal*, 5 March 1805.
34. *Freeman's Journal*, 15 March 1805; Koschnik, *Let a Common Interest Bind Us Together*, 66–69.
35. *Freeman's Journal*, 23 March 1805.
36. *Aurora*, 30 March 1805; Koschnik, *Let a Common Interest Bind Us Together*, 66–69.
37. *Aurora*, 30 March 1805.
38. *Aurora*, 15 March 1805. See also *Aurora*, 14 March, 1 April 1805.
39. *Freeman's Journal*, 14 June 1805.
40. *United States Gazette*, 19 April 1805.
41. *Journal of the Fifteenth House of Representatives*, 634–39.
42. For McKean's account, see *Aurora*, 3 June 1805, and *The Address of the Society of Constitutional Republicans*, 24–28. For another version, see *Aurora*, 29 March 1805, and Higginbotham, *Keystone in the Democratic Arch*, 84–86.
43. See, e.g., *Aurora*, 6 July 1805. The term "clodhopper" is a reference to the heavy-duty boots worn by farmers.
44. *Aurora*, 20 May 1805; *Pennsylvania Correspondent*, 16 April 1805; *Poulson's American Daily Advertiser*, 6 April 1805. Duane and Leib greeted Snyder's nomination coolly, and while they agreed to abide by the party's decision, rumors circulated that Leib had tried to undermine Snyder's candidacy. Nothing came of these whispers in 1805, but they did foreshadow future problems. Veritas, *Six Letters of the Intrigues*; Higginbotham, *Keystone in the Democratic Arch*, 88–89.
45. *Poulson's American Daily Advertiser*, 6 April 1805.
46. See, e.g., *Freeman's Journal*, 27 September 1805. See also *Freeman's Journal*, 15 April, 28 August 1805.
47. *Aurora*, 16 July 1805. See also *Aurora*, 26 June, 10 May 1805.
48. *Aurora*, 14, 15, 16, 18 May 1804.
49. *Aurora*, 7 July 1805; Koschnik, *Let a Common Interest Bind Us Together*, 140–46.
50. *Freeman's Journal*, 10 April 1805; Koschnik, *Let a Common Interest Bind Us Together*, 63.

51. *Philadelphia Evening Post,* 19 March 1804. Quids did hold Fourth of July celebrations in some parts of the state. See *Freeman's Journal,* 5, 6, 10 July 1805.
52. *Philadelphia Evening Post,* 16 May 1804; Shankman, *The Crucible of American Democracy,* 102.
53. *Freeman's Journal,* 5 September 1805.
54. It was originally given as a speech on 10 June 1805. The Society of Constitutional Republicans printed more than twenty-five thousand copies of the pamphlet in both German and English and had them dispersed throughout the state. *Freeman's Journal,* 28 June 1805.
55. *The Address of the Society of Constitutional Republicans; Freeman's Journal,* 28 June 1805; *Pennsylvania Correspondent,* 7 October 1805.
56. *Aurora,* 7, 9 May 1805.
57. *Aurora,* 15 July, 7 May 1805.
58. For an example of an author who challenged the concept of constitutions, see *Aurora,* 10 May, 21 August 1805. Democrats would back down from some of this more radical rhetoric as election day neared. See *Address of the Conferees of the City and County of Philadelphia,* and *Aurora,* 28 September 1805.
59. *Freeman's Journal,* 17 September 1805.
60. *Spirit of the Press,* 12 October 1805; *Kline's Carlisle Gazette,* 1 October 1805.
61. *Aurora,* 8 October 1805.
62. The official count for Snyder was lower due to a clerical error. Higginbotham, *Keystone in the Democratic Arch,* 100.
63. *Freeman's Journal,* 26 November 1805.
64. *Aurora,* 28 November 1805.
65. *Aurora,* 1 October 1805.
66. For more on the resurgence of Federalism during the Embargo Act, see Fischer, *The Revolution in American Conservatism.* See also Cunningham, *The Jeffersonian Republicans in Power.*
67. For an account that stresses personalities over principles, see Higginbotham, *Keystone in the Democratic Arch,* 136–45. Andrew Shankman, in contrast, portrays the split as rooted in conflicting visions of democracy, but his account does not take into consideration the different styles of political mobilization. See Shankman, *The Crucible of American Democracy,* 109–11, and *passim.*
68. *Narrative of Facts Relative to the Conduct of Some of the Members of the Legislature.* See also Veritas, *Six Letters of the Intrigues.*
69. *Democratic Press,* 7, 10, 11, 12, 15, 18, 21, 26 August 1807.
70. *Aurora,* 2 September 1807. The term "quadroon" was used to describe a person with one white parent and one half-Black/half-white parent. Interestingly, this would mean Duane saw Democrats as Black and Federalists as white.
71. *Aurora,* 1 September 1807.

72. *Aurora*, 19 August 1807.
73. *Aurora*, 1 September 1807; Higginbotham, *Keystone in the Democratic Arch*, 141–42.
74. *Aurora*, 4 September 1807.
75. *Aurora*, 23 September 1807.
76. *Democratic Press*, 24 November, 16 December 1807. See also *Democratic Press*, 9, 24 December 1807, and Higginbotham, *Keystone in the Democratic Arch*, 151.
77. Not everyone approved of the idea that the meetings could send instructions. One Democratic gathering, for example, concluded that everyone knew Snyder would be nominated and that "entering into a specific resolution to instruct members would shew a suspicion of their republican firmness and integrity." *Aurora*, 11 January 1808; Higginbotham, *Keystone in the Democratic Arch*, 153–54. For the account of the meeting that decided against sending instructions, see *Democratic Press*, 11 February 1808. Other Democratic gatherings had no qualms with issuing instructions. See, e.g., *Democratic Press*, 24 February 1808.
78. *Aurora*, 10 March 1808.
79. Higginbotham, *Keystone in the Democratic Arch*, 155; Joseph Hopkins to Unknown, 22 May 1808, as quoted in Shankman, *The Crucible of American Democracy*, 183; Fischer, *The Revolution in American Conservatism*, 76.
80. *Democratic Press*, 12, 17 May 1808; *Aurora*, 14 May, 7 June 1808.
81. *Democratic Press*, 3 August 1808. See also *Democratic Press*, 17 May, 3 June, 7 July 1808.
82. *Democratic Press*, 28 July, 3 August 1808.
83. *Democratic Press*, 11 May 1808. For another example of the efforts to distance Snyder from the challenge to the constitutions, see also *Kline's Carlisle Gazette*, 26 August 1808.
84. *Aurora*, 7 June 1808.
85. *Democratic Press*, 8 July 1808. See also *Commonwealth*, 6, 13, 20 July 1808.
86. *Kline's Carlisle Gazette*, 8 July 1808. For similar sentiments, see *Aurora*, 6 July 1808.
87. *Aurora*, 6 July 1808.
88. *Democratic Press*, 13 May, 28 July 1808; Higginbotham, *Keystone in the Democratic Arch*, 155.
89. *Freeman's Journal*, 6 April, 26 May, 22, 25, 26 July 1808; Higginbotham, *Keystone in the Democratic Arch*, 170–71.
90. *Kline's Carlisle Gazette*, 26 August 1808.
91. *Freeman's Journal*, 15, 16 August 1808.
92. *Democratic Press*, 28 September 1808.
93. *Democratic Press*, 25, 29 August 1808.
94. On Coxe, see, Shankman, *The Crucible of American Democracy*, 186–87.

95. *Pennsylvania Herald, and Easton Intelligencer,* 21 September 1808.
96. *Democratic Press,* 13 May, 28 July 1808; Higginbotham, *Keystone in the Democratic Arch,* 155.
97. On this point generally, see Fischer, *The Revolution in American Conservatism,* 95–109.
98. On the rumor that Spayd had dropped out, see *Democratic Press,* 7 September 1808, and Higginbotham, *Keystone in the Democratic Arch,* 173–74.

Conclusion

1. *Democratic Press,* 6 January 1809.
2. Pennsylvania Constitution (1776), in *Proceedings Relative to Calling the Conventions,* 55–56.
3. Pasley, "The Cheese and the Words," 45.
4. Koschnik, *Let a Common Interest Bind Us Together,* 184–227; Neem, *Creating a Nation of Joiners.*
5. Peart, *Era of Experimentation,* 73–107. On the Second Party System, see McCormick, *The Second American Party System;* Holt, *Political Parties and American Political Development;* Baker, *Affairs of Party;* and Howe, *What Hath God Wrought.* For a critical look at the role of political parties during this period, see Altschuler and Blumin, *Rude Republican.*
6. Polgar, *Standard-Bearers of Equality,* 211–60; Diemer, *The Politics of Black Citizenship,* 11–30. See also Bradburn, *Citizenship Revolution,* 235–71.
7. James Forten, "Series of Letters by a Man of Colour," in Newman, Rael, and Lapsanksy *Pamphlets of Protest,* 71.
8. Nash, *Forging Freedom,* 177.
9. Scudder, *Recollections of Samuel Breck,* 302.
10. As quoted in Smith, "The End of Black Voting Rights in Pennsylvania," 281.
11. Runcie, "'Hunting the Nigs' in Philadelphia," 190.
12. Smith, "The End of Black Voting Rights in Pennsylvania," 279–99; Nash, *Forging Freedom,* 246–79; Keyssar, *The Right to Vote,* 54–60.
13. Purvis, *Appeal of Forty Thousand Citizens; Pittsburgh Gazette,* 25 January 1838; Diemer, *The Politics of Black Citizenship,* 112–33.
14. Brown, "The Women's Rights Movement in Pennsylvania"; *The Proceedings of the Women's Rights Convention.*
15. U.S. Constitution, amendment 15, sec. 1.
16. Biddle and Dubin, *Tasting Freedom;* Smith, *Civic Ideals,* 383–90; Keyssar, *The Right to Vote,* 87–104, 263–75.
17. Keyssar, *The Right to Vote,* 172–221.

BIBLIOGRAPHY

Primary Sources

Newspapers (all published in Pennsylvania unless otherwise noted)

Aurora (Philadelphia)
Carlisle Gazette (Carlisle)
Claypoole's American Daily Advertiser (Philadelphia)
Commonwealth (Pittsburgh)
Democratic Press (Philadelphia)
Dunlap and Claypoole's American Daily Advertiser (Philadelphia)
Dunlap's American Daily Advertiser (Philadelphia)
Farmers Register (Chambersburg)
Federal Gazette (Philadelphia)
Freeman's Journal (Philadelphia)
Gazette of the United States (Philadelphia)
General Advertiser (Philadelphia)
Greenleaf's New York Journal (New York City)
Herald of Liberty (Washington)
Independent Gazetteer (Philadelphia)
Kline's Carlisle Gazette (Carlisle)
Mail; or, Claypoole's Daily Advertiser (Philadelphia)
National Gazette (Philadelphia)
North Carolina Gazette (New Bern, NC)
Oracle of Dauphin (Harrisburg)
Pennsylvania Correspondent (Doylestown)
Pennsylvania Evening Herald (Philadelphia)
Pennsylvania Evening Post (Philadelphia)
Pennsylvania Gazette (Philadelphia)
Pennsylvania Herald, and Easton Intelligencer (Easton)
Pennsylvania Journal (Philadelphia)
Pennsylvania Mercury and Universal Advertiser (Philadelphia)
Pennsylvania Packet (Philadelphia)
Philadelphia Evening Post (Philadelphia)
Philadelphia Gazette (Philadelphia)
Pittsburgh Gazette (Pittsburgh)
Porcupine's Gazette (Philadelphia)

Poulson's American Daily Advertiser (Philadelphia)
Reading Adler (Reading)
Spirit of the Press (Philadelphia)
Tree of Liberty (Pittsburgh)
United States Gazette (Philadelphia)
Western Telegraphe, and Washington Advertiser (Washington)

Manuscripts

HISTORICAL SOCIETY OF PENNSYLVANIA (PHILADELPHIA)

Broadside Collection
Cadwalader Family Papers, 1630–1900
Coxe Family Papers
George Mifflin Dallas Papers, 1792–1864
Irvine-Newbold Family Papers
Minutes of the Democratic Society of Pennsylvania
Minutes of the Northampton County Committee of Observation and Inspection
Thomas McKean Papers
Rawle Family Papers
James Wilson Papers

LIBRARY OF CONGRESS (WASHINGTON, DC)

George Washington Papers
Pennsylvania Whiskey Rebellion Collection

NEW-YORK HISTORICAL SOCIETY

Albert Gallatin Papers

PENNSYLVANIA STATE ARCHIVES (HARRISBURG)

General Assembly Petitions and Miscellaneous Records, 1776–1790
Records of the Proprietary Government, Executive Correspondence

UNIVERSITY OF PITTSBURGH

Jonathan Forman Papers

Pamphlets and Broadsides

Address of the Conferees of the City and County of Philadelphia. Philadelphia, 1805.
An Address of the Council of Censors to the Freemen of Pennsylvania. Philadelphia, 1784.
The Address of the Society of Constitutional Republicans, Established in the City and County of Philadelphia to the Republicans of Pennsylvania. Philadelphia, 1805.

The Alarm; or, An Address to the People of Pennsylvania, on the Late Resolve of Congress for Totally Suppressing All Power and Authority Derived from the Crown of Great-Britain. Philadelphia, 1776.

An Alarm. To the Freemen and Electors of Pennsylvania. Philadelphia, 1784.

Brackenridge, Hugh Henry. *Incidents of the Insurrection in the Western Parts of Pennsylvania in the Year 1794.* 3 vols. Philadelphia, 1795.

A Candid Examination of the Address of the Minority of the Council of Censors to the People of Pennsylvania. Philadelphia, 1784.

Carey, Matthew. *He Wou'd be a Poet; or, "Nature Will Be Still."* Philadelphia, 1796.

Carpenter, Thomas. *The Two Trials of John Fries, on an Indictment for Treason.* Philadelphia, 1800.

Cheetham, James. *A View of the Political Conduct of Aaron Burr, Esq.* New York, 1802.

Cobbett, William. *A Bone to Gnaw, for the Democrats; or, Observations on a Pamphlet, Entitled, "The Political Progress of Britain."* Philadelphia, 1795.

———. *History of American Jacobins: Commonly Denominated Democrats.* Philadelphia, 1796.

Dallas, Alexander J. *Features of Mr. Jay's Treaty. To Which Is Annexed a View of the Commerce of the United States, as It Stands at Present, and as It Is Fixed by Mr. Jay's Treaty.* Philadelphia, 1795.

———. *To the Citizens of the County of Philadelphia.* Philadelphia, 1799.

Declaration of the Reverend Mr. David Jones. Washington, PA, 1799.

Duane, William. *A Report of the Extraordinary Transactions.* Philadelphia, 1799.

Extract from the Minutes of the Proceedings of a General Meeting of the Citizens of Philadelphia, Held in the State House Yard. Philadelphia, 1792.

Findley, William. *History of the Insurrection in the Four Western Counties of Pennsylvania.* Philadelphia, 1796.

Gentlemen, Permit Us to Congratulate You upon the Establishment of a Constitution in Pennsylvania, Which Promises Security to Life, Liberty and Property, and Which Has Already Restored Harmony to Our Long Distracted State. Philadelphia, 1790.

Hopkinson, Francis. *An Account of the Grand Federal Procession: Performed at Philadelphia on Friday the 4th of July 1788.* Philadelphia, 1788.

In General Assembly of the State of Pennsylvania. Tuesday, June 17, 1777. Philadelphia, 1777.

Jackson, William. *An Oration to Commemorate the Independence of the United States.* Philadelphia, 1786.

Journal of the Fifteenth House of Representatives of the Commonwealth of Pennsylvania. Lancaster, PA, 1805.

MacPherson, William. *William MacPherson, Brigadier General in the Army of the United States, Commanding the Troops Destined to Act against the Insurgents in the Counties of Northampton, Montgomery and Bucks, in the State of Pennsylvania.* Philadelphia, 1799.

McKean, Thomas. *Fellow Citizens. The 2d Section of the 1st Article of the Constitution of the United States.* Carlisle, PA, 1798.

Minutes of the Third General Assembly. Philadelphia, 1779.

Minutes of the Third Session of the Thirteenth General Assembly of the Commonwealth of Pennsylvania, Which Commenced at Philadelphia, on Monday, the Twenty-Seventh Day of October, in the Year of Our Lord One Thousand Seven Hundred and Eighty-Eight. Philadelphia, 1789.

Muhlenberg, John Peter. *To the Republicans of Pennsylvania.* Philadelphia: 1799.

Narrative of Facts Relative to the Conduct of Some of the Members of the Legislature of Pennsylvania, Professing to Be Democrats, at the Election of a Senator to Represent This State in the Senate of the United States. Philadelphia, 1807.

Old Trusty. *To the Tories.* Philadelphia, 1776.

Philadelphia, May 27th. Sir, Deeply Interested in the Approaching Election. Philadelphia, 1799.

Porter, Robert. *An Oration to Commemorate the Independence of the United States of North America.* Philadelphia, 1791.

Proceedings of the General Town-Meeting, July 26–27, 1779. Philadelphia, 1779.

The Proceedings of the Women's Rights Convention Held at West Chester, PA June 2nd and 3rd, 1852. Philadelphia, 1852.

The Proceedings Relative to Calling the Conventions of 1776 and 1790: The Minutes of the Convention That Formed the Present Constitution of Pennsylvania. Harrisburg, PA, 1825.

Purvis, Robert. *Appeal of Forty Thousand Citizens, Threatened with Disenfranchisement, to the People of Pennsylvania.* Philadelphia, 1838.

Report of the Commissioners, Appointed by the President of the United States of America, to Confer with the Insurgents in the Western Counties of Pennsylvania. Philadelphia, 1794.

Republican State Committee Circular. Philadelphia, 1796.

Rogers, William. *An Oration, Delivered July 4, 1789 at the Presbyterian Church, in Arch Street, Philadelphia.* Philadelphia, 1789.

Sir, We Enclose a Copy of a Circular Letter Directed to Be Sent to the Gentlemen in Your County Who Have Been Nominated as a Committee to Promote the Ticket. Philadelphia, 1799.

Swanwick, John. *A Rub from Snub; or, A Cursory Analytical Epistle Addressed to Peter Porcupine, Author of the Bone to Gnaw, Kick for a Bite, &c, &c.* Philadelphia, 1975.

To [Blank] and Other Citizens in the County of [Blank]. Philadelphia, 1792.

To the Electors of Pennsylvania. Philadelphia, 1799.

To the Freemen of Pennsylvania. Friends and Countrymen, as the Sitting of the Council of Censors Is Now Nearly at an End. Philadelphia, 1784.

To the Freemen of the City of Philadelphia. Philadelphia, 1792.
To the Independent Electors of Pennsylvania. Philadelphia, 1792.
Veritas. *Six Letters of the Intrigues, Apostacy and Ambition of Doctor Michael Leib; Originally Published in "The Democratic Press."* Philadelphia, 1807.
Yates, William. *Rights of Coloured Men to Suffrage Citizenship and Trial by Jury*. Philadelphia, 1838.
York, 18th June 1779. A Meeting of the Inhabitants of This Town. Lancaster, PA, 1779.

Printed Sources

An Act in Addition to the Act, Entitled "An Act for the Punishment of Certain Crimes against the United States." Public Law 74. *U.S. Statutes at Large* 5 (1798): 596–97.
Allen, James. "Diary of James Allen, Esq. of Philadelphia, a Counsellor-at-Law, 1770–1778." *Pennsylvania Magazine of History and Biography* 9, no. 2 (July 1885): 176–96.
Binns, John. *Recollections of the Life of John Binns: Twenty-Nine Years in Europe and Fifty-Three in the United States*. Philadelphia: T. K. and P. G. Collins, 1854.
Bowling, Kenneth R., and Helen E. Veit, eds. *The Diary of William Maclay and Other Notes on Senate Debates, March 4, 1789–March 3, 1791*. Baltimore: Johns Hopkins University Press, 1988.
Boyd, Julian P., et al., eds. *The Papers of Thomas Jefferson*. 45 vols. to date. Princeton, NJ: Princeton University Press, 1950–.
Butterfield, L. H., ed. *Letters of Benjamin Rush*. 2 vols. Princeton, NJ: Princeton University Press: 1951.
Butterfield, L. H., et al., eds. *Adams Family Correspondence*. 14 vols. to date. Cambridge, MA: Belknap Press of Harvard University Press, 1963–.
Clitherall, James. "Extracts from the Diary of Dr. James Clitherall, 1776." *Pennsylvania Magazine of History and Biography* 22, no. 4 (1898): 469–70.
Cobbett, William. *Peter Porcupine in America: Pamphlets on Republicanism and Revolution*. Edited by David A. Wilson. Ithaca, NY: Cornell University Press, 1994.
Crane, Elaine Forman, ed. *The Diary of Elizabeth Drinker*. 3 vols. Boston: Northeastern University Press, 1991.
Dallas, George Mifflin. *The Life and Writings of Alexander James Dallas*. Philadelphia: J. B. Lippincott, 1871.
De Pauw, Linda Grant, et al., eds. *Documentary History of the First Federal Congress*. 22 vols. Baltimore: Johns Hopkins University Press, 1972–2017.
Duane, William, ed. *Extracts from the Diary of Christopher Marshall: Kept in Philadelphia and Lancaster during the American Revolution, 1774–1781*. Cambridge, MA: Harvard University Press, 1877.

Foner, Philip, ed. *The Democratic-Republican Societies, 1790–1800: A Documentary Sourcebook of Constitutions, Declarations, Addresses, Resolutions and Toasts.* Westport, CT: Greenwood Press, 1975.

Gawalt, Gerard W., ed. *Justifying Jefferson: The Political Writings of John James Beckley.* Washington, DC: Library of Congress, 1995.

Gibbs, George, ed. *Memoirs of the Administrations of Washington and John Adams, Edited from the Papers of Oliver Wolcott.* 2 vols. New York: W. Van Norden, 1846.

Gibson, James. "The Attack on Ft. Fisher, Oct. 4, 1779." *Pennsylvania Magazine of History and Biography* 5, no. 4 (1881): 475–76.

Hazard, Samuel, et al., eds. *Pennsylvania Archives.* 119 vols. Philadelphia and Harrisburg: Pennsylvania Historical and Museum Commission, 1852–1933.

Jensen, Merrill, et al., eds. *The Documentary History of the First Federal Elections.* 4 vols. Madison: University of Wisconsin Press, 1976–89.

———, eds. *The Documentary History of the Ratification of the Constitution.* 37 vols. to date. Madison: Wisconsin Historical Society, 1976–.

McMaster, J. B., and Frederick D Stone, eds. *Pennsylvania and the Federal Constitution, 1787–1788.* Philadelphia: Historical Society of Pennsylvania, 1888.

Michell, James T., et al., eds. *The Statutes at Large of Pennsylvania from 1682–1801.*17 vols. Harrisburg: C. M. Busch, 1896–1915.

Mitchell, Stewart, ed. *New Letters of Abigail Adams, 1788–1801.* Boston: Houghton Mifflin Company, 1947.

Newman, Richard, Patrick Rael, and Philip Lapsanksy, eds. *Pamphlets of Protest: An Anthology of Early African-American Protest Literature, 1790–1860.* New York: Routledge, 2001.

Parsons, Jacob Cox, ed. *Extracts from the Diary of Jacob Hiltzheimer of Philadelphia.* Philadelphia: William F. Fell, 1893.

Perkins, Bradford, ed. "A Diplomat's Wife in Philadelphia: Letters of Henrietta Liston, 1796–1800." *William and Mary Quarterly,* 3rd series, 11, no. 4 (October 1954): 592–631.

Pickering, Octavius, and Charles Wentworth Upham, eds. *The Life of Timothy Pickering.* 4 vols. Boston: Little, Brown, 1867.

Read, William T., ed. *The Life and Correspondence of George Read: A Signer of the Declaration of Independence with Notices of Some of His Contemporaries.* Philadelphia: J. B. Lippincott, 1870.

Reed, William B., ed. *Life and Correspondence of Joseph Reed: Military Secretary of Washington, at Cambridge, Adjutant-General of Continental Army, Member of the Congress of the United States, and President of the Executive Council of the State of Pennsylvania.* 2 vols. Philadelphia: Lindsay and Blakiston, 1847.

Ryden, George Herbert, ed. *Letters to and from Caesar Rodney, Member of the Stamp Act Congress and the First and Second Continental Congress; Speaker of the Delaware Colonial Assembly; President of the Delaware State; Major General of the Delaware Militia; Signer of the Declaration of Independence*. Philadelphia: Historical Society of Delaware, University of Pennsylvania Press, 1933.

Scudder, Horace, ed. *Recollections of Samuel Breck with Passages from His Note-Books, 1771–1862*. Carlisle, MA: Applewood Books, 1877.

Shapiro, Ian, ed. *The Federalist Papers*. New Haven, CT: Yale University Press, 2009.

Smith, Paul H., et al., eds. *Letters of Delegates to Congress, 1774–1789*. 26 vols. Washington, DC: Library of Congress, 1976–2000.

Smith, William Henry, ed. *The Life and Public Services of Arthur St. Clair*. Cincinnati: Robert Clarke, 1882.

Storing, Herbert J., ed. *The Complete Anti-Federalist*. Chicago: University of Chicago Press, 1981.

Syrett, Harold C., et al., eds. *The Papers of Alexander Hamilton*. 27 vols. New York: Columbia University Press, 1961–87.

Twohig, Dorothy, et al., eds. *The Papers of George Washington: Presidential Series*. 21 vols. Charlottesville: University of Virginia Press, 1987–2020.

Westcott, Thompson. *Names of Persons Who Took the Oath of Allegiance to the State of Pennsylvania between the Years 1777 and 1790 with a History of the "Test Laws" of Pennsylvania*. Philadelphia: John Campbell, 1865.

Electronic Sources

A New Nation Votes Database. American Antiquarian Society/Tufts University. https://elections.lib.tufts.edu/.

Pennsylvania Election Statistics Project. Wilkes University. http://staffweb.wilkes.edu/harold.cox/index.html.

U.S Congress. *Annals of Congress*. Library of Congress. https://memory.loc.gov/ammem/amlaw/lwaclink.html.

U.S Congress. *Journal of the House of Representatives of the United States*. Library of Congress. https://memory.loc.gov/ammem/amlaw/lwhjlink.html.

Secondary Sources

Adams, Willi Paul. *The First American Constitutions: Republican Ideology and the Making of the State Constitutions in the Revolutionary Era*. Translated by Rita and Robert Kimber. Chapel Hill: University of North Carolina Press, 1980.

Adelman, Joseph M. *Revolutionary Networks: The Business and Politics of Printing the News, 1763–1789*. Baltimore: Johns Hopkins University Press, 2019.

Alexander, John K. "The Fort Wilson Incident: A Case Study of the Revolutionary Crowd." *William and Mary Quarterly*, 3rd series, 31, no. 4 (October 1974): 589–612.

Altschuler, Glenn C., and Stuart M. Blumin. *Rude Republican: Americans and Their Politics in the Nineteenth Century*. Princeton, NJ: Princeton University Press, 2000.

Ammon, Harry. *The Genet Mission*. New York: Norton, 1971.

Anderson, Benedict. *Imagined Communities: Reflections on the Origin and Spread of Nationalism*. New York: Verso, 1983.

Appleby, Joyce. *Capitalism and a New Social Order: The Republican Vision of the 1790s*. New York: New York University Press, 1984.

———. *Inheriting the Revolution: The First Generation of Americans*. Cambridge, MA: Harvard University Press, 2000.

Arnold, Douglas M. *A Republican Revolution: Ideology and Politics in Pennsylvania, 1776–1790*. New York: Garland, 1989.

Bailyn, Bernard. *The Ideological Origins of the American Revolution*. Cambridge, MA: Belknap Press of Harvard University Press, 1967.

Baker, Jean H. *Affairs of Party: The Political Culture of Northern Democrats in the Mid-Nineteenth Century*. New York: Fordham University Press, 1998.

Banner, James, Jr. *To the Hartford Convention: The Federalists and the Origins of Party Politics in Massachusetts, 1789–1815*. New York: Knopf, 1970.

Banning, Lance. *The Jeffersonian Persuasion: Evolution of a Party Ideology*. Ithaca, NY: Cornell University Press, 1978.

Baumann, Richard. "The Democratic-Republicans of Philadelphia: The Origins, 1776–1797." Ph.D. diss., University of Pennsylvania, 1970.

———. "John Swanwick: Spokesman for 'Merchant Republicanism' in Philadelphia, 1790–1798." *Pennsylvania Magazine of History and Biography* 97, no. 2 (April 1973): 131–82.

———. "Philadelphia's Manufacturers and the Excise Taxes of 1794: The Forging of the Jeffersonian Coalition." *Pennsylvania Magazine of History and Biography* 106, no. 1 (January 1982): 3–39.

Beeman, Richard R. "Deference, Republicanism, and the Emergence of Popular Politics in Eighteenth-Century America." *William and Mary Quarterly*, 3rd series 49, no. 3 (July 1992): 401–30.

———. *The Varieties of Political Experience in Eighteenth-Century America*. Philadelphia: University of Pennsylvania Press, 2004.

Beeman, Richard R., Stephen Botein, and Edward Carter II, eds. *Beyond Confederation: Origins of the Constitution and American National Identity*. Chapel Hill: University of North Carolina Press, 1987.

Bemis, Samuel Flagg. *Jay's Treaty: A Study in Commerce and Diplomacy*. 2nd ed. Westport, CT: Greenwood Press, 1962.

Ben-Atar, Doron S., and Barbara Oberg, eds. *Federalists Reconsidered*. Charlottesville: University of Virginia Press, 1999.

Berkeley, Edmund, and Dorothy Smith Berkeley. *John Beckley: Zealous Partisan in a Nation Divided*. Philadelphia: American Philosophical Society, 1973.

Berkin, Carol. *The Bill of Rights: The Fight to Secure America's Liberties*. New York: Simon and Schuster, 2015.

———. *A Sovereign People: The Crises of the 1790s and the Birth of American Nationalism*. New York: Basic Books, 2017.

Biddle, Daniel R., and Murray Dubin. *Tasting Freedom: Octavius Catto and the Battle for Equality in Civil War America*. Philadelphia: Temple University Press, 2010.

Bockelman, Wayne L., and Owen S. Ireland. "The Internal Revolution in Pennsylvania: An Ethnic-Religious Interpretation." *Pennsylvania History* 41, no. 2 (1974): 124–59.

Bogin, Ruth. "Petitioning and the New Moral Economy of Post-Revolutionary America." *William and Mary Quarterly*, 3rd series, 45, no. 3 (July 1988): 391–425.

Bohman, James, and William Rehg, eds. *Deliberative Democracy: Essays on Reason and Politics*. Cambridge: Massachusetts Institute of Technology Press, 1997.

Boonshoft, Mark. *Aristocratic Education and the Making of the American Republic*. Chapel Hill: University of North Carolina Press, 2020.

Bouton, Terry. "'No Wonder the Times Were Troublesome': The Origins of the Fries Rebellion, 1783–1799." *Pennsylvania History* 67, no. 1 (2000): 21–42.

———. "A Road Closed: Rural Insurgency in Post-Revolutionary Pennsylvania." *Journal of American History* 87, no. 3 (December 2000): 855–87.

———. *Taming Democracy: The People, the Founders, and the Troubled Ending of the American Revolution*. New York: Oxford University Press, 2007.

Bowers, Douglas E. "From Caucus to Convention in Pennsylvania Politics, 1790–1830." *Pennsylvania History* 56, no. 4 (October 1989): 276–98.

Bowling, Kenneth R. "New Light on the Philadelphia Mutiny of 1783: Federal-State Confrontation at the Close of the War for Independence." *Pennsylvania Magazine of History and Biography* 101, no. 4 (October 1977): 419–50.

Bowling, Kenneth R., and Donald R. Kennon, eds. *Neither Separate nor Equal: Congress in the 1790s*. Athens: Ohio University Press, 2000.

Boyd, Steven R. "Antifederalists and the Acceptance of the Constitution: Pennsylvania, 1787–1792." *Publis* 9, no. 2 (Spring 1979): 123–37.

———, ed. *The Whiskey Rebellion: Past and Present Perspectives*. Westport, CT: Greenwood Press, 1985.

Bradburn, Douglas. *The Citizenship Revolution: Politics and the Creation of the American Union, 1774–1804*. Charlottesville: University of Virginia Press, 2009.

———. "A Clamor in the Public Mind: Opposition to the Alien and Sedition Acts." *William and Mary Quarterly*, 3rd series, 65, no. 3 (July 2008): 565–600.

Bradburn, Douglas, and Christopher R. Pearl, eds. *From Independence to the U.S. Constitution: Reconsidering the Critical Period in American History*. Charlottesville: University of Virginia Press, 2022.

Branson, Susan. *These Fiery Frenchified Dames: Women and Political Culture in Early National Philadelphia*. Philadelphia: University of Pennsylvania Press, 2001.

Breen, T. H. *American Insurgents, American Patriots: The Revolution of the People*. New York: Hill and Wang, 2010.

———. *The Marketplace of Revolution: How Consumer Politics Shaped American Independence*. New York: Oxford University Press, 2004.

———. *The Will of the People: The Revolutionary Birth of America*. Cambridge, MA: Belknap Press of Harvard University Press, 2019.

Brewin, Mark. "The History of Election Day in Philadelphia: A Study in American Political Ritual." Ph.D. diss., University of Pennsylvania, 2002.

Bric, Maurice. *Ireland, Philadelphia, and the Re-Invention of America, 1760–1800*. Dublin: Four Courts Press, 2008.

Brooke, John L. *Columbia Rising: Civil Life on the Upper Hudson from the Revolution to the Age of Jackson*. Chapel Hill: University of North Carolina Press, 2010.

Brown, Ira V. "The Women's Rights Movement in Pennsylvania, 1848–1873." *Pennsylvania History* 32, no. 2 (April 1965): 153–65.

Brown, Roger H. *Redeeming the Republic: Federalists, Taxation, and the Origins of the Constitution*. Baltimore: Johns Hopkins University Press, 2000.

Brunhouse, Robert Levere. *The Counter-Revolution in Pennsylvania, 1776–1790*. Harrisburg: Pennsylvania Historical Commission, 1942.

Bushman, Richard L. *King and People in Provincial Massachusetts*. Chapel Hill: University of North Carolina Press, 1985.

Caldwell, John. *William Findley from West of the Mountains: A Politician in Pennsylvania, 1783–1791*. Gig Harbor, WA: Red Apple, 2000.

———. *William Findley from West of the Mountains: Congressman, 1791–1821*. Gig Harbor, WA: Red Apple, 2002.

Calvert, Jane. "Liberty without Tumult: Understanding the Politics of John Dickinson." *Pennsylvania Magazine of History and Biography* 131, no. 3 (July 2007): 233–62.

———. *Quaker Constitutionalism and the Political Thought of John Dickinson*. New York: Cambridge University Press, 2009.

Carp, Benjamin L. *Rebels Rising: Cities and the American Revolution*. New York: Oxford University Press, 2007.

Carpenter, Daniel T. *Democracy by Petition: Popular Politics in Transformation, 1790–1870*. Cambridge, MA: Harvard University Press, 2021.

Carter, Edward C. "A 'Wild Irishman' under Every Federalist's Bed: Naturalization in Philadelphia, 1789–1806." *Proceedings of the American Philosophical Society* 133, no. 2 (1989): 178–89.

Carter, Katlyn. "Denouncing Secrecy and Defining Democracy in the Early American Republic." *Journal of the Early Republic* 40, no. 3 (Fall 2020): 409–33.

Charles, Joseph. *The Origins of the American Party System*. New York: Harper and Row, 1956.

Chervinsky, Lindsay M. *The Cabinet: George Washington and the Creation of an American Institution*. Cambridge, MA: Harvard University Press, 2020.

Churchill, Robert H. "Popular Nullification, Fries' Rebellion, and the Waning of Radical Republicanism, 1798–1801." *Pennsylvania History* 67, no. 1 (Winter 2000): 105–40.

———. *To Shake Their Guns in the Tyrants Face: Libertarian Political Violence and the Origins of the Militia Movement*. Ann Arbor: University of Michigan Press, 2011.

Clark, Mary Elizabeth. "Peter Porcupine in America: The Career of William Cobbett, 1792–1800." Ph.D. diss, University of Pennsylvania, 1939.

Cleves, Rachel Hope. *The Reign of Terror in America: Visions of Violence from Anti-Jacobinsim to Antislavery*. New York: Cambridge University Press, 2009.

Coleman, Billy. *Harnessing Harmony: Music, Power, and Politics in the United States, 1788–1815*. Chapel Hill: University of North Carolina Press, 2020.

Coleman, John M. *Thomas McKean: Forgotten Leader of the American Revolution*. Rockaway, NY: American Faculty Press, 1975.

Collins, Varnum L. *The Continental Congress at Princeton*. Princeton, NJ: Princeton University Library, 1908.

Combs, Jerald A. *The Jay Treaty: Political Battleground of the Founding Fathers*. Berkeley: University of California Press, 1970.

Conway, M. Margaret. "Political Parties and Political Mobilization." *American Review of Politics* 14 (Winter 1993): 549–63.

Cornell, Saul. "Aristocracy Assailed: The Ideology of Backcountry Anti-Federalism." *Journal of American History* 76, no. 4 (March 1990): 1148–72.

———. *The Other Founders: Anti-Federalism and the Dissenting Tradition in America, 1788–1828*. Chapel Hill: University of North Carolina Press, 1999.

Cotlar, Seth. *Tom Paine's America: The Rise and Fall of Transatlantic Radicalism in the Early Republic*. Charlottesville: University of Virginia Press, 2011.

Countryman, Edward. "The Problem of the Early American Crowd." *Journal of American Studies* 7, no. 1 (April 1973): 77–90.

Cunningham, Noble E. *Jeffersonian Republicans: The Formation of Party Organization*. Chapel Hill: University of North Carolina Press, 1957.

———. *The Jeffersonian Republicans in Power: Party Operations, 1801–1809*. Chapel Hill: University of North Carolina Press, 1963.

Cutterham, Tom. *Gentlemen Revolutionaries: Power and Justice in the New American Republic*. Princeton, NJ: Princeton University Press, 2017.

Daniel, Marcus L. *Scandal and Civility: Journalism and the Birth of American Democracy*. New York: Oxford University Press, 2009.

Davis, Jeffrey A. "Guarding the Republican Interest: The Western Pennsylvania Democratic Societies and the Excise Tax." *Pennsylvania History* 67, no. 1 (Fall 2000): 43–62.

Davis, Susan. *Parades and Power: Street Theater in Nineteenth-Century Philadelphia*. Berkeley: University of California Press, 1988.

Dawson, Matthew Q. *"Stop the Wheels of Government": Partisanship and the Birth of America's Second Party, 1796–1800*. Westport, CT: Greenwood Press, 2000.

DeConde, Alexander. *Entangling Alliance: Politics and Diplomacy under George Washington*. Westport, CT: Greenwood Press, 1958.

———. *The Quasi-War: The Politics and Diplomacy of the Undeclared War with France, 1797–1801*. New York: Scribner, 1966.

Diemer, Andrew K. *The Politics of Black Citizenship: Free African Americans in the Mid-Atlantic Borderland, 1817–1863*. Athens: University of Georgia Press, 2016.

Dimmig, Jeffrey S. "Palatine Liberty: Pennsylvania German Opposition to the Direct Tax of 1798." *American Journal of Legal History* 45, no. 4 (October 2001): 371–90.

Dinkin, Robert J. *Voting in Provincial America: A Study of Elections in the Thirteen Colonies, 1689–1776*. Westport, CT: Greenwood Press, 1977.

———. *Voting in Revolutionary America: A Study in Elections in the Original Thirteen States, 1776–1789*. Westport, CT: Greenwood Press, 1982.

Doerflinger, Thomas. *A Vigorous Spirit of Enterprise: Merchants and Economic Development in Revolutionary Philadelphia*. Chapel Hill: University of North Carolina Press, 1986.

Dunn, John. *Setting the People Free: The Story of Democracy*. London: Atlantic, 2005.

Durey, Michael. *Transatlantic Radicals in the Early American Republic*. Lawrence: University Press of Kansas, 1997.

Edling, Max M. *Perfecting the Union: National and State Authority in the US Constitution*. New York: Oxford University Press, 2020.

———. *A Revolution in Favour of Government: Origins of the US Constitution and the Making of the American State*. New York: Oxford University Press, 2003.

Einhorn, Robin L. *American Taxation, American Slavery*. Chicago: University of Chicago Press, 2006.

Elkins, Stanley, and Eric McKitrick. *The Age of Federalism: The Early American Republic, 1788–1800*. New York: Oxford University Press, 1993.

Elsmere, Jane S. "The Trial of John Fries." *Pennsylvania Magazine of History and Biography* 103, no. 4 (October 1979): 432–35.

Estes, Todd. *The Jay Treaty Debate, Public Opinion, and the Evolution of Early American Political Culture*. Amherst: University of Massachusetts Press, 2006.

———. "Shaping the Politics of Public Opinion: Federalists and the Jay Treaty Debate." *Journal of the Early Republic* 29, no. 3 (Fall 2000): 393–422.

Everett, Edward. "John Smilie, Forgotten Champion of Early Western Pennsylvania." *Western Pennsylvania Historical Magazine* 33, nos. 3–4 (September–December 1950): 77–89.

Fa, Bernard. "Early Party Machinery in the Unites States: Pennsylvania in the Election of 1796." *Pennsylvania Magazine of History and Biography* 60, no. 4 (October 1936): 375–90.

Fennell, Dorothy Elaine. "From Rebelliousness to Insurrection: A Social History of the Whiskey Rebellion, 1765–1802." Ph.D. diss, University of Pittsburgh, 1981.

Ferguson, E. James. "The Nationalists of 1781–1783 and the Economic Interpretation of the Constitution." *Journal of American History* 56 (1969): 241–61.

Ferguson, Russell J. *Early Western Pennsylvania Politics.* Pittsburgh: University of Pittsburgh Press, 1938.

Ferling, John. *Adams v. Jefferson: The Tumultuous Election of 1800.* New York: Oxford University Press, 2004.

Fischer, David Hackett. *The Revolution in American Conservatism: The Federalist Party in the Era of Jeffersonian Democracy.* New York: Harper and Row, 1965.

Foner, Eric. *Tom Paine and Revolutionary America.* New York: Oxford University Press, 1976.

Formisano, Ronald P. "Deferential-Participant Politics: The Early Republic's Political Culture, 1789–1840." *American Political Science Review* 68, no. 2 (June 1974): 473–87.

———. *For the People: American Populist Movements from the Revolution to the 1850s.* Chapel Hill: University of North Carolina Press, 2012.

———. *The Transformation of Political Culture: Massachusetts Parties, 1790s–1840s.* New York: Oxford University Press, 1983.

Foster, Joseph S. *In Pursuit of Equal Liberty: George Bryan and the Revolution in Pennsylvania.* University Park: Pennsylvania State University Press, 1994.

———. "The Politics of Ideology: The Pennsylvania Constitutional Convention of 1789–90." *Pennsylvania History* 59, no. 2 (1992): 122–44.

Frank, Jason. *Constituent Moments: Enacting the People.* Durham, NC: Duke University Press, 2010.

Frantz, John B., and William Pencak, eds. *Beyond Philadelphia: The American Revolution in the Pennsylvania Hinterland.* University Park: Pennsylvania State University Press, 1998.

Freeman, Joanne B. *Affairs of Honor: National Politics in the New Republic.* New Haven, CT: Yale University Press, 2001.

Fritz, Christian G. *American Sovereigns: The People and America's Constitutional Tradition before the Civil War.* New York: Oxford University Press, 2008.

Furstenberg, François. *In the Name of the Father: Washington's Legacy, Slavery, and the Making of a Nation.* New York: Penguin, 2006.

———. *When the United States Spoke French: Five Refugees Who Shaped a Nation*. New York: Penguin, 2014.

Furstenberg, François, and David Waldstreicher, eds. "Re-Introducing the Republican Court." Special issue, *Journal of the Early Republic* 35, no 2 (Summer 2015).

Geertz, Clifford. *Negara: The Theater State in Nineteenth Century Bali*. Princeton, NJ: Princeton University Press, 1980.

Gienapp, Jonathan. *The Second Creation: Fixing the American Constitution in the Founding Era*. Cambridge, MA: Harvard University Press, 2018.

Gilje, Paul A. "The Baltimore Riot of 1812 and the Breakdown of the Anglo-American Mob Tradition." *Journal of Social History* 13, no. 4 (Summer, 1980): 547–64.

———. *Rioting in America*. Bloomington: Indiana University Press, 1996.

———. *The Road to Mobocracy: Popular Disorder in New York City, 1763–1834*. Chapel Hill: University of North Carolina Press, 1987.

Goodman, Paul. *The Democratic-Republicans of Massachusetts: Politics in a Young Republic*. Cambridge, MA: Harvard University Press, 1964.

Gray, Edward G., and Jane Kamensky, eds. *The Oxford Handbook of the American Revolution*. New York: Oxford University Press, 2013.

Griffin, Patrick, et al., eds. *Between Sovereignty and Anarchy: The Politics of Violence in the American Revolutionary Era*. Charlottesville: University of Virginia Press, 2015.

Griffin, Paul. *American Leviathan: Empire, Nation, and Revolutionary Frontier*. New York: Hill and Wang, 2008.

Gustafson, Sandra M. *Imagining Deliberative Democracy in the Early American Republic*. Chicago: University of Chicago Press, 2011.

Habermas, Jürgen. *The Structural Transformation of the Public Sphere: An Inquiry into a Category of Bourgeois Society*. Translated by Thomas Burger and Frederick Lawrence. Cambridge: Massachusetts Institute of Technology, 1989.

Hale, Matthew Rainbow. "Neither Britons nor Frenchman: The French Revolution and American National Identity." Ph.D. diss., Brandeis University, 2002.

———. "Regenerating the World: The French Revolution, Civic Festivals, and the Forging of Modern American Democracy, 1793–1795." *Journal of American History* 103 (March 2017): 891–920.

Hall, Mark D. *The Political and Legal Philosophy of James Wilson, 1742–1798*. Columbia: University of Missouri Press, 1997.

Harper, R. Eugene. *The Transformation of Western Pennsylvania, 1770–1800*. Pittsburgh: University of Pittsburgh Press, 1991.

Harris, Tim. *London Crowds in the Reign of Charles II: Propaganda and Politics from the Restoration until the Exclusion Crisis*. New York: Cambridge University Press, 1990.

Hattem, Michael. *Past and Prologue: Politics and Memory in the American Revolution*. New Haven, CT: Yale University Press, 2020.

Hawke, David Freeman. *In the Midst of a Revolution.* Philadelphia: University of Pennsylvania Press, 1961.

Hazen, Charles F. *Contemporary American Opinion of the French Revolution.* Baltimore: Johns Hopkins University Press, 1897.

Henderson, Amy Hudson. "Furnishing the Republican Court: Building and Decorating Philadelphia Homes, 1790–1800." Ph.D. diss., University of Delaware, 2008.

Higginbotham, Sanford W. *The Keystone in the Democratic Arch: Pennsylvania Politics, 1800–1816.* Harrisburg: Pennsylvania Historical and Museum Commission, 1952.

Higginson, Stephen A. "A Short History of the Right to Petition Government for the Redress of Government." *Yale Law Journal* 96, no. 1 (November 1986): 142–66.

Hoffman, Ronald, and Peter J. Albert, eds. *Launching the Extended Republic: The Federalist Era.* Charlottesville: University Press of Virginia, 1996.

Hofstadter, Richard. *The Idea of a Party System: The Rise of the Legitimate Opposition in the United States, 1740–1840.* Berkeley: University of California Press, 1969.

Hogeland, William. *The Whiskey Rebellion: George Washington, Alexander Hamilton, and the Frontier Rebels Who Challenged America's Newfound Sovereignty.* New York: Scribner, 2006.

Holt, Michael F. *Political Parties and American Political Development: From the Age of Jackson to the Age of Lincoln.* Baton Rouge: Louisiana State University Press, 1992.

Holton, Woody. "An Excess of Democracy—or a Shortage? The Federalists' Earliest Adversaries." *Journal of the Early Republic* 25, no. 3 (2005): 339–82.

———. *Liberty Is Sweet: The Hidden History of the American Revolution.* New York: Simon and Schuster, 2021.

———. *Unruly Americans and the Origins of the Constitution.* New York: Hill and Wang, 2007.

Horn, James, Jan Ellen Lewis, and Peter Onuf, eds. *The Revolution of 1800: Democracy, Race, and the New Republic.* Charlottesville: University of Virginia Press, 2002.

Houpt, David W. "Contested Election Laws: Representation, Elections, and Party Building in Pennsylvania, 1788–1794." *Pennsylvania History* 79, no. 3 (Summer 2012): 257–83.

Howe, Daniel Walker. *What Hath God Wrought: The Transformation of America, 1815–1848.* New York: Oxford University Press, 2007.

Howe, John. *Language and Political Meaning in Revolutionary America.* Amherst: University of Massachusetts Press, 2004.

Howe, John R., Jr. "Republican Thought and the Political Violence of the 1790s." *American Quarterly* 19, no. 2 (Summer 1967): 147–65.

Hunt, Lynn. *Politics, Culture and Class in the French Revolution*. Berkeley: University of California Press, 1984.

Hutchins, Catherine E., ed. *Shaping a National Culture: The Philadelphia Experience, 1750–1800*. Winterthur, DE: Winterthur, 1994.

Innes, Joanna, and Mark Philip, eds. *Re-Imagining Democracy in the Age of Revolutions: America, France, Britain, Ireland, 1750–1850*. Oxford: Oxford University Press, 2013.

Ireland, Owen S. "The Crux of Politics: Religion and Party in Pennsylvania, 1778–1789." *William and Mary Quarterly*, 3rd series, 42 (October 1985): 463–75.

———. "The Ethnic-Religious Dimension of Politics." *William and Mary Quarterly*, 3rd series, 30 (July 1973): 423–28.

———. "The Invention of American Democracy: The Pennsylvania Federalists and the New Republic." *Pennsylvania History* 67, no. 1 (Winter 2000): 161–71.

———. "The People's Triumph: The Federalist Majority in Pennsylvania, 1787–1788." *Pennsylvania History* 56, no. 2 (April 1989): 93–113.

———. "The Ratification of the Federal Constitution in Pennsylvania." Ph.D. diss., University of Pittsburgh, 1966.

———. *Religion, Ethnicity, and Politics: Ratifying the Constitution in Pennsylvania*. University Park: Pennsylvania State University Press, 1995.

Irvin, Benjamin H. *Clothed in Robes of Sovereignty: The Continental Congress and the People Out of Doors*. New York: Oxford University Press, 2011.

———. "The Streets of Philadelphia: Crowds, Congress, and the Political Culture of Revolution, 1774–1783." *Pennsylvania Magazine of History and Biography* 129 (January 2005): 7–44.

James, Edmund J. "The First Apportionment of Federal Representatives in the United States." *Annals of the American Academy of Political and Social Science* 9 (1897): 1–41.

Jensen, Merrill. *The Articles of Confederation: An Interpretation of the Social-Constitutional History of the American Revolution, 1774–1781*. Madison: University of Wisconsin Press, 1970.

John, Richard R. *Spreading the News: The American Postal System from Franklin to Morse*. Cambridge, MA: Harvard University Press, 1995.

Johnson, Daniel F. *Occupied America: British Military Rule and the Experience of Revolution*. Philadelphia: University of Pennsylvania Press, 2020.

Jones, Mark H. "Herman Husband: Millenarian, Carolina Regulator, and Whiskey Rebel." Ph.D. diss., Northern Illinois University, 1983.

Karter, Diana. *The Glorious Fourth: An American Holiday, an American History*. New York: Facts on File, 1989.

Kazin, Michael. *The Populist Persuasion: An American History*. Ithaca, NY: Cornell University Press, 1995.

Keller, Clair W. "The Rise of Representation: Electing County Officeholders in Colonial Pennsylvania." *Social Science History* 3, nos. 3–4 (October 1979): 139–66.

Keller, Kenneth W. "Diversity and Democracy: Ethnic Politics in Southeastern Pennsylvania, 1788–1799." Ph.D. diss., Yale University, 1971.

———. "Rural Politics and the Collapse of Pennsylvania Federalism." *Transactions of the American Philosophical Society* 72, no. 6 (1982): 1–73.

Kelly, Catherine E., and Joshua Piker, eds. "Writing to and from the Revolution: A Joint Issue with the *Journal of the Early Republic*." *William and Mary Quarterly*, 3rd series, 74, no. 4 (2017).

———. "Writing to and from the Revolution: A Joint Issue with the *William and Mary Quarterly*." *Journal of the Early Republic* 37, no. 4 (Winter 2017).

Kenny, Kevin. *Peaceable Kingdom Lost: The Paxton Boys and the Destruction of William Penn's Holy Experiment*. New York: Oxford University Press, 2009.

Kerber, Linda. *The Federalists in Dissent: Imagery and Ideology in Jeffersonian America*. Ithaca, NY: Cornell University Press 1980.

Kertzer, David I. *Ritual, Politics, and Power*. New Haven, CT: Yale University Press, 1988.

Keyssar, Alexander. *The Right to Vote: The Contested History of Democracy in the United States*. Revised edition. New York: Basic Books, 2000.

Klarman, Michael. *The Framers' Coup: The Making of the United States Constitution*. New York: Oxford University Press, 2016.

Kleppner, Paul, et al., eds. *The Evolution of American Electoral Systems*. Westport, CT: Greenwood Press, 1981.

Kohn, Richard H. "The Washington Administration's Decision to Crush the Whiskey Rebellion." *Journal of American History* 59, no. 3 (December 1972): 571–73.

Koschnik, Albrecht. "The Democratic Societies of Philadelphia and the Limits of the American Public Sphere, circa 1793–1795." *William and Mary Quarterly*, 3rd series, 58, no. 3 (2001): 615–36.

———. *Let a Common Interest Bind Us Together: Associations, Partisanship and Culture in Philadelphia, 1775–1840*. Charlottesville: University of Virginia Press, 2007.

———. "Political Conflict and Public Contest: Rituals of National Celebration in Philadelphia, 1788–1815." *Pennsylvania Magazine of History and Biography* 118, no. 3 (July 1994): 209–48.

Kramer, Larry D. *The People Themselves: Popular Constitutionalism and Judicial Review*. New York: Oxford University Press, 2004.

Krotoszynski, Ronald J., Jr. *Reclaiming the Petition Clause: Seditious Libel, "Offensive" Protest, and the Right to Petition the Government for a Redress of Grievances*. New Haven, CT: Yale University Press, 2012.

Kruman, Marc W. *Between Authority and Liberty: State Constitution Making in Revolutionary America.* Chapel Hill: University of North Carolina Press, 1997.

Kurtz, Stephen G. *The Presidency of John Adams: The Collapse of Federalism.* Philadelphia: University of Pennsylvania Press, 1957.

Leibiger, Stuart, ed. *A Companion to James Madison and James Monroe.* New York: Wiley, 2012.

Lemon, James T. *The Best Poor Man's Country: A Geographical Study of Southeastern Pennsylvania.* Baltimore: Johns Hopkins University Press, 1972.

Leonard, Gerald, and Saul Cornell. *The Partisan Republic: Democracy, Exclusion, and the Fall of the Founder's Constitution, 1780s–1830s.* New York: Cambridge University Press, 2019.

Leonard, Sister Joan de Lourdes. "Elections in Colonial Pennsylvania." *William and Mary Quarterly,* 3rd series, 11, no. 3 (July 1954): 385–401.

Link, Eugene P. *The Democratic-Republican Societies, 1790–1800.* New York: Columbia University Press, 1942.

List, Karen K. "The Role of William Cobbett in Philadelphia's Party Press, 1794–1799." Ph.D. diss., University of Wisconsin–Madison, 1980.

Lohman, Laura. *Hail Columbia! American Music and Politics in the Early Nation.* New York: Oxford University Press, 2020.

Longmore, Paul K. *The Invention of George Washington.* Berkeley: University of California Press, 1988.

Loughran, Trish. *The Republic in Print: Print Culture in the Age of U.S. Nation Building, 1770–1870.* New York: Columbia University Press, 2007.

Lurie, Shira. "Liberty Poles and the Fight for Popular Politics." *Journal of the Early American Republic* 38, no. 4 (Winter 2018): 673–97.

Lynd, Staughton, and David Waldstreicher. "Reflections on Economic Interpretation, Slavery, the People Out of Doors, and Top Down versus Bottom Up." *William and Mary Quarterly,* 3rd series, 68, no. 4 (October 2011): 649–56.

Lynn, Joshua A. *Preserving the White Man's Republic: Jacksonian Democracy, Race and the Transformation of American Conservatism.* Charlottesville: University of Virginia Press, 2019.

Maier, Pauline. *American Scripture: Making the Declaration of Independence.* New York: Vintage, 1998.

———. *From Resistance to Revolution: Colonial Radicals and the Development of American Opposition to Britain, 1765–1776.* New York: Knopf, 1972.

———. "Popular Uprisings and Civil Authority in Eighteenth-Century America." *William and Mary Quarterly,* 3rd series, 27, no. 1 (January 1970): 3–35.

———. *Ratification: The People Debate the Constitution, 1787–1788.* New York: Simon and Schuster, 2010.

Main, Jackson Turner. *Political Parties before the Constitution.* Chapel Hill: University of North Carolina Press, 1973.

Mark, Gregory A. "The Vestigial Constitution: The History and Significance of the Right to Petition." *Fordham Law Review* 66, no. 6 (1998): 2153–231.
Martin, Robert W. T. *Government by Dissent: Protest, Resistance, and Radical Democratic Thought in the Early American Republic.* New York: New York University Press, 2013.
McConville, Brendan. *The King's Three Faces: The Rise and Fall of Royal America, 1688–1776.* Chapel Hill: University of North Carolina Press, 2006.
McCormick, Richard P. *The Second American Party System: Party Formation in the Jacksonian Era.* Chapel Hill: University of North Carolina Press, 1966.
McCoy, Drew. *The Elusive Republic: Political Economy in Jeffersonian America.* Chapel Hill: University of North Carolina Press, 1980.
McDonnel, Michael A. *The Politics of War: Race, Class, and Conflict in Revolutionary Virginia.* Chapel Hill: University of North Carolina Press, 2007.
Miller, Joshua. "The Ghostly Body Politic: The *Federalist Papers* and Popular Sovereignty." *Political Theory* 16 (1988): 99–119.
Miller, Richard G. *Philadelphia—The Federalist City: A Study of Urban Politics, 1789–1801.* Port Washington, NY: Kennikat Press, 1976.
Moats, Sandra. *Celebrating the Republic: Presidential Ceremony and Popular Sovereignty from Washington to Monroe.* DeKalb: Northern Illinois University Press, 2010.
Monroe, James A. *The Democratic Wish: Popular Participation and the Limits of American Government.* New Haven, CT: Yale University Press, 1998.
Morgan, Edmund. *Inventing the People: The Rise of Popular Sovereignty in England and America.* New York: Norton, 1988.
Moyer, Paul B. *Wild Yankees: The Struggle for Independence along Pennsylvania's Revolutionary Frontier.* Ithaca, NY: Cornell University Press, 2007.
Myers, Minor. *Liberty without Anarchy: A History of the Society of the Cincinnati.* Charlottesville: University Press of Virginia, 1983.
Myrsidaes, Linda. "A Tale of a Whiskey Rebellion Judge: William Paterson, Grand Jury Charges, and the Trials of the Whiskey Rebels." *Pennsylvania Magazine of History and Biography* 140, no. 2 (April 2016): 129–65.
Nash, Gary B. "The American Clergy and the French Revolution." *William and Mary Quarterly*, 3rd series, 22, no. 3 (July 1965): 392–412.
———. *Forging Freedom: The Formation of Philadelphia's Black Community, 1720–1840.* Cambridge, MA: Harvard University Press, 1988.
———. "Philadelphia or Boston: Who Is the 'Cradle of Liberty?'" Constitution Center. http://blog.constitutioncenter.org/2011/06/philadelphia-or-boston-who-is-the-cradle-of-liberty/.
———. *The Unknown American Revolution: The Unruly Birth of Democracy and the Struggle to Create America.* New York: Penguin, 2006.

Nash, Gary, and Jean R. Soderlund. *Freedom by Degrees: Emancipation in Pennsylvania and Its Aftermath*. New York: Oxford University Press, 1991.

Neem, Johann N. *Creating a Nation of Joiners: Democracy and Civil Society in Early National Massachusetts*. Cambridge, MA: Harvard University Press, 2008.

———. "Freedom of Association in the Early Republic: The Republican Party, the Whiskey Rebellion, and the New York Cordwainers Cases." *Pennsylvania Magazine of History and Biography* 127, no. 3 (July 2003): 259–90.

Nelson, Dana D. *Commons Democracy: Reading the Politics of Participation in the Early United States*. New York: Fordham University Press, 2016.

Newman, Paul Douglas. "The Federalists' Cold War: The Fries Rebellion, National Security, and the State, 1787–1800." *Pennsylvania History* 67, no. 1 (Winter 2000): 63–104.

———. *Fries's Rebellion: The Enduring Struggle for the American Revolution*. Philadelphia: University of Pennsylvania Press, 2004.

Newman, Simon P. *Parades and the Politics of the Street: Festive Culture in the Early American Republic*. Philadelphia: University of Pennsylvania Press, 1997.

———. "Principles or Men? George Washington and the Political Culture of National Leadership, 1776–1801." *Journal of American History* 12, no. 4 (Winter 1992): 477–507.

Nolt, Stephen M. *Foreigners in Their Own Land: Pennsylvania Germans in the Early Republic*. University Park: Pennsylvania State University Press, 2002.

Novak, William J. "The Myth of the Weak American State." *American Historical Review* 113 (June 2008): 752–72.

Oaks, Robert F. "Philadelphians in Exile: The Problem of Loyalty during the American Revolution." *Pennsylvania Magazine of History and Biography* 96, no. 3 (July 1972): 298–325.

Olton, Charles S. *Artisans for Independence: Philadelphia Mechanics and the American Revolution*. Syracuse, NY: Syracuse University Press, 1975.

Ousterhout, Ann M. "Controlling the Opposition in Pennsylvania during the American Revolution." *Pennsylvania Magazine of History and Biography* 105, no. 1 (January 1981): 3–34.

Owen, Kenneth. *Political Community in Revolutionary Pennsylvania, 1774–1800*. New York: Oxford University Press, 2018.

Ozouf, Mona. *Festivals and the French Revolution*. Cambridge, MA: Harvard University Press, 1988.

Parker, John, and Carol Urness, eds. *The American Revolution: A Heritage of Change*. Minneapolis: Associates of the James Ford Bell Library, 1975.

Parkinson, Robert G. *The Common Cause: Creating Race and Nation in the American Revolution*. Chapel Hill: University of North Carolina Press, 2016.

Pasley, Jeffrey L. *The First Presidential Contest: 1796 and the Founding of American Democracy*. Lawrence: University Press of Kansas, 2013.

———. "'A Journeyman, Either in Law or Politics': John Beckley and the Social Origins of Political Campaigning." *Journal of the Early Republic* 16, no. 4 (Winter 1996): 531–69.

———. *"The Tyranny of Printers": Newspaper Politics in the Early American Republic.* Charlottesville: University of Virginia Press, 2001.

Pasley, Jeffrey L., Andrew W. Robertson, and David Waldstreicher, eds. *Beyond the Founders: New Approaches to the Political History of the Early American Republic.* Chapel Hill: University of North Carolina Press, 2004.

Pearl, Christopher. "Becoming Patriots: The Struggle for Inclusion and Exclusion on Pennsylvania's Revolutionary Frontier." *Pennsylvania History* 88, no. 3 (Summer 2021): 362–401.

———. *Conceived in Crisis: The Revolutionary Creating of an American State.* Charlottesville: University of Virginia Press, 2020.

Peart, Daniel. *Era of Experimentation: American Political Practices in the Early Republic.* Charlottesville: University of Virginia Press, 2014.

Peart, Daniel, and Adam I. P. Smith, eds. *Practicing Democracy: Popular Politics in the United States from the Constitution to the Civil War.* Charlottesville: University of Virginia Press, 2015.

Pencack, William. *Jews and Gentiles in Early America: 1654–1800.* Ann Arbor: University of Michigan Press, 2005.

———, ed. *Pennsylvania's Revolution.* University Park: Pennsylvania State University Press, 2010.

Pencak, William, Matthew Dennis, and Simon Newman, eds. *Riot and Revelry in Early America.* University Park: Pennsylvania State University Press, 2002.

Pfleger, Birte. "'Miserable Germans' and Fries's Rebellion: Language, Ethnicity, and Citizenship in the Early Republic." *Early American Studies* 2, no. 2 (2004): 343–61.

Phillips, Kim T. "William Duane, Philadelphia's Democratic Republicans, and the Origins of Modern Politics." *Pennsylvania Magazine of History and Biography* 101, no. 3 (July 1977): 356–87.

Pole, J. R. *Political Representation in England and the Origins of the American Republic.* New York: Macmillan, 1966.

Polgar, Paul. *Standard-Bearers of Equality: America's First Abolition Movement.* Chapel Hill: University of North Carolina Press, 2019.

Potter, Kathleen O. *The Federalist's Vision of Popular Sovereignty in the New American Republic.* New York: LFP Scholarly, 2002.

Rakove, Jack N. *Original Meanings: Politics and Ideas in the Making of the Constitution.* New York: Random House, 1996.

Rappaport, George David. *Stability and Change in Revolutionary Pennsylvania: Banking, Politics, and Social Structure.* University Park: Pennsylvania State University Press, 1996.

Rasmussen, Ethel. "Capital on the Delaware: The Philadelphia Upper Class in Transition, 1789–1801." Ph.D. diss., Brown University, 1962.
Ray, Thomas R. "'Not One Cent for Tribute': The Public Address and American Popular Reaction to the XYZ Affair, 1798–1799." *Journal of the Early Republic* 3, no. 4 (Winter 1983): 389–412.
Ridgway, William H. "Fries in the Federalist Imagination: A Crisis of Republican Society." *Pennsylvania History* 67, no. 1 (Winter 2000): 141–60.
Ridner, Judith. *The Scotch Irish of Early Pennsylvania: A Varied People*. Philadelphia: Temple University Press, 2018.
———. *A Town In-Between: Carlisle, Pennsylvania, and the Early Mid-Atlantic Interior*. Philadelphia: University of Pennsylvania Press, 2010.
Robertson, Andrew W. *The Language of Democracy: Political Rhetoric in the United States and Britain, 1790–1900*. Ithaca, NY: Cornell University Press, 1995.
Robinson, Donald L. *Town Meetings: Practicing Democracy in Rural New England*. Amherst: University of Massachusetts Press, 2011.
Ron, Ariel, and Gautham Rao. "Taking Stock of the State in Nineteenth-Century America." *Journal of the Early Republic* 38, no. 1 (Winter 2018): 61–118.
Roney, Jessica. *Governed by a Spirit of Opposition: The Origins of American Political Practice in Colonial Philadelphia*. Baltimore: Johns Hopkins University Press, 2014.
Rossman, Kenneth R. *Thomas Mifflin and the Politics of the American Revolution*. Chapel Hill: University of North Carolina Press, 1952.
Rosswurm, Steven. *Arms, Country, and Class: The Philadelphia Militia and the "Lower Sort" during the American Revolution*. New Brunswick, NJ: Rutgers University Press, 1987.
Rowe, G. S. *Thomas McKean: The Shaping of an American Republicanism*. Boulder, CO: Associated Faculty Press, 1978.
Rude, George. *The Crowd in History: A Study of Popular Disturbances in France and England, 1730–1840*. New York: Serif, 2005.
Runcie, John. "'Hunting the Nigs' in Philadelphia: The Race Riot of August 1834." *Pennsylvania History* 39, no. 2 (April 1972): 187–218.
Ryerson, Richard A. "Political Mobilization and the American Revolution: The Resistance Movement in Philadelphia, 1765 to 1776." *William and Mary Quarterly*, 3rd series, 31, no. 4 (October 1974): 565–88.
———. *The Revolution Is Now Begun: The Radical Committees of Philadelphia, 1765–1776*. Philadelphia: University of Pennsylvania Press, 1978.
Scharff, J. Thomas, and Thompson Westcott. *History of Philadelphia, 1609–1884*. Volume 1. Philadelphia: L. H. Everts, 1884.
Schoenbachler, Matthew. "Republicanism in the Age of Democratic Revolution: The Democratic-Republican Societies of the 1790s." *Journal of the Early Republic* 18, no. 2 (Summer 1998): 237–61.

Schwartz, Barry. *George Washington: The Making of an American Symbol.* New York: Cornell University Press, 1987.

Schweitzer, Mary M. "The Spatial Organization of Federalist Philadelphia, 1790." *Journal of Interdisciplinary History* 24, no. 1 (Summer 1993): 31–57.

Selsam, John Paul. *The Pennsylvania Constitution of 1776: A Study in Revolutionary Democracy.* New York: Oxford University Press, 1936.

Seymour, Joseph. *The Pennsylvania Associators, 1747–1777.* Yardley, PA: Westholme, 2012.

Shaeffer, John N. "Public Consideration of the 1776 Pennsylvania Constitution." *Pennsylvania Magazine of History and Biography* 98, no. 4 (October 1974): 415–37.

Shade, William. "'Corrupt and Contented': Where Have the Politicians Gone? A Survey of Recent Books on Pennsylvania Political History, 1787–1877." *Pennsylvania Magazine of History and Biography* 132, no. 4 (October 2008): 433–51.

Shankman, Andrew. *The Crucible of American Democracy: The Struggle to Fuse Egalitarianism and Capitalism in Jeffersonian Pennsylvania.* Lawrence: University Press of Kansas, 2004.

Sharp, James Roger. *American Politics in the Early Republic.* New Haven, CT: Yale University Press, 1993.

Sheehan, Colleen A. "The Politics of Public Opinion: James Madison's 'Notes on Government.'" *William and Mary Quarterly*, 3rd series, 49, no. 4 (1992): 609–21.

Sioli, Marco M. "The Democratic Republican Societies at the End of the Eighteenth Century: The Western Pennsylvania Experience." *Pennsylvania History* 60, no. 3 (July 1993): 288–304.

Slaughter, Thomas P. "Crowds in Eighteenth-Century America: Reflections and New Directions." *Pennsylvania Magazine of History and Biography* 115, no. 1 (January 1991): 3–34.

———. "The Tax Man Cometh: Ideological Opposition to Internal Taxes, 1760–1790." *William and Mary Quarterly*, 3rd series, 41, no. 4 (October 1984): 566–91.

———. *The Whiskey Rebellion: Frontier Epilogue to the American Revolution.* Oxford: Oxford University Press, 1986.

Smelser, Marshall. "The Jacobin Phrenzy: Federalism and the Menace of Liberty, Equality and Fraternity." *Review of Politics* 13, no. 4 (October 1951): 457–82.

———. "The Jacobin Phrenzy: The Menace of Monarchy, Plutocracy, and Anglophilia, 1789–1798." *Review of Politics* 21, no. 1 (January 1959): 239–58.

Smith, Barbara Clark. "Beyond the Vote: The Limits of Deference in Colonial Politics." *Early American Studies* 3, no. 2 (Fall 2005): 341–62.

———. *The Freedoms We Lost: Consent and Resistance in Revolutionary America.* New York: New Press, 2010.

Smith, Billy G. *The "Lower Sort": Philadelphia's Labouring People, 1750–1800.* Ithaca, NY: Cornell University Press, 1990.

Smith, C. Page. "The Attack on Fort Wilson." *Pennsylvania Magazine of History and Biography* 78, no. 2 (April 1954): 177–88.

Smith, Don L. "The Right to Petition for Redress of Grievances: Constitutional Development and Interpretations." Ph.D. diss., Texas Tech University, 1971.

Smith, Eric Ledell. "The End of Black Voting Rights in Pennsylvania: African Americans and the Pennsylvania Constitutional Convention of 1837–1838." *Pennsylvania History* 65, no. 3 (Summer 1998): 279–99.

Smith, James Morton. *Freedom's Fetters: The Alien and Sedition Laws and American Civil Liberties.* Ithaca, NY: Cornell University Press, 1956.

Smith, Rogers M. *Civic Ideals: Conflicting Visions of Citizenship in U.S. History.* New Haven, CT: Yale University Press, 1997.

Spero, Patrick. *Frontier Country: The Politics of War in Early Pennsylvania.* Philadelphia: University of Pennsylvania Press, 2016.

Splitter, Wolfgang. "The Germans in Pennsylvania Politics, 1754–1790: A Quantitative Analysis." *Pennsylvania Magazine of History and Biography* 122, nos. 1–2 (April 1998): 39–76.

Squire, Peverill. *The Rise of the Representative: Lawmakers and Constituents in Colonial America.* Ann Arbor: University of Michigan Press, 2017.

Stewart, Brice E. *Redemption from Tyranny: Herman Husband's American Revolution.* Charlottesville: University of Virginia Press, 2020.

Sullivan, Aaron. *The Disaffected: Britain's Occupation of Philadelphia during the American Revolution.* Philadelphia: University of Pennsylvania Press, 2019.

Thayer, Theodore. *Pennsylvania Politics and the Growth of Democracy, 1740–1776.* Harrisburg: Pennsylvania Historical and Museum Commission, 1953.

Thompson, E. P. *The Making of the English Working Class.* New York: Vintage, 1966.

———. "The Moral Economy of the English Crowd in the Eighteenth Century." *Past and Present* 50, no. 1 (1971): 76–136.

———. "Patrician Society, Plebian Culture." *Journal of Social History* 7 (1974): 382–405.

Thompson, Peter. *Rum Punch and Revolution: Tavern-Going and Public Life in Eighteenth-Century Philadelphia.* Philadelphia: University of Pennsylvania Press, 1998.

Tiedmann, Joseph S. "A Tumultuous People: The Rage for Liberty and the Ambiance of Violence in the Middle Colonies in the Years Proceeding the American Revolution." *Pennsylvania History* 77, no. 4 (Autumn 2010): 387–431.

Tinkcom, Harry M. *The Republicans and Federalists in Pennsylvania, 1790–1801: A Study in National Stimulus and Local Response.* Harrisburg: Pennsylvania Historical and Museum Commission, 1950.

Tolles, Frederick B. *George Logan of Philadelphia.* New York: Oxford University Press, 1953.
Travers, Len. *Celebrating the Fourth: Independence Day and Rites of Nationalism in the Early Republic.* Amherst: University of Massachusetts Press, 1997.
Tully, Alan. *Forming American Politics: Ideals, Interests and Institutions in Colonial New York and Pennsylvania.* Baltimore: Johns Hopkins University Press, 1994.
Van Cleve, William. *We Have Not a Government: The Articles of Confederation and the Road to the Constitution.* Chicago: University of Chicago Press, 2017.
Waldstreicher, David, ed. *A Companion to John Adams and John Quincy Adams.* Malden, MA: Wiley-Blackwell, 2013.
———. *In The Midst of Perpetual Fetes: The Making of American Nationalism, 1776–1820.* Chapel Hill: University of North Carolina Press, 1997.
Walters, Raymond, Jr. *Albert Gallatin: Jeffersonian Financier and Diplomat.* Pittsburgh: University of Pittsburgh Press, 1957.
———. *Alexander James Dallas: Lawyer, Politician, Financier, 1759–1817.* Philadelphia: University of Pennsylvania Press, 1943.
Walton, Joseph S. "Nominating Conventions in Pennsylvania." *American Historical Review* 2, no. 2 (January 1897): 262–78.
Warner, Sam Bass *The Private City: Philadelphia in Three Periods of Its Growth.* Philadelphia: University of Pennsylvania Press, 1968.
Watkins, William J., Jr. *Reclaiming the American Revolution: The Kentucky and Virginia Resolutions.* New York: Palgrave Macmillan, 2004.
Weigley, Russell F., ed. *Philadelphia: A 300-Year History.* Philadelphia: Barra Foundation, 1982.
Wendel, Thomas. "The Keith-Lloyd Alliance: Factional and Coalition Politics in Colonial Pennsylvania." *Pennsylvania Magazine of History and Biography* 92, no. 3 (July 1968): 289–305.
Wilentz, Sean. *The Rise of American Democracy: Jefferson to Lincoln.* New York: Norton, 2005.
Wilf, Steven. *Imagined Republic: Popular Politics and Criminal Justice in Revolutionary America.* New York: Cambridge University Press, 2010.
Winch, Julie. "Free Men and 'Freemen': Black Voting Rights in Pennsylvania, 1790–1870." *Pennsylvania Legacies* 8, no. 2 (November 2008): 14–19.
Wood, Gordon S. *The Creation of the American Republic, 1776–1787.* New York: Norton, 1972.
———. *Empire of Liberty: A History of the Early Republic.* New York: Oxford University Press, 2009.
———. "A Note on the Mobs in the American Revolution." *William and Mary Quarterly,* 3rd series, 23, no. 4 (1966): 635–42.
———. *The Radicalism of the American Revolution.* New York: Knopf, 1991.

Wood, Nicholas. "'A Sacrifice on the Alter of Slavery': Doughface Politics and Black Disenfranchisement in Pennsylvania, 1837–1838." *Journal of the Early Republic* 31, no. 1 (Spring 2011): 75–106.

Young, Alfred F., ed. *The American Revolution: Explorations in the History of American Radicalism*. DeKalb: Northern Illinois University Press, 1976.

———. *The Democratic Republicans of New York: The Origins, 1763–1797*. Chapel Hill: University of North Carolina Press, 1967.

———. "The Framers of the Constitution and the 'Genius' of the People." *Radical History Review* 42 (Fall 1988): 8–18.

———. *Liberty Tree: Ordinary People and the American Revolution*. New York: New York University Press, 2006.

Young, Alfred F., Gary Nash, and Ray Raphael, eds. *Revolutionary Founders: Rebels, Radicals, and Reformers in the Making of the Nation*. New York: Knopf, 2011.

Young, Christopher J. "Connecting the President and the People: Washington's Neutrality, Genet's Challenge, and Hamilton's Fight for Public Support." *Journal of the Early Republic* 31, no. 3 (Fall 2011): 435–66.

Young, Ralph F. *Dissent: The History of an American Idea*. New York: New York University Press, 2015.

Zagarri, Rosemarie. *Revolutionary Backlash: Women and Politics in the Early American Republic*. Philadelphia: University of Pennsylvania Press, 2007.

INDEX

Early American Histories

Plain Paths and Dividing Lines: Navigating Native Land and Water in the Seventeenth-Century Chesapeake
Jessica Lauren Taylor

The Travels of Richard Traunter: Two Journeys through the Native Southeast in 1698 and 1699
Edited by Sandra L. Dahlberg

Making the Early Modern Metropolis: Culture and Power in Pre-Revolutionary Philadelphia
Daniel P. Johnson

The Permanent Resident: Excavations and Explorations of George Washington's Life
Philip Levy

From Independence to the U.S. Constitution: Reconsidering the Critical Period of American History
Douglas Bradburn and Christopher R. Pearl, editors

Washington's Government: Charting the Origins of the Federal Administration
Max M. Edling and Peter J. Kastor, editors

The Natural, Moral, and Political History of Jamaica, and the Territories thereon Depending, from the First Discovery of the Island by Christopher Columbus to the Year 1746
James Knight, edited by Jack P. Greene

Statute Law in Colonial Virginia: Governors, Assemblymen, and the Revisals That Forged the Old Dominion
Warren M. Billings

Against Popery: Britain, Empire, and Anti-Catholicism
Evan Haefeli, editor

Conceived in Crisis: The Revolutionary Creation of an American State
Christopher R. Pearl

Redemption from Tyranny: Herman Husband's American Revolution
Bruce E. Stewart

Experiencing Empire: Power, People, and Revolution in Early America
Patrick Griffin, editor

Citizens of Convenience: The Imperial Origins of American Nationhood on the U.S.-Canadian Border
Lawrence B. A. Hatter

"Esteemed Bookes of Lawe" and the Legal Culture of Early Virginia
Warren M. Billings and Brent Tarter, editors

Settler Jamaica in the 1750s: A Social Portrait
Jack P. Greene

Loyal Protestants and Dangerous Papists: Maryland and the Politics of Religion in the English Atlantic, 1630–1690
Antoinette Sutto

The Road to Black Ned's Forge: A Story of Race, Sex, and Trade on the Colonial American Frontier
Turk McCleskey

Dunmore's New World: The Extraordinary Life of a Royal Governor in Revolutionary America—with Jacobites, Counterfeiters, Land Schemes, Shipwrecks, Scalping, Indian Politics, Runaway Slaves, and Two Illegal Royal Weddings
James Corbett David

Creating the British Atlantic: Essays on Transplantation, Adaptation, and Continuity
Jack P. Greene

The Evil Necessity: British Naval Impressment in the Eighteenth-Century Atlantic World
Denver Brunsman

Early Modern Virginia: Reconsidering the Old Dominion
Douglas Bradburn and John C. Coombs, editors

Printed in the USA
CPSIA information can be obtained
at www.ICGtesting.com
LVHW091535281023
762365LV00003B/404